GERMAN TELEVISION

Film Europa: German Cinema in an International Context
Series Editors: **Hans-Michael Bock** (CineGraph Hamburg); **Tim Bergfelder** (University of Southampton); **Sabine Hake** (University of Texas, Austin)

German cinema is normally seen as a distinct form, but this series emphasizes connections, influences, and exchanges of German cinema across national borders, as well as its links with other media and art forms. Individual titles present traditional historical research (archival work, industry studies) as well as new critical approaches in film and media studies (theories of the transnational), with a special emphasis on the continuities associated with popular traditions and local perspectives.

The Concise Cinegraph: An Encyclopedia of German Cinema
General Editor: Hans-Michael Bock
Associate Editor: Tim Bergfelder

International Adventures: German Popular Cinema and European Co-Productions in the 1960s
Tim Bergfelder

Between Two Worlds: The Jewish Presence in German and Austrian Film, 1910–1933
S. S. Prawer

Framing the Fifties: Cinema in a Divided Germany
Edited by John Davidson and Sabine Hake

A Foreign Affair: Billy Wilder's American Films
Gerd Gemünden

Destination London: German-speaking Emigrés and British Cinema, 1925–1950
Edited by Tim Bergfelder and Christian Cargnelli

Michael Haneke's Cinema: The Ethic of the Image
Catherine Wheatley

Willing Seduction: *The Blue Angel,* **Marlene Dietrich, and Mass Culture**
Barbara Kosta

Dismantling the Dream Factory: Gender, German Cinema, and the Postwar Quest for a New Film Language
Hester Baer

Belá Balázs: Early Film Theory. *Visible Man* and *The Spirit of Film*
Bela Balazs, edited by Erica Carter, translated by Rodney Livingstone

Screening the East: Heimat, Memory and Nostalgia in German Film since 1989
Nick Hodgin

Peter Lorre: Face Maker. Constructing Stardom and Performance in Hollywood and Europe
Sarah Thomas

Turkish German Cinema in the New Millennium: Sites, Sounds, and Screens
Edited by Sabine Hake and Barbara Mennel

Postwall German Cinema: History, Film History and Cinephilia
Mattias Frey

Homemade Men in Postwar Austrian Cinema: Nationhood, Genre and Masculinity
Maria Fritsche

The Emergence of Film Culture: Knowledge Production, Institution Building, and the Fate of the Avant-Garde in Europe, 1919–1945
Edited by Malte Hagener

Imperial Projections: Screening the German Colonies
Wolfgang Fuhrmann

Cinema in Service of the State: Perspectives on East German and Czech Film Culture, 1945–1960
Edited by Lars Karl and Pavel Skopal

German Television: Historical and Theoretical Perspectives
Edited by Larson Powell and Robert Shandley

German Television

Historical and Theoretical Perspectives

Edited by
Larson Powell and Robert Shandley

berghahn
NEW YORK · OXFORD
www.berghahnbooks.com

Published in 2016 by
Berghahn Books
www.BerghahnBooks.com

© 2016, 2018 Larson Powell and Robert Shandley
First paperback edition published in 2018

All rights reserved. Except for the quotation of short passages
for the purposes of criticism and review, no part of this book
may be reproduced in any form or by any means, electronic or
mechanical, including photocopying, recording, or any
information storage and retrieval system now known or to be
invented, without written permission of Berghahn Books.

Library of Congress Cataloging-in-Publication Data
Names: Powell, Larson, 1960- editor. | Shandley, Robert R., editor.
Title: German television : historical and theoretical approaches / edited by Larson Powell and Robert Shandley.
Description: New York : Berghahn Books, 2016. | Series: Film Europa: German cinema in an international context | Includes bibliographical references and index.
Identifiers: LCCN 2016026101 | ISBN 9781785331121 (hardback) | ISBN 9781785338373 (paperback)
Subjects: LCSH: Television broadcasting--Germany--History. | Television--Social aspects--Germany.
Classification: LCC PN1992.3.G4 G465 2016 | DDC 791.450943--dc23
LC record available at https://lccn.loc.gov/2016026101

British Library Cataloguing in Publication Data
A catalogue record for this book is available from the British Library.

ISBN 978-1-78533-112-1 (hardback)
ISBN 978-1-78533-837-3 (paperback)
ISBN 978-1-78533-113-8 (ebook)

Contents

List of Figures and Tables — vii

Introduction. German Television: Culture, Technology, or Cultural Technology? — 1
   Larson Powell and Robert Shandley

Part I. Technical Prehistory and Theoretical Approaches

1. The Third Image: Contingencies and Ruptures in the Technological History of Television — 17
   Wolfgang Hagen

2. Boredom, War, and Paradox: German Theories of Television — 33
   Larson Powell

Part II. GDR Television

3. "Just Like in the West, Except Different": Television and Its Relationship to Film in the Context of 1950s GDR Development — 53
   Thomas Beutelschmidt

4. Adventures in Stagnation: Gottfried Kolditz's Unfilmed Project *Zimtpiraten* — 63
   Evan Torner

Part III. Television in the Federal Republic: Auteurist TV

5. "A Challenge, Maybe the Greatest for a Filmmaker": Televisual Perspectives on Rainer Werner Fassbinder's *Martha* (1974) — 87
   Brad Prager

6. *Nah am Fern*: Kluge TV — 110
   Stefanie Harris

Part IV. Present and Future Perspectives

7. Television History in Germany: Media-Political and
   Media-Ethical Aspects 133
   Rüdiger Steinmetz

8. Germany as TV Show Import Market 155
   Lothar Mikos

9. Heritage, *Heimat*, and German Historical "Event
   Television": Nico Hofmann's teamWorx 175
   Paul Cooke

10. Once Upon a Crime: *Tatort*, Germany's Longest Running
    Police Procedural 193
    Bärbel Göbel-Stolz

Bibliography 215

Index 232

Figures and Tables

Figures

1.1. Vibrating plate of the kind developed by acoustician Ernst Florenz Chladni. Image courtesy of the Smithsonian Institution. — 21

1.2. Early drawing of the telephone by Alexander Graham Bell, 1876. Image courtesy of the Library of Congress, Manuscript Division. — 25

5.1. Above: A hand reaches for an unattended purse in *Martha*. Directed by Rainer Werner Fassbinder and produced by Westdeutscher Rundfunk (WDR) in 1974. Below: A purse beneath Tippi Hedren's arm in the opening moments of *Marnie*. Directed by Alfred Hitchcock and produced by Alfred J. Hitchcock Productions in 1964. — 97

5.2. Helmut touches Martha's sunburned abdomen in R. W. Fassbinder's *Martha* (1974). — 102

5.3. Above: The patio railing and the horizon in R. W. Fassbinder's *Martha* (1974). Below: A closed window, looking out at the horizon in Alfred Hitchcock's *Marnie* (1964). — 103

10.1. Hypermasculine homicide detective Horst Schimanski. — 196

10.2. A fifteen-year-old Nastassya Kinski portraying student Sina in the episode "Reifezeugnis" (1977). — 198

10.3. Detective Charlotte Lindholm with Selda Özkan in "Wem Ehre Gebührt" (2007). — 204

10.4. *Tatort* general audience ratings percentages, September 2010. — 213

10.5. *Tatort* ratings percentages for ages 14–49, September 2010. — 213

10.6. 2010 *Tatort* ratings, general audiences. 213
10.7. 2010 *Tatort* ratings, Ages 14–49. 213

Tables

10.1. *Tatort* withdrawn episodes. 201

Introduction

German Television: Culture, Technology, or Cultural Technology?

Theorizing television has proven an elusive matter. After decades of being incorporated into mass communication studies, television was largely bypassed by the first wave of poststructuralist German *Medientheorie* in the 1980s and 1990s. The reasons for this are multiple. On the one hand, the medium itself, and not only in Germany, "remains more comfortably pathologized as a cultural symptom than explored as a cultural form," as William Uricchio (1998a) has it.[1] As no other medium, television embodies the tension between technology and culture, a tension many have seen as antagonistic, with television playing the historical role of chief villain, as it did in Neil Postman's widely read *Amusing Ourselves to Death* (1985). Ambitious attempts in English to give television a philosophical dimension, like Richard Dienst's *Still Life in Real Time* (1994), or Paddy Scannell's recent *Television and the Meaning of 'Live'* (2014), which both (like *Medientheorie*) draw on Heidegger, have thus been the exception rather than the rule. On the other hand, *Medientheorie* defined itself through a polemical opposition not only to Frankfurt School concerns with the (mediated) public sphere, but also to traditional mass media studies' culturalist perspective. "The objects of research that defined communication studies (press, film, television, radio—that is, primarily mass media) were never of great interest" to *Medientheorie* (Siegert 2013: 49; see also Siegert 1996). We are thus faced with the paradox that although all manner of techniques and technologies may be and have been seen as "media," one of the schoolbook examples of a medium still awaits the sophisticated treatment recently given to spinning wheels, servants, or bureaucratic paper trails. Since traditional television studies were historically tied to an older sociological concept of media, whether indebted to Frankfurt or Birmingham, that newer *Medientheorie* wanted to avoid at all costs, television as object of study has suffered from its association with a certain methodological perspective. The opposition of a certain kind of theory to television has also a particularly German stamp about it, however.

This book seeks to correct this split between television and theory, although it does not attempt to do so in monolithic fashion, which would do violence to the field of television studies. There exists no unified field theory for television, any more than there does for physics. Television studies are characterized by a wide range of approaches, some empirical, others more speculative (and indebted to poststructuralism), and the present volume seeks to give a sense of that variety. Although the contributors to this volume do not all subscribe to one methodology, there are nonetheless recurring themes and conceptual tensions within the field. One hint as to how we might conceptualize television as medium in a way different from traditional mass media studies is given by the recent post-Kittlerian turn in Germany to what is known as *Kulturtechniken* or cultural techniques.[2] This is more than a mere shotgun wedding between two influential concepts in the humanities, and offers an important corrective to or expansion of earlier *Medientheorie*. Whereas Kittler's own programmatic antihumanism, transposing the medium of Foucault's disappearance of Man from sand to silicone (Winthrop-Young 2000: 402), insisted that "there is no software," so that computer programming would eventually eliminate "so-called Man," other media theoreticians since Kittler have become increasingly interested in media technology's cultural embedding. This has not meant a return to familiar ideas of subject or "agency," however, for the technical a priori—the priority of technology to any human instance—remains in force; it is techniques like ploughing, writing, or even the use of doors and gates that first produce the actor who then seems instrumentally to use them. Scholars of *Kulturtechnik* therefore operate with a model of "culture" somewhat distinct from the familiar one of Raymond Williams (1981). In a nutshell: Williams' "technology and cultural form" becomes "technology as cultural form." *Kulturtechnik* as a method is also different from the cultural studies model used by Heather Gumbert (2014) in her recent book on East German television. Gumbert's book, while informative and important in its analyses, nonetheless remains within the social-science-defined context of American communication studies. The present book seeks to widen that context, without, however, indulging in the anathemas hurled against communications by Kittler and his followers. The notion of *Kulturtechnik* may help this process of broadening. If Sybille Krämer has argued for seeing computer usage as cultural, why not that of television? So Geoffrey

Winthrop-Young notes in his introduction to a recent issue of *Theory, Culture and Society* dedicated to *Kulturtechnik*:

> Watching television, for instance, requires specific technological know-how (identifying the on/off button, mastering the remote, programming the VCR) as well as equally medium-specific mental and conceptual skills such as understanding audiovisual referentiality structures, assessing the fictionality status of different programs, interacting with media-specific narrative formats, or the ability to distinguish between intended and unintended messages. All these skills, aptitudes and abilities are part of the *Kulturtechniken des Fernsehens*, the cultural techniques of television. (Winthrop-Young 2013: 5–6)

In other words: to see television as a cultural technique means including its effects (its specific form of medial subjectivity) together with its technical and social dispositive. It also means recognizing that the development of television is incomprehensible without consideration of its embedding in cultural techniques, including "nets and networks" (the subject of several recent German publications). According to Sebastian Giessmann (2005: 424), the blind spot of German media theory has lain less in the storage function of media than in their embedding in networks of transmission, which can be seen as cultural techniques.[3] This is, it should be noted, a different model of "television culture" than that proposed by older scholars in the 1980s, which was still bound up with a "traditional middle-class understanding of culture that links culture to humanist educational imperatives" (Siegert 2015: 57).[4] An interesting question brought up by current discussions of *Kulturtechnik* is how to define the latter: what makes a technique "cultural?" Culture, according to Kittler's media-informed view of it, is defined by its recursivity: that is, culture is self-referential and builds up its own world of meaning via this feedback loop. Opinions differ, however, on precisely where techniques become cultural; if Thomas Macho believes "cultural techniques" must be recursive and symbolic, Bernhard Siegert (2013: 59) disagrees. Wolfgang Hagen's argument in his chapter for this book suggests that TV's "third image" might be an instance of an internal, technical recursivity, contradicting the usual notion of the medium as mere transparent window on the world. One need only add that these "cultural techniques" are, like all culture, historical to arrive at the third coordinate of this book. Germany has been not only a country with a specific culture of science and technology (one with at times serious political consequences), but it has also a very particular culture of television, one born of the peculiar historical circumstances of empire, National Socialism, and the Cold War. As Richard Dienst put it, the "techniques" for implementing TV "were borrowed from the existing discourses of state and cultural authority that immediately informed the creation of broadcasting institutions," (1994: 7)[5] and we will find these political and cultural discourses again and again in German television.

The Ariadne's thread running through this volume is thus a shared concern with the specific historical manifestations of these German circumstances, whether in the overall evolution of television in Germany or in specific cases of productions for TV. The first part of the book offers a look at some current German theoretical and historiographical views of television. For Wolfgang Hagen, the "cultural techniques" in question are that of knowledge and science as specific discursive formations,[6] tied to the medium of book printing. Hagen's chapter is thus very much in the Foucauldian tradition of a historiography of ruptures (*Zäsuren*), or what in German is known as *Medienarchäologie*. It may thus seem "jumpy" or speculative to readers accustomed to more traditional histories of technology. A comparison with English-language histories of television's development can highlight Hagen's subtle differences: where R. W. Burns (1998: 76) lists three periods of television prehistory, beginning roughly with Bell's telephone in the 1870s,[7] Hagen begins earlier on. He thus goes even further than generalizations about the genesis of science in early modernity, to situate the origins of televisual thinking in the context of German Romantic *Naturphilosophie*. This might contradict Kittler's apodictic assertion in *Optical Media* (2010: 207) that "there were no dreams of television before its development"—although what interests Hagen is not the old dream of "seeing at a distance" so much as Romantic ideas about electrical transmission. Another difference from Kittler is the larger role given to book printing in Hagen's historical model. For Hagen, scientific culture serves, following Niklas Luhmann, as a storage function to preserve improbable technical inventions. His chapter well illustrates the difference between media history written from a perspective kin to that of *Kulturtechnik* and that of traditional historiography, for it stresses the discontinuities and divergences between different social instances—science, culture, economics—rather than subsuming them under any hermeneutical totality. As Hagen puts it: "culture as the memory of society would not exist without the contingency of the medial." In the terms of the influential historian of science Hans-Jörg Rheinberger (2010), scientific culture serves to frame what are at first only poorly understood "epistemic objects" as matters that have discursive consequences. Until the mid-twentieth century, television remained only an epistemic object, not fully realized and thus partly latent in the history of media. The historical reasons for this latency are not solely technological. But Hagen's chapter also has even larger consequences for media and cultural history, for his account of the delay between the preconditions of television's invention circa 1900 and the final stabilizing of the medium in 1939 implies also that television may be seen as culturally regulating and controlling a potentially destructive "rupture in epistemology" as Hagen puts it in his chapter. The larger cultural shift from an alienated and protesting avant-garde before World War II and a "cooler," more distanced media culture after 1945 may be directly linked to television.

Larson Powell's chapter seeks to give an overview of several currents within contemporary German television theory. Thus German theory about television must be itself as historicized as the medium. Powell begins by examining the reasons why earlier variants of German media theory tended to marginalize television. With its seeming transparency, television did not suit the urge of media theorists like Kittler to give technological invention more weight than its social embedding in driving media history, nor did it tally with Kittler's emphasis on the constructivist and antimimetic dimension of media. TV's tendency to center its representations on individual persons also does not fit Kittler's antihumanism. In Kittler's view of media history (as also in that of Siegfried Zielinski), television is doomed to vanish into the black hole of the digital. However, as Hagen's previous chapter already showed, television's "third image" might be seen as an instance of recursivity within televisual technology, thus as a moment of *Kulturtechnik*. Powell's chapter concludes by considering the television theory of Lorenz Engell—the most important theoretician of TV in Germany today, but still little known to English readers—as an alternative mode of approaching TV technology, one indebted to Niklas Luhmann's sociological systems theory, but which also makes room for specific program analysis. Both Powell's and Hagen's chapters thus propose ways in which the transatlantic divide between older sociological theories of television and more recent *Medientheorie* might be bridged. If this does not yet mean a single unified Theory of Television, it does at least seek to mediate between differing theoretical approaches.

The next two chapters are concerned with GDR television and the tension between political demands made by the state and the imperative to develop a popular entertainment culture that could compete with that of West Germany and its television. (They also broach the topic of film and television, to be taken up both by Torner's chapter on GDR made-for-TV film and in Part III.) Thomas Beutelschmidt shows how the relations of television to film in the GDR were determined by political oppositions at the height of the Cold War in the 1950s; the relatively conservative and controlled function of television as mouthpiece of the Socialist Unity Party may be seen as the medium-specific manifestation of the GDR's hardline position relative to other, more liberal Eastern Bloc states like Poland or Hungary. Yet his chapter shows how the internal logic of the medium as dispositive nonetheless succeeded in establishing itself by the early 1960s, thanks to dramatic and literary adaptations, detective series, and increased live coverage of sports and other events. (In this, Beutelschmidt's conclusions are close to those of Heather Gumbrecht.) Early GDR television remained in tension between the "high cultural" claims of the first socialist German state to be the heir of its great bourgeois and Enlightenment ancestors on the one hand, and the need for popular acceptance on the other. If television remained "the medium of the fathers" (Henning Wrage) in the GDR, it had still to provide entertainment for the workers' and peasants' state and provide some degree of coverage of the everyday. In this tension, specific technical limitations—such as the inability of early TV to record and store its performances—worked together with a specifically German high cultural "heritage." Beutelschmidt's chapter ends circa 1960, at the time when TV became a mass medium in the GDR. Beutelschmidt's ideas could also be extended further into comparative Eastern Bloc television studies. For instance: was the comparatively liberal situation in Poland linked to specific TV policies?[8]

Evan Torner's contribution moves from a panoramic perspective to a close up on one particular production seen as emblematic of a moment in GDR TV history: Gottfried Kolditz's unfilmed project of 1984, *Zimtpiraten*, a swashbuckler adventure to have been made in collaboration between the FRG and the GDR. As does Beutelschmidt's chapter, Torner's also places GDR TV in the historical context of German-German relations and the pressures of the international market. Torner discusses the global and local forces affecting GDR film at the beginning of the 1980s, a time of "crisis" via confrontation with television. In the early 1980s, commercial television was introduced in the FRG and American blockbusters and series appeared on West German stations. In the end, cinema and television had to support each other on either side of the Wall with "safe" genre entertainment. Again we see here a tension between statist political imperatives and those of economic profitability within a larger Cold War nexus. Torner's chapter shows that the event TV discussed in Paul Cooke's chapter was already on the horizon by the 1980s, and that new entertainment and sports formats in television put considerable pressure on the politicized concept of East German broadcasting. The historical break of the *Wende* in 1989–90 thus needs to be understood as linked to changes in the media landscape occurring earlier in the decade. Torner's characterization of the relations between television and film in the GDR contrasts sharply with Brad Prager's discussion of those relations in the West.

In the third part of the book, we move to West German television and its relation to auteurist filmmaking, zooming in from broad panoramas to a closer focus on individual directors and their television projects. The example of Fassbinder and Kluge proves that—contrary to many commentators who have written off TV as a "zero degree style"—the medium does not forbid more politically and formally reflective approaches. Brad Prager's piece considers the early television work of Rainer Werner Fassbinder, whose 1972–73 television melodrama, *Eight Hours Are Not a Day*, was intended to influence working-class consciousness. Fassbinder then employed television as a medium to "engage dominant voices such as Hitchcock and Chabrol, and to bring out what was unspoken in their work." Scholars have long been aware of the crucial role played by television in New German Cinema, but Prager's intervention reveals both Fassbinder's engagement with expanding the possibilities of what television programming could mean and do as well as the filmmaker's own leftist political commitments. The chapter provides a detailed formal reading of *Martha*'s (and Fassbinder's) critique of marriage that doubles as a critique of the constraints of the medium.

In the next chapter Stefanie Harris turns to Alexander Kluge's television and, more recent, Internet projects. In *Public Sphere and Experience* (1993), Oskar Negt and Kluge already argued that television participates in the bourgeois public sphere in its contradictory attempt both to representatively reflect the entire world and to eliminate any information that disturbs this image of completeness. What forms of critique, they asked, might then serve to confront the apparatus of the television industry if the critique of television cannot be formulated in the predominant medium of the bourgeois public sphere (literature or journalism)? Kluge's own foray into alternative television productions in the 1980s (with the introduction of private television broadcasting) functions as a performative television criticism, constructed both to reveal latent forms of the industrial organization of consciousness and to interrupt them, and this within and alongside familiar broadcast material and programming. Through an analysis of individual television broadcasts and the dctp.tv Internet site, Harris examines how Kluge's work takes up the technological, industrial/economic, and political forces that shape the material conditions of production and distribution; the links between television and larger symbolic orders of social and political lives (or the public sphere); and the construction of meaning in traditional (and now Internet-based) television programming and production. With its theoretical dimensions, Harris's chapter also links back with the two chapters of the book's first part.

The final part of the book looks at German television after 1989, with an emphasis on the global and economic forces that have intensified since then, and the consequences these have had in terms of change in content and format exports. Rüdiger Steinmetz, too, treats of German cultural particularities in television usage, among them the strong tradition of communitarian ethics (something common to both East and West Germany during the Cold War) and the public role of churches in regulating media. One of peculiar features of television in divided Germany was the claim made by both sides to be representative of German *Kultur* as an undivided whole; this representative claim, despite its irreality in the face of actual political division and opposition, played a constitutive role in the self-understanding of the respective broadcasting systems (as it did with the BBC). The concept of culture had, in the German context, a strong ethical stamp, like the concept of *Bildung*; its practical realization was legally underpinned by crucial court decisions mentioned in Steinmetz's survey. The evolution of TV might be correlated to legal developments such as the new GDR constitution of 1968. The component of state and public regulation shared by both Germanies had thus a moral foundation in the country's cultural past. Again, in Steinmetz's chapter we can see how technical developments like the introduction of cable in the late 1970s changed the cultural conditions of TV programming. The conflicts Steinmetz delineates between cultural and business-driven models of television will seem familiar to the English-speaking reader who knows the similar opposition from the history of the BBC. What becomes clear from Steinmetz is that the commercial and not cultural model taken for granted by Americans was, in Germany, only a later development, and one that continues to meet with considerable bourgeois resistance.

Lothar Mikos's piece analyzes how German television imports were modeled on Great Britain and the United States. Major broadcasters ARD and ZDF acquired new stock from Great Britain and the United States, such as *Dallas* and *Dynasty*. ARD's *Lindenstrasse* and ZDF's *Die Schwarzwaldklinik* were modeled on these hit imports, establishing a new programming trend. In 1999, the popularity of *Who Wants to Be a Millionaire?* led to more quiz shows on all major networks. In 2000,

Big Brother marked the beginning of the trend towards "reality" shows. Thus the German television market developed a momentum driven mainly by licensing and imitating standardized international formats. Mikos contextualizes this import structure via the globalization of the TV market and media politics in Germany. If Hagen's chapter could be called technically hard-wired in its close attention to the evolution of inventions, Mikos's is the chapter most aware of economic factors and of television's function as global entertainment. The conclusions reached in this chapter are similar to those of recent work done on global television in English by Joseph Straubhaar (2007, especially chapters 7 and 8 on international genre markets) and Tim Havens (2006). The new series and shows Mikos discusses may have become popular through their specifically German themes or topics, yet their debt to US or UK models betrays an international fingerprint.

Paul Cooke's contribution moves beyond readings of recent German "historical event television" in terms of authentic German history. Instead he situates television productions by the successful studio *teamWorx* such as *Dresden* (2006) or *Die Flucht* (2007) in terms of Daniel Dayan und Elihu Katz's work on "media events." In this analysis, historical veracity gives way to a producing a sense of community and identity in a transnational context. The reenacted spectacle of the firebombing of Dresden allows Germans to identify with a sense of victimhood, whether of catastrophes or war. Television thus has an important part in the refashioning of Germans' self-understanding as a nation after unification. The shift in German memory often registered with some concern by professional historians—from the critical self-examinations of the 1970s to a normalized reconciliation with the past via empathy since the 1980s (Jarausch and Geyer 2003: 10–11)—thus has its specific medial coefficient.

Bärbel Stolz's concluding chapter on *Tatort* contextualizes this most famous of all German television series, which involved cooperation between regional broadcasters to give individual episodes local specificity, right from its inception in 1971. Thus the federal structure of German broadcasting left its mark on the way the entire series has been conceived. Detective series played an important role in establishing television as a popular mass medium in both Germanies, and *Tatort* has survived the media upheavals of unification to remain an emblematic show for the entire nation, including former DEFA stars like Manfred Krug. Due to its longevity, *Tatort* has created a visual archive of German society, making it an ideal case study for how German public television has represented politics, gender norms, and societal evolution over time, thus proving itself a culturally adaptable medium. Recent episodes illustrate *Tatort*'s relevance to the politics of tolerance in Germany, while revealing the series' audience-driven censoring process.

Although the present volume covers many different aspects of German television, it cannot hope to be exhaustive. The field of television research in Germany continues to evolve: while more sociological studies of programming are published, practitioners of *Medientheorie* are beginning to overcome their long aversion to the medium (Grisko and Münker 2009), and the changes in the medium itself effected by digitalization and pay TV are being analyzed (Kretzschmar and Mundhenkel 2012). Readers with knowledge of German will want to complement the historical chapters here with Knut Hickethier's encyclopedic *Geschichte des Fernsehens in Deutschland*; the extensive German literature on television also includes books dedicated to specific televisual genres, such as news broadcasting (with its specifically German subgenre of the *Magazin*) or situation comedies, which we have not had space to discuss in detail here. Another important topic is the role of national (and transnational) television within the European Union, and its function in defining a public sphere for the latter. Thanks to their shared German language, Germany's ZDF (Second Channel), Austria's ORF (Austrian Broadcasting), and Swiss SRG SSR (Swiss Broadcasting) were able to team up as 3sat in 1984, joined in 1990 by former East German broadcaster DFF. The resulting public TV network, with its focus on advertising-free cultural programming, is unique in Europe as a forum reaching across national boundaries.

Future Perspectives

The literature on television in German is already hard to grasp in its entirety and thus difficult to sum up in generalizations. (Larson Powell's chapter suggests some of the larger tendencies within the field.) Theoretically speculative approaches coexist with more empirical and sociological research. Specific genres, from the characteristic political *Magazin* to comedy and advertisement, have received detailed treatment, as has the overall generic system.[9] Many publications have been concerned with audience research, political fallout, or other social effects of television; others deal with legal or economic questions. If one includes industry publications and the metadiscourse of TV guides (like *Hör zu*), the field expands even further. From a North American

Germanist or media historical perspective, there are, however, certain possibilities that immediately come to mind.

Firstly, more studies of the interdependence of film and television, following the example of Jane Shattuc's 1990s work on Fassbinder, could be done.[10] Our view of East German cultural figures such as Jurek Becker and Frank Beyer might be changed by greater attention to the work both of them did for GDR TV. Literature, too, could be freshly illuminated by putting it in intermedial context: Henning Wrage's *Die Zeit der Kunst* offers an example of how one might link the study of literature and film to that of television. Frank Kelleter's recent anthology *Populäre Serialität* (2012) also traces the origins of TV's serial formats back to nineteenth-century literature. What effects did the broadcasting of *Das literarische Quartett* (1988–2001) have on West German literary production, and how did its functions as arbiter of taste differ from those of older print literary magazines?[11] Secondly, as Heather Gumbert has noted, cultural history in general has not often included television, either. Could one imagine work on television and music or literature that would make the connections Kittler did among the gramophone, film, radio, and the written word? Is there something televisual about the aesthetic of the postwar *nouveau roman*? How did television aid in disseminating the work of the Frankfurt School, whose members (despite their skepticism about the medium) were more present on TV than Heidegger or Jaspers? What role did TV play in May '68?[12]

Including television would, at very least, mean a different marking of epochal boundaries in German postwar cultural history. Thus the television theorist Lorenz Engell (Engell et al. 2004) has argued that 1950 marks a decisive caesura in the history of the twentieth century. Finally, the inclusion of television in media theory and history requires that one revise some of the assumptions of the best-known German *Medientheorien*, including that of Friedrich Kittler (as Larson Powell argues in this volume). Part of the difficulty with television studies has been its disciplinary location in communication studies departments (where knowledge of German is not always common, and where older cultural-studies models of media studies from the 1970s still dominate); the project Germans call *Medienkulturwissenschaft* would thus have no self-evident *Sitz im Leben* in North American universities. That literary and cultural theories in US humanities have become increasingly anti-sociological—while American sociology departments are ever more quantitative and antitheoretical—is another obstacle to the cross-disciplinary work needed for television. But the popular word "culture" in US Germanist scholarship will remain blindly attached to traditional notions of culture as long as television is not included. Paradoxically, the inclusion of television (as a *Kulturtechnik*) might imply an expansion of "culture" without Kittler's polemical "expulsion of the spirit from humanities."[13] In many ways, Kittler's work can be seen as a last-ditch attempt of High Theory to defend itself against the disseminatory effects of television;[14] such a view would make his later turn to Greece and Homer less surprising than it first seemed. Whether the future of German television studies will lie with speculative syntheses such as Fahle and Engell's *Philosophie des Fernsehens*, or with an incorporation of television into overarching historical analyses of cultural techniques,[15] remains to be seen. An English-language perspective on German television theory may, however, be able to bridge over, or at least reflect on, some of the divisions within this theory more easily than an inner-German one. Since this is the first volume in English covering so many different aspects of German television, and since the chapters cover not only technical or media-specific features of television, but also its larger cultural context, it is hoped that the book may be useful both for media historians and also those interested in German cultural and social history. Television, arguably one of the driving forces of post-1945 modernization, indeed offers an inclusive lens or prism through which to view twentieth- and twenty-first-century Germany.

Larson Powell is Professor of German at the University of Missouri, Kansas City. His latest book, *The Differentiation of Modernism: Postwar German Media Arts,* was published by Camden House in 2013. Other recent work includes a volume on classical music in East Germany co-edited with Kyle Frackman (Rochester, NY: Camden House, 2015), and essays on film music, musicology, and Eastern European film. Current research includes a monograph on Konrad Wolf and a book on German-Polish relations.

Robert Shandley is Professor of German and Head of the Department of International Studies at Texas A&M University. His work includes *Hogan's Heroes* (Detroit: Wayne State University Press, 2011 TV Milestone Series), *Runaway Romances: Hollywood's Postwar European Tour* (Philadelphia: Temple University Press, 2009) and *Rubble Films: German Cinema in the Shadow of the Third Reich* (Philadelphia: Temple University Press, 2001).

Notes

1. Stanley Cavell made the same diagnosis (1982).
2. For discussion, see the first issue of the periodical *Kulturtechnik: Zeitschrift für Medien- und Kulturforschung* (2010), especially 101–220. This journal is associated with the Bauhaus University in Weimar and edited by Lorenz Engell and Bernhard Siegert.
3. See also Giessmann 2006 and Barkoff, Böhme, and Riou 2004.
4. An instance of this transitional use of the term "culture" would be Doelker 1989.
5. A similar statement is made by Fahle and Engell (2006: 9).
6. English readers might compare Hagen's essay to the work of Bruno Latour and Steve Woolgar on scientific cultures (1986), although Hagen does not share the politicized perspective of many practitioners of STS (Science and Technology Studies).
7. Burns's three distinct periods are: the era of "speculation (1877 to c. 1922)," low definition television (1926–1935), and high definition television (1936 onward). Hagen's choice of historical landmarks for television's development—Alexander Bain, the discovery of selenium, Nipkow's rotating disc, the cathode ray tube—can however all be (empirically) correlated with Burns's history. See also Abramson 1987.
8. See Haltof 2002, which discusses the TV work of Wajda (120) and Zanussi (128); in Polish, among other works, Trzynadlowski 1992.
9. For a cognitive-psychological look at how audiences identify genres (as opposed to traditional textual genre studies), see Gehrau 2001.
10. On Wenders and television: Beier 1996 and Deeken 2004. On recent film and television, see Halle 2008, esp. chapter 6; Cooke 2012, esp. chapter 1, discussing television's role in film financing; also Elsaesser 2005.
11. On the representation of TV journalism in German fiction, see Nitsch 2011.
12. See Klimke and Scharloth 2007.
13. As John Durham Peters's wittily titled "Die Zurücktreibung der Medien in die Geisteswissenschaften" (2010) implies: Kittler's antihumanism could paradoxically only have had the shock value it did in the German context, where *Medientheorie* had much less contact with the social sciences than in the United States, and where "Geisteswissenschaften" were traditionally more media-blind.
14. The link between television and dissemination (in Derrida's sense) is a central topic of Dienst's book, which—like Lorenz Engell's work—seeks to show how television is "theoretical" without making its theory explicit. This is the reason why Alexander Kluge has asserted that television cannot be "criticized" outside its own form.
15. An interesting possibility would be to see television as one among modern "cultural techniques of synchronization," as a recent German book has it (Kassung and Macho 2013; Michael Wedel's chapter, "Risse im 'Erlebnis-System,' Tonfilm, Synchronisation, Audiovision um 1930" (309–38) is particularly relevant to TV). This is another way of viewing James Beniger's "control revolution" (1986), but it also links up with Luhmann's central notion of the simultaneity of systems.

PART I

TECHNICAL PREHISTORY AND THEORETICAL APPROACHES

Chapter 1

THE THIRD IMAGE

Contingencies and Ruptures in
the Technological History of Television

Wolfgang Hagen

Seen from the viewpoint of the history of science, television history is marked by three breaks [*Zäsuren*], and it would certainly exceed the limits of this paper to trace each of them in detail. We may, however, at least give a brief sketch of them in order to explicate the context of the present chapter's thesis. This paper argues that television, the beginnings of which may be dated to 1939, depended on the technical construction and technological realization of a third image that has remained epistemologically largely ungrasped. This means that television begins its triumphal procession through history from just that point in time when the knowledge that makes it technically possible lags after the artifacts it has construed. In a certain sense, this knowledge lag persists even today.

With this, we have named one of the three breaks already—namely, the last up to now, which can be dated to the year 1939. In that year, the first comprehensive electronic television system in the world was presented to the world by RCA in New York at the world exhibition. Camera systems, production of receivers, and broadcasting chains were simultaneously launched. It was the last world exhibition before the atomic bomb, and also one of the largest and most forgotten, if one measures it against the illusions it generated. In the same year, its traces were effaced by wars in Europe and Japan. All that remained of its visions was television.

It may be surprising that—from the perspective of this essay—there have been no further caesuras, even in the domain of digital optics. In fact, the digital chip found since the 1980s in all cameras, whether for photography or TV, does not constitute a further epistemological caesura with regard to television. This digital CCD-chip, which admittedly opens completely new operative dimensions to our photography and films, is, from the point of view of industry history, itself the child of TV research, and thus presumes the medium of TV already. What digital images everywhere offer us today was developed as the optimization of an element already defined by electronic television in 1939, namely, the "stored picture," also named in some patents the "electrical image." The Charged Coupled Device (CCD-chip for short), first described in 1970, was the result of the organized research of an applied and developed domain of knowledge, the quantum mechanics of solid state physics. From the beginning this chip served the purpose of building a video or still-image storage for TV cameras. The electronic cameras of 1939 already contained a "stored image," i.e. a third stored image, albeit not in this now scientistically [*szientivisch*] perfectly conceived form of the CCD-chip.

In the image technology of the twentieth century, it is not digitalization that constitutes the decisive caesura, but rather the first, purely electronically produced image of television from 1939. Only in a further step, which is only logical from the point of view of the history of science, does one fall back on digitalization's concept and technology. (Digitalization, as a mathematical "sampling of frequencies," goes back to Fourier's work of 1823.)

Defining Technical Media

These introductory considerations have already given some preliminary hints about the concepts of contingency and caesura, which are decisive for understanding the history of technology. Since TV marks a very late medial caesura in modernity, a cursory look back at its origins may be helpful. Technical media emerge from the history of knowledge as a contingent caesura, usually as an act of considerable, surprising, and often completely unrecognized improbability. Precisely for this reason technical media are "technical." It would be imprecise, to say the least, to call the alphabetic script already a technical medium. Certainly the qualification of contingency and extreme improbability holds true for the formation of Western alphabets. But what we call knowledge first arose together with this last. If we declare the subsequent arisal of media from 1600 on to be contingent in the sense of a caesura of knowledge, then a concept of knowledge, structured and ordered according to book-form writing, is already assumed. We can only speak of technical media with reference to modern media [*Medien der Neuzeit*], which, as is well known, begin with book printing.

Niklas Luhmann is entirely right to maintain that book printing, circa 1450, would never have been able to expand without its embedding in an already developed money economy and a differentiated European trade system. Other cultures already had printed books, but precisely no book printing. In Europe, it took nearly 150 years for book printing as a medium to make its mark as a caesura in science. That process began around 1600 with the formatting of knowledge as a modern science, which is strictly coupled to this originary medium of the book to this day. The technical medium of book printing thus establishes an expanded frame for the contingency of all subsequent medial caesuras. From this point on, technical media mark caesuras not only in knowledge, but also, in the same way, in that formation of knowledge called science. This is especially true for the double invention of photography and telegraphy around 1830, with which—in the strict sense of a media-scientific marking of caesurae—modernity already begins. The contingence of this is first perceived when one identifies its entry into the field of knowledge and science, already stamped by book printing.

To use Luhmann's terms: technical media are, after their highly unlikely arisal, converted into the likelihood of preservation ensured by a culture of knowledge and science. Here it is a question neither of positive knowledge nor of scientific truth. In the case of telegraphy, for instance, it took decades to implement it in cultural, economic, and political terms as a superior form of communication, despite all its incomprehensible flaws and functional weaknesses. This was done without understanding, in the sense of a scientific truth function, why and how telegraphy actually functioned. Telegraphy functioned for decades—in fact, for almost the entire nineteenth century—as a "blind" knowledge, and produced within its force field a parallel discursive world in the form of "modern spiritism." To speak of contingent caesuras in knowledge means also to speak of caesuras in ignorance and uncertainty. It is a matter of contingencies that open up new contexts in which—without further grounds and often quite suddenly—"something" appears and exists and may be described on the level of perception and world, may be built and used while remaining at the same time scientifically "untrue," inconsistent, uncertain, and approximate. This "something" is technical, and it exists materially and functionally, but cannot be addressed with a truth function within the discourses coupled in the field of science. Nonetheless this "something" is anchored in a function, economically, militarily, and politically, and thus also in the memory of a culture. Modern media [*Medien der Neuzeit*] are, since they are contingent caesuras in knowledge, as irreversible as writing. Their entropy is irreversible and thus not a negentropy.[1] Culture as the memory of society would not exist without the contingency of the medial. Yet no one knows what this has achieved. Only one thing is sure: technical media can only be destroyed together with the culture and society in which they contingently arose. In this far-reaching sense, one can also call them artifacts of articulation or—in a narrow sense of history of science—"epistemic things," to use an expression of Hans-Jörg Rheinberger (1997).

First Caesura: Photography/Electricity/Telegraphy

The history of tele-media begins with just such an "epistemic thing," a completely contingent artifact. This beginning lies much further back in the past than most histories of television would have one believe. The first caesura that is decisive for television history is marked by what Georg Christoph Lichtenberg offered to the scientific world in 1777 in six sensationally illustrated essays—those peculiar figures of resinous dust that he found by chance, due to the presence of resinous dirt in his laboratory. The arisal of these figures is thus completely contingent. They show figures of positive and negative charges of static electricity.

These were images of the discharge of an electrophorus, a device well known in the scientific world of its day, and found in hundreds of labs in all of Europe. Through experiments with this electrophorus, Alessandro Volta, who worked closely with Lichtenberg, found his way quite logically to his discovery of the electrochemical production of a flowing current in 1800—that is, what we now call a battery. There is no space here to explicate the connection between electrophorus and battery, but it is anything but improbable or uncertain. Sooner or later, the discovery of small currents from electrolytic sources made by Volta would have been likely, as long as one refined the electrophorus as an instrument to measure atmospheric currents, as Volta and Lichtenberg did. But Lichtenberg's figures remained completely improbable, uncertain, not understood, and contingent, both in 1777 and afterward.

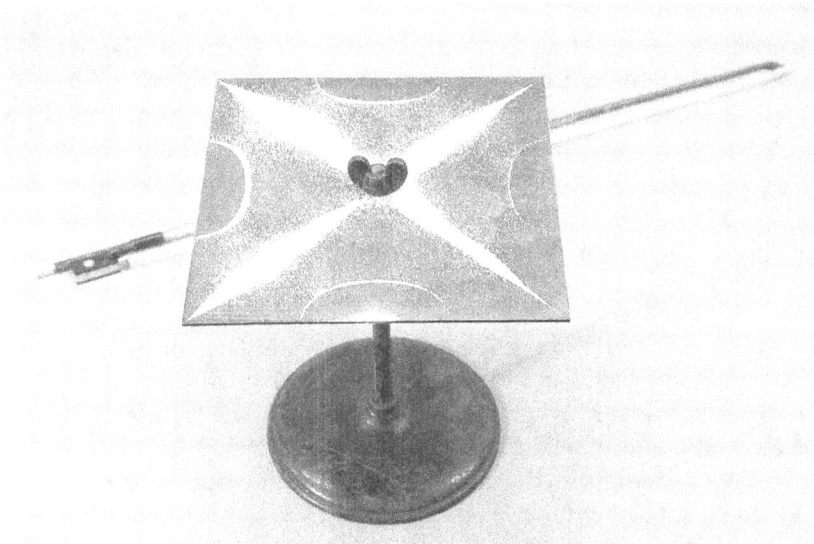

Figure 1.1. Vibrating plate of the kind developed by acoustician Ernst Florenz Chladni. Image courtesy of the Smithsonian Institution.

Twenty years later, Novalis included these figures of Lichtenberg in the "great ciphered writing" of nature's self-description, once the acoustician Ernst Florenz Chladni, following Lichtenberg, had placed the self-description of tones and sound on the agenda of Romantic philosophy of nature.[2] How could photography and telegraphy, the most important new media of the nineteenth century, arise in such temporal proximity to each other, almost simultaneously in the 1830s? One answer would be that they both sprang from the same insistent epistemological uncertainty, and mark their caesuras in it nearly at the same time. For, the uncertainty generated by Lichtenberg's figures from 1777 did not lead to their explanation. Only atomic physics could clarify and explain them in the twentieth century. The uncertainty of Lichtenberg's figures, and thus of a self-describing ciphered writing of nature, remained a constant in Romantic philosophy of nature, namely in the so-called speculative physics of early Schelling and German idealism as a whole. While searching for self-imagings of electricity and its polar, dual-dialectical qualities, Christian Oerstedt, a Romantic philosopher and physicist, discovered the electrodynamic effects of electrical currents in 1820. With this, the decisive epistemological precondition for telegraphy was found, namely that a constant electrical current has a magnetic effect.

The simultaneity of appearance of these two main media of the nineteenth century, photography and electricity, followed a characteristic tendency of Romantic philosophy of nature to self-similar[3] experiments with the uncertainty of techniques for nature's self-inscription. Thus Oersted discovered the electrodynamic effect that Andre-Marie Ampere immediately addressed[4] as the first electrodynamic law of modernity. From this there followed immediately the construction of the first pointer telegraph by Ampere himself. The self-similar experiment with the uncertainty of a self-transcribing nature is, however, also the reason why photography was brought into the world by the two leading scientific academies of Europe in 1839—in Paris, Daguerre's invention, presented by Arago; and in London, shortly thereafter so as not to be shown up, Talbot's invention, presented by Michael Faraday. For both the Paris Academy and the Royal Society in London, photography is above all a scientific medium, something since then all too often forgotten due to an overemphasis on culture and art.

This inner epistemological coupling of photography and telegraphy explains how the Scottish clockmaker and instrument builder Alexander Bain was already able in 1843, thus simultaneously with Morse's telegraph in the United States, to exhibit the first machine for transmission of images. Telegraphy was from the beginning not only a matter of writing and Morse code. Charles Wheatstone, the founder of the English telegraph system, had also already developed such a patent in 1940.

Here is—once more from the early years of telegraphy—the image telegraph of Frederick Bakewell from 1848. Its principle is the burning-in of a picture with nonconducting ink, which is then electromagnetically scanned in order to appear on the receiver's end as a stamped image.

The whole was perfected in the 1860s by the pan-telegraph of Giovanni Caselli, with which handwritten texts, written with nonconducting ink, could be transmitted, along with other images etched in copper.

Among the heirs of the uncertainty of Lichtenberg's figures in the knowledge of Romantic philosophy of nature, we may also count, of course, the connection between light and electricity. That which remained still unclear in Lichtenberg's figures was out of the question for photography. That photography was obviously due to a chemical light effect had been described by the academies in Paris und London. However, one had no explanation for the brute fact of it, as the secretary Arago had to admit.

Edmond Becquerel's discovery resulted inexorably from these self-similar, uncertain experiments with light and electricity that had been initiated by the Romantic philosophy of nature. His discovery of 1839 was that light causes a photovoltaic reaction. The incursion of light into a chemical flow cell brings forth a flowing current, which is very weak and thus unusable. But it belonged henceforth to the formatted knowledge of the community of researchers. It is the same effect that today converts light into electrical energy on our roofs, in the form of solar cells.

This all still belongs to that first large epistemological caesura to which TV owes its existence. TV arises, with regard to this first enabling caesura, from the coupling of uncertainty about the connection of light, self-ciphering of nature, and electricity. For the uncertainty about the origin of electrical currents in Becquerel's electrolytic apparatus was not greater than that in the electricity-theoretical origin of Lichtenberg's figures in 1777. Today it has been established in the history of science that the development of the theory of electricity did not arise from the certainties offered by the classical theories of Newton or analytical mechanics, but rather from the great and even catastrophic uncertainties occurring with the application of the medium of telegraphy. At the end of the 1860s, England had numerous oceanic cables at its disposal, crossing over the entire world, and could thus base its financial power and the Commonwealth-Empire upon this. These same ocean cables, however, functioned rather badly in a technical sense. Measured by today's standards, they were more or less dysfunctional. They operated with signal errors that could not be explained theoretically. Signals either disappeared or only arrived in weak and distorted form. The search for the causes of these defects—once again an operation in the realm of uncertainty—were what helped Maxwell's theory of electricity to its breakthrough at the end of the century. Generations of electricians and physicists were occupied with looking for the cause of bad transmissions from 1850 on, and one of them found a further building block that would be essential for the development of television—namely, selenium.

Selenium was first described in 1873 as a semiconductive metal that conducts a current especially well when sun shines on it and particularly badly when stored in the dark. Werner von Siemens developed a photometer from this, and we can imagine what significance this element would have for television.

The last and most significant element found through experimental research in the extremely uncertain context of light and electricity came from Heinrich Hertz. While systematically exploring a chance discovery that led finally to the discovery of radio waves, Hertz discovered that sparks discharged at the tip of a metal rod were especially strong and bright when ultraviolet light fell on them. Hertz could not explain this effect, but he described beyond all doubt how it occurred in his first publication of 1887. It was the experimental working out of this effect that would lead to the establishment of the completely electronic television in 1939. At first, however, smaller devices were built, called photocells, which technically exploited the effect. If light falls on the light-sensitive metal on the right side of the small glass bulb, a measurable current arises, which can be conducted out through the wire circle on the left side.

Second Caesura: Telephony and Mechanical TV

The second caesura to which television is due has a name from the history of technology: the "mechanical television." Mechanical television makes its entry onstage (via the elements just described) only when the telephone begins to conquer the world, after 1876 and no earlier.

Alexander Graham Bell was, however, anything but a physicist, as we should remember; instead he was an autodidactic researcher of deaf-mutes and a language teacher. The experimental history of the telephone is thus one of the most curious and improbable developmental narratives in the field of scientific uncertainty that the nineteenth century can offer us. Whoever wants to find out more precisely how extrascientific knowledge, confusions, and gross misunderstandings force their way into science and allow a scientific outsider the most improbable thing, namely the discovery of the telephone, should read Bell's lab books. When Bell presented his completed discovery, however, he thereby proved the theory of electricity that had previously been at once the most exotic and also the sole correct one, without himself having the slightest inking of it: the theory of James Clerk Maxwell. Only twelve years later did Heinrich Hertz prove the experimental validity of this theory. Shortly before his death, none other than Maxwell himself honored the teacher Bell in a great lecture. Bell suddenly became even more famous than Maxwell himself had been during his lifetime.

With the contingent "invention" of the Bell telephone, extrascientific knowledge (press articles, "public opinions") decisively intervened via the person of the inventor into the science and technology of the nineteenth century. After tele-hearing and tele-speech, which Bell introduced to physics and the history of technology, television became a relevant motivation and reason for research in a general cultural sense,

The Third Image 25

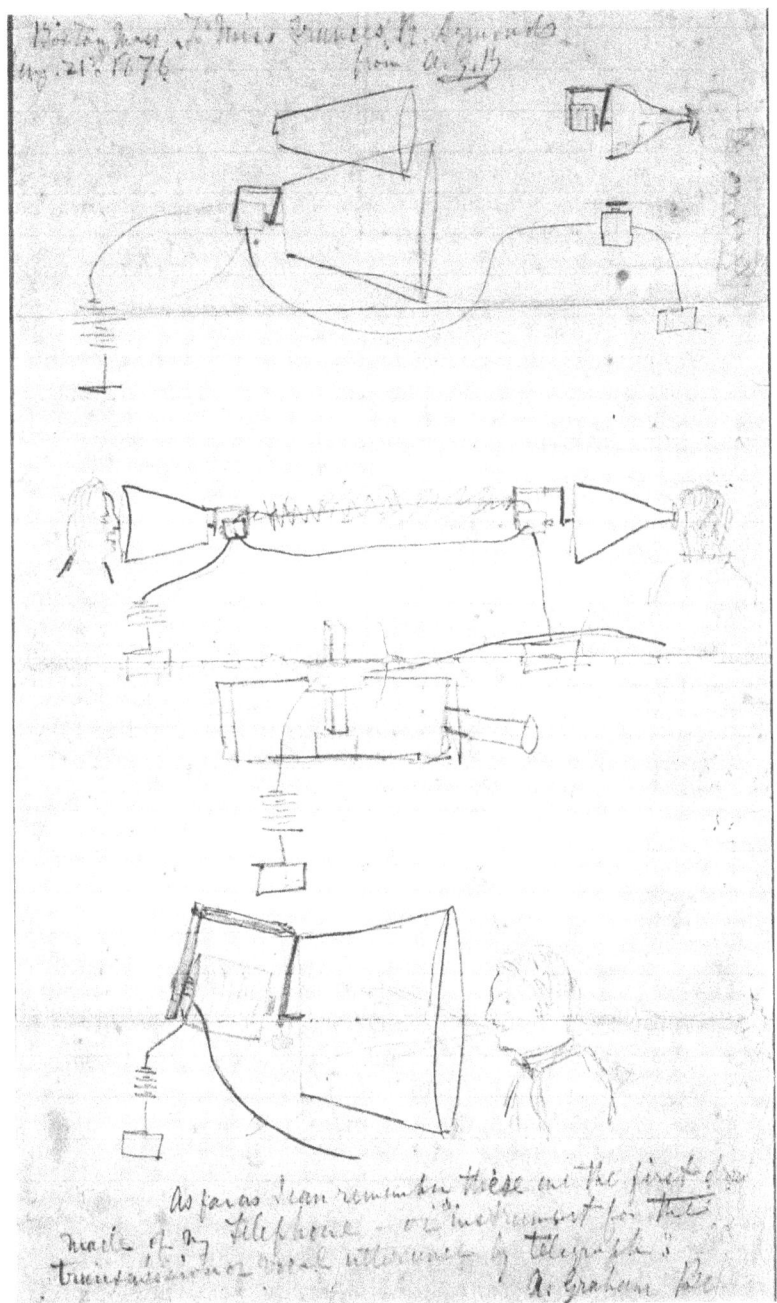

Figure 1.2. Early drawing of the telephone by Alexander Graham Bell, 1876. Image courtesy of the Library of Congress, Manuscript Division.

as we can see from Paul Nipkow's patent. Television became relevant in the sense of the construction of a telephone-like apparatus.

> Since the task of transmitting tones and even articulated sounds across vast distances has been solved in such an astonishingly simple way by Reis, Bell and other distinguished researchers, certain inventively gifted men have set themselves a further task well suited to arouse the same interest. It is the task of creating a device which, just as the telephone does for the ear, gives the eye the possibility of perceiving things far outside its natural sphere of activity. (Nipkow 1885)

To this end, he made use of "familiar things," such as perforated discs, which were only too familiar from acoustical physics since Seebeck's overtone experiments of 1841. Nipkow literally turned these acoustic discs around into the optical domain. The same device that was once built for hearing siren tones was now meant to enable the electromagnetic viewing of images.

Spiral-shaped holes are made on the Nipkow disc, rotating in front of the object to be transmitted, which in this way is sampled, hole for hole. Behind each hole that lets through a brief light pulse, selenium is mounted, which produces a current proportional to the strength of light, and then produced on the receiver's end by a light bulb. This receiving bulb must itself stand behind a perforated disc that revolves synchronously with that of the transmitter. Mechanical television, reckoned from its beginnings in 1884, remained for some fifty years—until the mid-1930s—the dominant paradigm of development. But even before World War I, scientists and engineers had described the instability of this undertaking clearly enough.

In order to reach a resolution that would produce a moving image sufficiently coherent for the human eye, the English electrical engineer Alan Archibald Campbell Swinton calculated in 1908 that one would need 160,000 synchronous sampling operations per second. Yet with even the best application of mechanical techniques, 160,000 sampling and reproductive operations could never be exactly synchronized via means such as rotating perforated irises and carefully worked out mirror reflex constructions. However, the mechanical epistemologies prevalent in England and Germany, and deeply ingrained in the minds of hundreds of thousands of engineers and scientists, were for long decades deaf to these objections. In the prevalent thinking about mechanics and ontology, Europeans continued for another quarter century to understand television as a pendant to telephony, trying to force their way towards it with mechanical means.

The Third Image: A Hidden Epistemological Paradox

This dead end was already corrected one year later, on the occasion of the Berlin Olympics, by the import of an American receiving tube called the Iconoscope. This latter had no mechanical parts. It constructed, purely electronically, a "third" image within the receiving tube of the TV camera. With this, we have arrived at the third and decisive caesura that enables TV in its present form. Its object is nonobjectivity, pure and simple.

We are speaking of the electron, that subatomic particle J. J. Thomson had discovered in 1897 in a cathode ray tube of the same type that Ferdinand Braun had presented to the world in Karlsruhe, at the same time. With this combination of measurable invisibility and an immeasurable effect of visibility, which is bound up with a logic and phenomenology of the non-unobservable, television arises. As concerns the electron, it was true from the day of its discovery that one could measure it and weigh it (as Thomson already did), and determine its charge, therefore its energy, along with its place, via the traces it left behind. But one cannot see the electron in question when measuring it. Its appearance is, according to our contemporary knowledge, a quantum effect, dependent on a probability function. It is certainly ironic that in the same year, in two different tubes in different places in the world, the electron's measurable existence and, parallel to this, its directable visibility became a part of our knowledge. One can only see the electron if one is not measuring it, and can thus only determine one of its local qualities. It was with the electron that Heisenberg proposed his uncertainty principle. This latter states that in the measuring process of the electron, at least one quality must remain undefined. For television and its technical arisal, the uncertainty principle plays no role. But for the epistemology of the particles, on the interdependency of which it is based, that principle indeed plays a part. Braun's invention described the cathode ray tube as a screen, a describable and paintable surface, which produces as its effect a cathode ray that is free of inertia and magnetically directable. With this, we still watch television today. Braun had put fluorescent materials on the inner right edge of the bulb that briefly made the discharge ray of the cathode tube glow. Thomson's discovery had the same tube as Braun's, but not prepared for seeing, rather for measuring. There is nothing to see here.

Thomson measured the energy of the ray that he sent through the tube and determined through its various angles of deflection the energy and mass of the particles of which it consisted. It was a brilliant experiment, but within the knowledge of the science of which Thomson was the child, it was only consequential and logically determined. It was only the result of this experiment that made an epistemological world first crumble and then collapse. For from now on, since 1897, seeing meant measuring, and the ontology of the electric meant that either the measurable exists, or nothing at all. Around the turn of the century, we might say, a constructed world began to dawn. It is in the process of losing its basis in being, if in an important part of its knowledge seeing is replaced by measuring (and without alternative)—or, in simple English, if the world disappears in favor of a construction of the world through observation. This is not to maintain that constructivism is established in intellectual history around 1900. Precisely through not asserting this, we can point to the unimaginably huge and destructive forces in the intellectual and cultural world of the first half of the twentieth century. Eccentricity, madness, suffering from alienation, the excesses of death and destruction, but also that otherworldly force of the avant-garde in art—this may be explained by the fact that from 1900 on, there is a rupture in epistemology that remained unremarked for decades, up to the 1950s, although it is based already in this rupture in Thomson's experiment.

Thomson introduced an energetically exactly measurable and almost inertia-free particle into the world of science and technology around 1900. This particle was nonetheless easily manipulable according to traditional laws of electrical currents, while remaining invisible, and interacting with light—the matter of the visible—in the most exquisite fashion. A hectic activity arose among the physicists who were concerned with photographic cells. Could light actually produce electrons from metals? Yes, it could, as Philipp Lenard, the assistant to Heinrich Hertz, already definitely proved in 1910. Before World War I, the two fundamental empirical laws of photoelectrics were already founded on his measurements, which were in no way inferior to Thomson's:

1. The number of electrons per temporal unit that stream out of a photoelectric surface is proportional to the intensity of light.
2. The energy, i.e., speed of the electrons given off by a photoelectric surface is not dependent on light intensity, but rather on its frequency, thus on its color.

With these two laws, electronic television could be realized. We owe the medium of 1939 to a Russian who had immigrated to the United States, Vladimir Kozmich Zworykin.[5] Zworykin, a deeply educated physicist from the school of Thomson and Lenard, had on the basis of both of Lenard's laws already written a patent in 1923 that would make television possible. It is the patent for the third image, an image stored between the others and constructed from electrons, which must arise in order that distant light become televisual light. If one proceeds determinedly enough to construct the visible from the invisible, the structure of Zworykin's camera is quickly understood. Light rays from an image fall through a lens onto a very fine mosaic of photocells. There are roughly 370,000 small cells on this mosaic, to be precise: silver drops containing cesium. These droplets react to light by discharging electrons (according to Lenard's laws), and they flow over the signal plate. Now the cathode ray tube comes into play, set up at an open angle to the plate of droplets. In precisely two seconds, it sweeps exactly 525 times over the plate of droplets, from left to right, with millimeter precision, and leads the electron charge they had lost from the light back to the droplets with a deft switching. Proportional to this, the discharged electrons flow out of the signal plate in the form of definite quantities of charge. On the receiver end, on the screen—that is, a Braun tube—a cathode ray sweeps, completely synchronous and at the same interval [*Takt*], 525 times every two seconds over the screen, line by line. In doing so, this ray is regulated with utmost precision by the outflowing charges on the camera's signal plate.

With this we have a televisual image based on the construction of a third, unseen image. Period. The World Exposition is opened. Contrast and sharpness may still be improved. Quantum effects play no role in any of this. In Zworykin's books, which explain his invention in detail for anyone else to reconstruct, there is no mention of quantum mathematics. He had no need for them. Television does not need atomic physics. One need understand nothing of the double-slit experiment to understand television. One also need understand nothing of the uncertainty principle, nothing of Einstein, Bose, Fermi, or Dirac, in order to grasp how television in its epistemology radically calculates the electronic down to the electric, addresses electron flows as quantities of charge, and thereby gets by with nineteenth-century mathematics. This is the secret of its rapid success, for the armies of technicians around 1940, who had all been educated according the state of knowledge of telegraphic electricity from the nineteenth century, did not have to relearn in order to apply the characteristics of TV in hundreds of factories and workshops and to build televisions and cameras on an assembly line.

And yet there remains a break in the epistemology of the electronic. One can apply the mutual reactions of light photons and electrons and their reconversion into light impulses on the fluorescent screen without the slightest knowledge of the phenomenological lag that remains. This is the scandal of the epistemology of the electronic in the twentieth century. It permits and enables technique of medial image construction and thereby hides its epistemological impact at the same time. If one asks more closely, persistently, and fundamentally than is necessary for the foreground technical function of TV, why and exactly how light photons interact with silver electrons that are mixed with cesium atoms, then there is no getting around quantum mechanics and their foundation in quantum physics. But then one finds oneself epistemologically already amid the virulent argument between analytic philosophy and philosophy of science that still goes on today, as Richard Rorty (2000) resumed it in his speech for the hundredth birthday of Gadamer. The "techies," like Saul Kripke and David Lewis, view electrons and elementary particles as ontologically given, as irrefutable facts in nature, which are not given *de dicto,* but rather *de re.*[6] The "fuzzies," like David Putnam, Ian Hacking, Bruno Latour, and others, believe that the definition of elementary particles is a construction of observation and designation, to which one could add others that might be different, but equally valid. It is beyond dispute that the descriptions we now have of the electron are the only successful ones (in the sense of technical construction). The "techies" among American philosophers are thus downright enthusiastic about these successes and their consequences. They would like to enchant us with cosmologies of the Big Bang, or trouble us with possible conclusions as to really existing parallel universes. The "fuzzies," among them Rorty himself, practice a looser nominalism and look for a more balanced discourse, for anti-metaphysical consensus and linguistic solidarity.

In media epistemological terms, there are two consequences to be drawn from the considerations presented here. First, we may state again that the televisual image, as it arose in 1939, was based on the technical construction of a third image. Television's third image is a pure construction of electrical effects and thus no continuation of the image of the camera obscura. The light falling into the camera and the image that results no longer come out, nor do they cast any illumination or glow (in the sense of illumination) upon anything. What we see on the flickering screen of our sets is not that which enters the camera. It is rather the sampling and electrical measuring of an intermediary image, an invisible storage, a technical icon—to formulate it precisely, television operates as an electronic iconoscope. The constructors of this technology [*Technik*] turned *expressis verbis* away from the preceding attempts at mechanical television that still depended on the mechanistic idea of reproducing light at its source directly at the place of the distant goal. Zworykin always insisted, on the contrary, that his iconoscopic television was not mechanical, and that there could be no talk of a direct transmission of light and images. Zworykin's nonmechanical television, however, still pretends very convincingly that it is mechanical.

TV is the construction of a third image from electronic effects. These are due to a knowledge and an epistemology that is never troubled by the questions—paradoxical in a quantum-mechanical sense—of how the reciprocal effects between light photons and electrically charged particles might be described physically or even ontologically. Television is a technology that integrates a new knowledge about the fundamental constructedness of the world, but only by overlaying it with the application of an old knowledge about the natural continuity of reality.

Thus, in the case of TV, we have, in terms of a history of knowledge, to do with an overlaying that has a distortion as its consequence. For a long time, people thought they were transmitting a reality, since the invention is assembled by means of an epistemology that is completely satisfied by an idea of the continuity of world and nature. In fact, however, television is from its beginnings a construction and can thus only be understood by means of constructivist theories of perception and communication. The present remarks should contribute to a deconstruction of these, and to a keeping open of the folds of their discourses.

Wolfgang Hagen is a professor of media studies at the Leuphana University in Lueneburg, Germany. He has been a visiting scholar and lecturer at several institutions, including the University of California, Santa Barbara; the University of St. Gallen, Switzerland; and the Humboldt University in Berlin. In 2012 he finished his professional career in radio as head of the cultural departments of Deutschlandradio Kultur, Berlin. He is the author of numerous works on the history and epistemology of media, with emphasis on radio and the computer. His most recent publication is "Discharged Crowds—On the Crisis of a Concept," Zürich 2016.

Notes

Translated by Larson Powell.
  1. Translator's note: the concept of entropy, originally from thermodynamics, was introduced into information theory by Claude Shannon; Hagen is however applying it

to the evolution of science. (Entropy has also been used as a sociological concept: see Bailey 1990.) It is typical of Hagen's version of media history that all three of these meanings are in play here.
2. Translator's note: compare the discussion of Chladni in Benjamin's *Ursprung des deutschen Trauerspiels* (1980).
3. Translator's note: Self-similarity (*Selbstähnlichkeit*) is the property of an object that preserves its structure even in expanded size; it is most familiar from fractal geometry (see Mandelbrot 1982).
4. Translator's note: the author intends "address" in the technical sense developed by media theory, meaning the destination of a discovery within scientific discourse (on this concept, see Andriopoulos, Schabacher, and Schumacher 2001). For media theory, the address (*Anschrift*) of a medium determines its content.
5. Translator's note: on Zworykin, see Abramson 1995.
6. Translator's note: for a discussion of this, see Soames 2015.

Chapter 2

BOREDOM, WAR, AND PARADOX

German Theories of Television

Larson Powell

On the Margins of Media Theory

> Fernsehen, das einmal überholt schien, erhält sich am Leben, weil der Augenblick seiner Verwirklichung versäumt ward. Das summarische Urteil, es habe die Welt bloss interpretiert, sei durch Resignation vor der Realität verkrüppelt auch in sich, wird zum Defaitismus der Vernunft, nachdem die Veränderung der Medien misslang.[1]

The deliberate parody of the famous opening of Adorno's *Negative Dialektik* is meant as more than a joke, and least of all one at Adorno's expense. For television has indeed been passed over by a great deal of media theory as somehow unworthy of interpretation, as less theoretically glamorous than digitalization or the Internet—as, thus, merely a kind of poor relative of film, best left to the sociological and statistics-gathering efforts of communication departments. Just as televisual style was long dismissed by filmmakers and film historians as an unwitting realization of Writing Degree Zero, the form of the medium itself has proven slippery to theorize. Moreover, some of the major theoretical tendencies in German media theory have appeared to leap over television altogether, skipping from film to video or the digital and the computerized without much attention to the age of television. Friedrich Kittler, for instance, devoted relatively little attention to television, which may in fact be an inescapable effect of the entire design of his theory. As Bernhard Siegert (1996) categorically declared two decades ago, in opposition to the Frankfurt School: *es gibt keine Massenmedien*—a dictum moreover justified with reference to digital technology. This elision of television is moreover often justified with grand teleological prophecies of television's end, as in the work of Siegfried Zielinski. Might there be an element of wishful thinking in these prophecies? For despite the inattention of these media theorists, television remains a real existing *Leitmedium*, more powerful than ever, and apparently capable of absorbing technological innovations into its structure or medial *dispositif*. Might television be a latency or blind spot of media theory? Does studying television inherently require a more "culturalist" approach than the often techno-centered, Foucault- or discourse-theory-inspired Grand Media Theories so important in Germany would admit? Or are culturalist approaches only taking the seeming transparency of the televisual medium *à la lettre*?

On the other end of the theoretical spectrum, Niklas Luhmann, whose sociological systems theory remains a powerful presence in Germany, although less so in the United States, was one of the roughly 2 percent of the population without a TV in his house. Wolfgang Hagen quite logically asked the question: "How can a man who has no television write" — as Luhmann did in *The Reality of the Mass Media* — that "whatever we know about the society we live in, indeed, about the world we inhabit, we know through the mass media?" In Hagen's formulation, Luhmann's answer would have been: "whoever wants to evaluate the mass media does not have to consume them" (Hagen 2004: 9). This is necessary so that we may — to borrow the witty title of a book by Heidemarie Schumacher — *Fernsehen fernsehen* (Schumacher 2000) see television from a distance, from what Luhmann called an "incongruent perspective." The following introduction to German television theory offers an overview of some of the directions that German research on television has taken, along with some of those it might take. There have been nearly 300 German publications on the subject of television in the last five years alone, and though what follows cannot cover all of them, it will at least sketch in a few broad contours.

Theoretical Approaches

One may roughly divide television research in Germany into three groups, following a by now familiar distinction made in German between *Medienanalyse, Mediengeschichte,* and *Medientheorie*. The first — television reception analysis — would be largely made up of sociological studies of the sort sufficiently familiar in the United States and United Kingdom, devoted to questions of politics, gender, power, violence in the media, effects on children, and so on. On *Tatort* alone one may find over ten books. There are many others concerning violence on TV, terrorism, sports, politicians, women, television's educational use, TV personalities, and even a special volume on German reception of Star Trek. There are volumes devoted to strictly economic descriptions (Berger 2008), or to the history of institutional policies (Künzler 2009), certainly aspects not to be neglected. Another important historical subfield is the domain of literary adaptations for television, on which Thomas Beutelschmidt and Henning Wrage (2004) have worked. Many of these approaches may link up to cultural studies work as well, although it should be pointed out that what in Germany is called *Medienkulturwissenschaft* is very different from Anglo-American cultural studies.[2]

The most important example of the second group, *Mediengeschichte*, would be Knut Hickethier and Peter Hoff's standard reference work, *Geschichte des deutschen Fernsehens* (1998), which offers a panoramic perspective of the medium from its origins to the present. Also offering a synthetic overview is Rüdiger Steinmetz and Reinhard Viehoff's *Deutsches Fernsehen Ost* (2008). Hickethier's work, along with his standard teaching reference works such as *Film- und Fernsehanalyse*—now in its fourth edition—are important enough to merit individual discussion. Hickethier himself (2000, 2001, 2003) has designated his approach as the "Hamburger Modell" and profiled it against other methods of media and television theory.

The introduction to *Geschichte des deutschen Fernsehens*, titled "Fernsehgeschichte als Mediengeschichte," programmatically states the position. Television is, as film once was, a "motor of modernity" understood in that word's broadest sense. Even more strongly formulated: "Fernsehen stellt ... die avancierteste und deshalb auch die umstrittenste Form der Moderne dar" (1). Yet this process of modernity and modernization is neither monolithic nor entirely rationally controllable: its unintended side effects show themselves most clearly "wo es um die Organisation von Wahrnehmung, Beobachtung und Verhalten geht" (2). This happens in despite of the apparently rational planning of programs. Already we can see here—to borrow a distinction from Luhmann that Hickethier himself does not use[3]—that coding and programming are, in the case of television, only loosely coordinated. In Hickethier's own words, "es entwickelt auch eine Eigendynamik, die sich nicht immer funktional zur Rolle des Fernsehens als Agenten des soziokulturellen Wandels verhält" (2). The unpredictable effects of television are thus not simply to be described in terms of traditional narratives of sociocultural modernization or functionalism. Nonetheless, Hickethier acknowledges a debt to Raymond Williams's idea of television as "technology and cultural form," and emphasizes that his history "versteht sich als eine programmgeschichtlich akzentuierte Darstellung" (5). We will need to look elsewhere to grasp the split of television's code and program.

Space permitting, one would need to discuss other important contributions to *Mediengeschichte,* including Irmela Schneider's (2002, 2003, 2004) multivolume series titled *Medienkultur der Fünfziger, Sechziger* and *Siebziger Jahre,* subtitled *Diskursgeschichte der Medien nach 1945.* But we need to go on to the next category, namely *Medientheorie.* It should be kept in mind that the opposition between *Theorie* and *Geschichte* is somewhat problematic. Even *Medientheorie* also needs *Geschichte,* albeit of a more archaeological, thus Foucauldian, sort. As we will see, the history written by *Medientheorie*—synoptic, multi- and intermedial, and encompassing not only the history of modern media, but increasingly their prehistory as well—is illustrative, if not to say occasionally tendentious.

Either/Or: *Medientheorie*'s War with Television

Es gibt keine Medientheorie[4]—except via the exclusion of television. The apodictic and deliberately exaggerated statement is not only an homage to Kittler, but also largely of his own making. It implies two corollaries: first, that there is no one unified media theory, and second, that *Medientheorie* in Kittler's version is not *Wissenschaft* in the ordinary sense. The eccentric or marginal position of television relative to *Medientheorie* offers a good touchstone by which to show why.

A little over a decade ago, Geoffrey Winthrop-Young (2000) asked if German media theory might not offer a "posthuman merger" of Luhmann and Kittler, in the form of a "silicon sociology" of Hegelian character. In this, Winthrop-Young was following on the lead of Rudolf Maresch and others attempting to forge links between *Medientheorie* and systems theory, complementing Luhmann's blindness to "materialities of communication" with Kittler's hardware. Yet the commonalities found between Kittler and Luhmann were chiefly negative: a shared opposition to Habermas, hermeneutics, and humanism. (In a sense, Winthrop-Young was taking the denunciations of Kittler and Luhmann by the German Left as a common denominator and viewing it more neutrally.) Winthrop-Young's conclusion was thus skeptical about any grand media-theoretical synthesis, and had to point out significant differences between the two theoretical approaches, most significantly in their approaches to Shannon's information theory and second-order cybernetics. Although Kittler included Luhmann among his gallery of "Unsterbliche," Luhmann himself was much more circumspect about returning the compliment, and his most important students, such as Dirk Baecker (1999) and Elena Esposito (2002), have been open in their criticisms of Kittler's version of *Medientheorie*. Moreover, the development of an at least partly Luhmann-inspired media theory of television by Lorenz Engell, who has repeatedly and polemically criticized Kittler, has further widened the breach between the fronts. The case of television will help show why this is so.

It may be argued, with Rainer Leschke (2003), that the two theories ultimately belong to logically different types of approach to media. In Leschke's broader perspective on media theories, Luhmann belongs, together with Adorno, Habermas, and Siegfried Schmidt's constructivism, among the "general media theories." These latter are chiefly concerned with media's social effects and functions, and less with media in and of themselves. Since general media theories only approach media through the lens of particular theoretical questions—Habermas's and Luhmann's opposed conceptions of communication, Schmidt's of cognition—they inevitably subordinate media to the role of examples illustrative of those questions. Leschke's specific critique of *Die Realität der Massenmedien* (215–23) points up weaknesses in Luhmann's conception of the media resulting from this subordination, to which we will need to return.

Kittler, on the other hand, belongs to what Leschke calls "general media ontologies," along with McLuhan, Baudrillard, Virilio, and Flusser. The common denominator of these last lies in a crisis of Grand Theories once popularly termed "postmodern" (a word for which Luhmann, significantly, had nothing but disdain). It was the then-sensed inadequacy of metanarratives—chief among them Marxism, Kittler's bête noire—that opened up a place for *Medientheorie* to fill with its hints of technodeterminism, whether affirmed (Kittler) or bewailed (Virilio), the end of "society," or the replacement of words with images (McLuhan and Flusser), and the simulacrum (Baudrillard). If general media theories like Luhmann's and Habermas's shared a belief in the social functionality of media, Kittler's Neronic joy in the ultimate senselessness (or Foucauldian *folie*) of war-driven technological development has to be described as antifunctional. The opposition to functionality affects not only his view of "so-called society"[5]—a term he deliberately avoids in much of his writing—but also the very design of his own work, which is deliberately anticonceptual and prefers rhetorical mimesis and storytelling to the dry sobriety of Luhmann's paradoxes. Habermas's (1985) old accusation that poststructuralism leveled the generic distinction between philosophy and literature, while less than entirely fair in the case of Derrida, may have more relevance to Kittler. The ironic paradox or re-entry (to use Luhmann's terms) of Kittler's writing is that the constant reference to technology, hardware, and numbers remains partly metaphorical or rhetorical—in Nietzsche's famous formulation, "a mobile army of metaphors, metonymies and anthropomorphisms, in short a sum of human relations." Just as Derrida's deconstruction can never escape the metaphysical double-bind it endlessly accuses, so Kittler's reference to number can never get out of the rhetorical clothing of language and (human, all-too-human) meaning it denounces as outdated.[6] The result is that Kittler's histories of media technology end up repeating the same military anecdotes presented in entertaining form: *Geschichte* as a sum of *Geschichten*. "The core of media histories is thus this collection of surprising media historical details" (Leschke 2003: 292), selected according to a Foucauldian principle of singular rarity, and promptly followed up with a wittily epigrammatic point or maxim. The jerky discontinuity of Kittler's narratives is thus born of a deliberate antifunctionalism at the root of his thinking; the code words for this are *Rausch* and mathematics. Without function, what remains is less a theory than an effect.[7]

What does this overall conception mean for the place of television in Kittler's *Medientheorie*? If it is easy to see how television might function for Habermas (as generator of a problematic public sphere) or for Luhmann (as generator of "irritation" in the form of information and *Sinn*), how could it have a nonfunctional role in a theory the motto of which would have to be "stop making sense" (Schreiber 1994)?

Unsurprisingly, television is accorded a very reduced place in Kittler's version of media history. The synoptic history of *Optical Media* is a good example. Even in the prehistory of modern media, television was not even a fantasy: "Unlike film, there were no dreams of television before its development. ... Television was and is not a desire of so-called humans, but rather it is largely a civilian by-product of military electronics" (2010: 207–8). Commenting on Paul Nipkow's pioneering inventions in the 1880s, Kittler cannot resist adding that television "is not an entertainment medium, as our current misunderstanding might assume, but rather a channel in Claude Shannon's literal sense of the word" (209). A distinct whiff of the attitude of Kittler's nemesis Adorno toward entertainment is detectable here. Rather than entertainment, television "functions according to its own principle as a weapon" (215–216), and "always also remains a form of worldwide surveillance" (221)—a formulation reminding one of Virilio. Stripped of its real and unabated commercial popularity, television can thus disappear into the digital: HDTV's data compression technology MUSE "is no longer concerned with genuine optical processes," and so "visible optics must disappear into a black hole of circuits" (225). This fate, or medial-Heideggerian *Seinsgeschick*, was again built into television from the beginning. "In contrast to film, television was already no longer optics. ... Digital image processing thus represents the liquidation of this last remnant of the imaginary" (226).

There are a number of motives within Kittler's thinking that motivate this tendentious marginalization of television from media history. One is Kittler's idiosyncratic reading of Lacan through the lens of Claude Shannon. Kittler always favored Lacan's Real—meaning gramophone—and Symbolic—meaning first typewriter and then computer—over the Imaginary—meaning film. Had Kittler chosen to devote more attention to Lacan's middle period of the 1960s, centered on the Imaginary, he would have had to give more place to problems of culture, programming, and, in general, historical semantics. That would, however, have meant less opposition to the cultural studies Kittler so abhorred, which drew precisely on this idea of the Imaginary (to the point of neglecting the Real).[8] We may see Kittler's reception of Lacan as diametrically opposed to the one made popular in English language film studies via Laura Mulvey's famous refunctioning of "the gaze" in a politicized manner far from Lacan's original conception. Mulvey and her followers (including Homi Bhabha, whose Lacan was borrowed secondhand from film theory's) forgot about the Real and reduced Lacan to a binary opposition between Imaginary and Symbolic. Kittler, by contrast, has stressed the Real (madness, analog media) and the Symbolic (mathematics, computer) over the Imaginary (ideology, film and television). In Lacan's trinity of RSI, the Imaginary is that which patches over the rupture between unsymbolizable Real and the supraindividual Symbolic with subjective fictions; thus precisely what Kittler's mad hero Daniel Paul Schreber lacks is the Imaginary.[9] If Kittler denies subjectivity any reality, the Imaginary must be denounced or excluded as well. And a discontinuous, Foucauldian model of media history that has to posit epistemological and discursive breaks between the Discourse Networks of 1800 (writing), 1900 (gramophone, film, typewriter), and 2000 (computer) cannot leave much room for a medium that does not fit those models and can therefore only be "transitional."

Second: one of the centers of Kittler's antimimetic, antifunctional media history is time manipulation, as Sybille Krämer (2004) has noted. Television's focus on immediacy and simultaneity, its seeming transparency as "degree zero," seems unable to link up to this concern. Third: Kittler's original training as a *Literaturwissenschaftler*, typical for his 1980s generation of media theorists, may have predisposed him to minimize television, the technology of which may be harder to textualize than that of other media (on this, see Winthrop-Young 2005: 81). Fourth and finally: television may not be antihumanist enough for Kittler's taste. The famous disappearing of the face of man in Foucault's sand does not appear on TV screens; quite the contrary. And if dehumanizing physical handicaps like deafness or aphasia, accidents and war wounds are at the origin of media for Kittler, one does not know what sort of handicap would play this role for television. Entertainment is fine for Kittler in the form of rock music, but not that of television; that TV played a large role in disseminating and defining his beloved rock 'n' roll apparently did not faze him.[10]

These various aspects help show up the complexity of Kittler's thought, yet remain still slightly disparate; can they be linked to any one common denominator? Simply to note their antipopulist, antidemocratic implications, along with their ironic kinship to Adorno's attack on mass culture (which Geisler 1999 has noted), would be too convenient, leaving us reassured of our own *bien-pensant* political rightness in too commonsensical a way. Kittler is not "merely a continuation of the Frankfurt School debunking of the mass media by other means" (Geisler 1999: 104). In fact, he is, from a Frankfurt perspective, much worse—or from a Heideggerian one, much more fundamental. It is arguable that, for Kittler, the entire dispositive of television, like the concept of a public sphere (for which he never had much time), is linked to an illusory conception of society. Kittler's Discourse Network 1800 had already been a subversion of the Scholars' Republic (*république des lettres*): in a telling apothegm he spills the beans not only on this, but on the idiosyncratic "methodology" from which he has never deviated: "Acculturation in 1800 short-circuited the circuit of discourse" (Kittler 1990: 50). The short circuit is Kittler's master trope in all his works, and it is what produces *Rauschen* and *Rausch*, noise and madness. TV, by contrast, does no more than reproduce and generate the normal "circuit of discourse," the wires of which Kittler-the-tinkerer would happily cross. If it produces its own version of senselessness, it is only one of chatter—*das Man, das Uneigentliche*—not one in which Kittler is interested. Just as the individual Imaginary serves as discursive glue to hold together the fiction of the subject, so the collective Imaginary of ideology or imagined communities functions in society.[11] Of all of this Kittler will have nothing. Television merely perpetuates the illusion that "Werkzeuge immer von ihrem Benutzer her definiert sind" (Kittler 1996). The medial a priori is incompatible with a user-driven idea of TV as *Werkzeug*, as programming. *Es gibt kein Fernsehen* for Kittler because there is no software, no society, no observer, and no mass media. We are thus left with an aporetical opposition between television and *Medientheorie*.

The position of Siegfried Zielinski shares some of Kittler's approaches to media historiography. *Audiovisions*, first published in 1989, has the telling subtitle: *Cinema and Television as Entr-Actes in History*—and indeed, by the penultimate chapter, set in the 1970s, we are already at "the beginning of a new historical and cultural form of the audiovisual discourse," "no longer cinema, no longer television." Zielinski is not content with Umberto Eco's (1984) more modest distinction between paleo-TV and neo-TV (the latter beginning roughly in the 1980s). Rather, television must be *aufgehoben* (sublated) by the digital, whether in the form of the computer or the video game. Even the VCR was "no longer television in the sense of the central organization of circular effects" (Zielinski 1989: 239): the ability to record and replay undermined "the immediacy of address of the television medium" (240), the essential liveness of its classical broadcasting age. Despite Zielinski's occasional qualification of this assertion, implicitly acknowledging (14) what Bolter and Grusin (1999) later termed "remediation," his point is that "traditional television is fast losing its hegemonial function" (16). In its place, we have a general "discourse" of the "audiovisual" in which television, like film, is disseminated. This general dissemination of media in Zielinski means that the boundaries between media and other technological phenomena are extremely blurred. What organizes Zielinski's history is, alternately, what he calls "audiovisual discourse" (18), or a dispositive, or an apparatus (187), or "signifying praxes" (232).

Zielinski's claim of television's obsolescence is less than entirely convincing. The fact that television, far from going into eclipse, revitalized itself with new links to the Web like Hulu, can find no explanation here. There is space here to mention only methodological problems with his approach. First, if media have always been embedded in a larger system of interrelations, as none other than Kittler has admitted—"there are no media, but rather always only intermedial systems," as he puts it with typical trenchancy in *Optical Media* (2010: 133)—then Zielinski's claim that the fusion or synthesis of individual media in the "audiovisual" is specifically postmodern loses its distinction. Second, Zielinski's depiction of the utopian, decentralized potential of audiovision, rather like the exaggerated claims once made for hacker culture, seems overdrawn. Third, he never really defines what "audiovisual discourse" might be, and his book thus often has something of the vaguely metaphorical quality of certain brands of New Historicism—as if Stephen Greenblatt's "social energy" had been converted into circuitry or a stream of digital bits. An example is his sketchy analogy between the acceleration of international financial transactions and media development: "On the stock market, movement had become everything ... In the world of electronic audiovisions, movement had become everything too" (220–21). This is too unspecific to be helpful, and here as with Kittler, one suspects that media have become a late modern form of the aesthetic Sublime.

More important than these problems, however, is Zielinski's weighting of television's description between technology and management (a word he significantly does not use). "With regard to the materiality of the media, [television] wrought deeper changes in the spheres of production and distribution than for sensory perception" (1989: 186).[12] Yet television, for Zielinski, *already bears within it the seeds of its own digital dissolution.* If, in Stewart Brand's phrase, "information wants to be free," media, for Zielinski, want to be disseminated in the audiovisual. His history of the media is therefore a somewhat tendentious one. Zielinski places the origins of the "audiovisual" before cinema or television, so that its eventual triumph becomes inevitable. And as in so much Foucauldian historiography, the traditional notion of *Verstehen* is bracketed out, in favor of a media-theoretical "happy positivism" consisting, as in the German news magazine *Focus,* of masses of *Fakten, Fakten, Fakten.* It is characteristic that Zielinski devotes little attention to television *programming,* which is at the center of *Medienanalyse* and to some extent of *Mediengeschichte* as well.

The Paradoxical Function of the Mass Media (Luhmann)

The opening of Luhmann's *Reality of the Mass Media* is just as categorical as the famous first sentence of *Gramophone Film Typewriter.* Yet whereas Kittler's "Media determine our situation" refers to a technological a priori of which no hermeneutical sense can be made, Luhmann's statement is solidly centered on sense (*Sinn*), the key category for a sociology of communication: "Whatever we know about our society, or indeed about the world in which we live, we know through the mass media" (Luhmann 1996: 9). The sentence is in fact as hyperbolic as Kittler's, for what a scientist knows in a lab, a student in a classroom, a listener at a chamber music concert, or even a person walking on a city street is all hardly reducible to mass media information. Precisely this overstatement is meant to bring out the function of the mass media for Luhmann, which lies in the diffusion of "knowledge" in the form of information and meaning (these two latter tending, as Luhmann's critics have pointed out, to blur into each other).[13] Mass media, for which television is in fact representative, do this through "reduction of complexity," a euphemism for what Kittler trenchantly called "Dummheit:" they simplify, personalize, and above all, repeat. These simplifications or reductions are termed "schemata," and their function is to assure that things continue as they have; they are a form of what the younger Luhmann called "trust" (*Vertrauen*). Mass media are thus a form of second-order observation, despite their semblance of real time and immediacy, which tends to collapse information and communication in what other media theorists (Virilio, Baudrillard) denounce as a simulacrum. Luhmann only escapes the trap of the latter through an insistence on the temporal dimension of mass media: their need for a constant supply of novelty means that they are forced to correct themselves, and this self-correction is what assures they are not mere illusion or manipulation. In his own terms, this is the "unfolding" of paradoxes by temporalization. (There is an interesting structural similarity here to the way Habermas makes his version of communication inevitably point toward an eventual consensus, although in Luhmann's case, what guarantees a "reality" outside the system of the mass media is its inability ever to close entirely in on itself.)

To extend Winthrop-Young's helpful contrast between Kittler's and Luhmann's divergent receptions of information theory: a key difference from Kittler is that Luhmann is more attentive to the role of redundancy in communication. Mass media do nothing else but ensure an adequate supply of redundancy (or *Dummheit*). This means that their "function" is a stabilizing one. In the chapter on advertising, Luhmann states that mass media have their own function, "which may lie in the stabilizing of the relation between redundancy and variety in everyday culture" (1996: 94; the sentence is italicized in the original). The result is "a sort of best of all possible worlds with as much order as necessary and as much freedom as possible." Luhmann is sounding very much like his teacher Parsons here: even though Parsons is criticized in *The*

Reality of the Mass Media for treating mass media in too integrative a fashion, Luhmann himself does little else. Mass media in fact seem to take over the "function" that culture—in Parsonese, the "pattern maintenance system"—had for Parsons. The trust in meaning they underpin is as much a Bentham-like social fiction as Lacan's Imaginary, yet still an inevitable one. The only difference lies in Luhmann's "old European" sense of irony and skepsis relative to this integrative function, relative to Parsons's optimistic New Dealer belief in "value commitments." Where Kittler relishes the sense-confounding madness and *Rausch* of the short circuit, Luhmann adopts an almost Taoist position of ironic distance from the fundamental paradox of mass media as a system: how can something so patently absurd continue to function? Yet at bottom, mass media do for Luhmann what culture did for Parsons, stripped of the latter's Weberian concept of substantive values. (Kittler, by contrast, keeps function and culture strictly distinct: as in Adorno, culture is the subversion of function and meaning for Kittler.) This also implies that mass media cannot lie outside the social system, as culture had to in Parsons's conception.

As Leschke has noted, Luhmann's book on the mass media is much less systematic and more informal than his works devoted to other social subsystems (such as law, economy, or art). Given the centrality of communication to his theory, it is hard to see how the mass media could not have been reduced to a merely instrumental role; as technological bearers of *Sinn*, they and the book devoted to them are in the awkward position of a frame supporting a picture, and one could easily imagine a deconstructive reading that would show how meaning and communication could be more dependent on media technology than Luhmann allows (see Stäheli 2000). As a system, the mass media seem to possess less of the autopoietic flexibility and adaptability than other systems, since there is something mechanical (and not biological) in their underlying conception.[14] To return to our typical Kittlerian trope, the technology of media, excluded by the *Supermedium Sinn*, seem nonetheless to be short-circuiting Luhmann's usual elegant separation of functional levels of operation.

Philosophy of Television: Boredom and Contradiction

When we turn to our last category, which fits neither into *Mediengeschichte*, nor *Medienanalyse*, nor *Medientheorie*, the question of social function changes again. We may dub this last variant *Medienphilosophie*, following the lead of its own practitioners. (A recent publication from this group [Fahle and Engell 2006] is titled *Philosophie des Fernsehens*.) The term "philosophy" marks a difference from *Medientheorie* as practiced by Kittler and others, which prefers rhetorical figurality to traditional discursive argument (as Leschke has noted). The chief representative of this tendency would be Lorenz Engell, arguably the most important German theorist of television. Engell has written or edited many books on media theory; we will concentrate here on his first book, titled *Vom Widerspruch zur Langeweile: Logische und Temporale Begründungen des Fernsehens* (Engell 1989).

As the philosophical title suggests, Engell attempts here no less than a foundational study on the specificity of television as medium. Television is as central to Engell as it is for Luhmann: "television is no longer only *one* window onto the world, but rather ... it regulates access to the world as a whole" (67; see also 285: "the world is television itself"). His point of departure is a critique of Neil Postman's *Amusing Ourselves to Death* (1985), read even more widely in Germany than in the United States. Against Postman's cultural critique of the idiot box, Engell calls on Heidegger. He does so in a different way than most others, relying not on "Die Frage nach der Technik"—as did Kittler—but on *Sein und Zeit*, expanding the definition of television beyond even a *dispositif* to a particular relationship between *Dasein* and its world (9). There is thus a phenomenological aspect to Engell's work, referring back to Husserl as well as to Heidegger; this Husserlian reference links him to Luhmann. Television, for Engell, discovers a pre-logical way of being-in-the-world: "Media ... do nothing other than undo the constitution of objects via a disregard of logical prescriptions, leading back to the reality of a hermeneutical relation to the world" (72). Therefore "a critique of television that proceeds logically is something ontologically impossible," and "the proper medium and theory of critique of television would thus have to be television itself"(82). Alexander Kluge might well be pleased by this assertion. For Engell is not suggesting that all critique is impossible, that media can only produce "Dummheit," as Kittler gleefully puts it; he still believes in a chance at an emancipatory media pedagogy, although not of Postman's stamp (so to speak); modern media-critical Catos who declaim that *media delenda sunt* will find no consolation here. Critique, however, cannot remain on the surface of television's content, but must look at the way in which it restructures time and perception.

Engell explains this with reference to the difference between *Vorstellung* and *Wahrnehmung*, and here he must refer to communication theory and semiotics as well. Contrary to usual understandings of TV as mere passive recorder or window onto the world, he insists that television works with *Vorstellungen*, however closely they may be modeled on perceptions (198).[15] Television has thus the character of *Schrift* (223), as Adorno already recognized. But television structures its signifiers differently. Whereas in face-to-face communication, "the communications partners are perceivable and the objects [referred to] are represented, with television the reverse holds true" (199). Whereas in verbal communication, the "perceptible sound form" or *Lautgestalt* and the thought-representation are two distinct aspects, the same distinction is less clear in television (201). Saussure, in other words, does not quite apply here. (The same observation, by the way, may be found in Luhmann's *Die Realität der Massenmedien*.) Television offers a mirror less of the outer world than of consciousness itself (203), and thereby breaks down the usual duality of subject-object: it is, in Engell's words, "at once subject and object of perception" (197). Moreover, what it represents is chiefly time itself, in its pre-logical form, which Engell links to Heidegger's notion of *Weltzeit*. Engell does not hesitate to draw philosophical consequences from this: the functioning of television has thus similarities to deconstruction, for its constant displacement of meaning can be seen as a form of *différance* (145), and its endless stream of allusion is disseminatory (220). As mentioned earlier, this link of television and dissemination may be found in Zielinsky as well; the idea would help explain why television has proven so resistant to theory. He also fleshes out his definition of television's mediality through a historical comparison to film, and suggests, in his speculative concluding section, that whereas film had been a provider of integrative meaning to early modernity through its narrative closure and theatrically defined space of reception, television, in contrast, is a corroder of social meaning (308–9). Here he has indeed learned a lesson from Postman.

By this point, when he is writing of media history, Engell's theoretical frame of reference has shifted from Heidegger to Luhmann. This greater embedding in sociology allows him to see television, computers, and video as part of one larger, encompassing paradigm, and not as disjunct technological phases that must supersede each other (as Kittler and Zielinski do). Yet Engell also dissents from Luhmann in significant ways. For Luhmann, society is based on communication, and its non-negatable "Supermedium" is meaning; thus mass media, too, cannot do other than produce meaning, thereby serving a social need for the latter. As many critics have pointed out, Luhmann did not himself reflect much on the technological a prioris of his own conception of meaning, that is, on its "materialities of communication." But rather than putting Luhmann on his technological feet—as Kittler did with Foucault—Engell takes another tack. He suggests that television, rather than reinforcing the dominance of meaning typical of information society, offers a counterpoint to it. Although television owed its domination to the historical discovery of information as a productive force (320), it nonetheless is "the opposing force to the production of meaning" and is practically a "meaning-free space" (309). Television thus destabilizes the social production of sense, is a permanent *Störenfried* or "irritation" in Luhmann's sense.[16] Engell's argument implies that television is not so much *within* the social system as in some way outside, as the *Umwelt* or environment to meaning. This also allows him to conceptually profile TV's medial particularity more sharply than could Hickethier's *Mediengeschichte* model. Paradoxically, Engell argues this through allowing television to represent the entirety of the world within itself (as a kind of microcosm) in a way Luhmann would not have permitted. Television's "paradoxical achievement [*Leistung*]" is "to present the wholeness of the world within the world [*Weltganzheit innerweltlich vorzustellen*]" (158). But this world-wholeness is not one of meaning, rather one of absurdity and boredom. Luhmann implicitly made information nearly equivalent to meaning (insofar as it is socially believed and used as departure for further communication), so that the observer of television can only smile in ironic detachment at the absurdities TV passes off for meaning (*Sinn*)—without, however, being able to alter this pattern at all. Television becomes an allegory for the empty paradox of social meaning-production, a game of mirrors now just as it was for one of Luhmann's most-cited authors, the Spanish Baroque Jesuit Balthasar Gracian. Kittler, by contrast, abhors television precisely for its production of noise-taken-for-meaning, and longs for television's disappearance in order to reveal the ultimately military command structure of media hidden beneath its deceptive appearance. Engell, finally, accepts the emptiness of television as boredom and meaninglessness, neither aestheticizing it as violence (as Kittler) nor seeing it as the inevitable social glue of the "Supermedium Sinn" (as Luhmann). The differences among these three approaches to television may also (again extending Winthrop-Young) be read through the different appropriations of information theory each pursue, specifically the role of redundancy. Kittler is not much interested in redundancy, since it interferes with his reduction of information to terse military command. Luhmann has a classical liberal's view of redundancy as an inevitable compromise paradoxically generating social stability. Finally, Engell sees redundancy as nonsense and boredom. One might be tempted to see the differences between boredom, war, and paradox as linked up to specifically generational experiences: paradox as a defense against the lawless disorder Luhmann experienced under the Nazis, war as object of Kittler's 68er "hunger for experience," and boredom as typical of the neoliberal 1980s with their "end of history" (Engell's dissertation appeared in 1989).

Where does our overview leave us? Does German television theory only offer the seductive prospect of putting another new king on Hegel's old high theoretical throne—as Winthrop-Young (2000) wrote of Luhmann and Kittler a decade ago? This would be too simple a view. The wish for a more ambitious theoretical approach to TV is not only German; American scholars like Richard Dienst have also worked with Heidegger and the medium.[17] And Engell's ambitious philosophical model does not exclude closer-grained case studies, either—which gives him an advantage over Kittler and Zielinski. In his most recent work, Engell (2009) has viewed television as an inherently experimental medium—something also far removed from any teleological grand narratives of media history. We thus need neither abandon TV to content analysis alone, nor make it disappear as an embarrassment to the sublimities of Kittler's mathematical sublime. Even some of the insights of Adorno from 1953 may be reexamined, if we disembed them from the totalizing historico-philosophical paradigm of *Kulturindustrie*. Recent developments in German media theory, whether going under the moniker of *Kulturtechnik* or the synoptic umbrella term of *Medienkulturwissenschaft*, tend to bear out Adorno's claim that "die gesellschaftlichen, technischen, künstlerischen Aspekte des Fernsehens können nicht isoliert behandelt werden."[18] We would only need to add to this that the insights of media and television theories up to now have been inseparable from their frequent one-sidedness; any attempt at a more ecumenical theory of TV ought to preserve something of the provocative nature of those earlier views and not merely tone them down in reasonable, generalizing moderation, if it is to do justice to the novelty of TV as a medium.

Larson Powell is Professor of German at the University of Missouri, Kansas City. His latest book, co-edited with Kyle Frackman, *Classical Music in the German Democratic Republic* was published by Camden House in 2015. Other recent work includes *The Differentiation of Modernism: Postwar German Media Arts* (Camden House, 2013), and essays on film music, musicology, and Eastern European film. Current research includes a monograph on Konrad Wolf and a book on German-Polish relations.

Notes

1. Adorno 1997a 6:15, modified. "Television, which once seemed obsolete, lives on because the moment to realize it was missed. The summary judgment that it had merely interpreted the world, that resignation in the face of reality had crippled it in itself, becomes a defeatism of reason after the attempt to change the world miscarried." (modified from E.B. Ashton's translation, *Negative Dialectics* [London: Routledge, 2004, 3]).
2. On the difference, see Musner 2001.
3. Luhmann's work on mass media is cited here, on p. 540, and one wonders if there may be systems-theoretical resonances in the choice of the word *Beobachtung*.
4. As Bernhard Siegert puts it (2013: 49), "What arose in the 1980s in Freiburg and has come to be associated with names such as Friedrich Kittler, Klaus Theweleit, Manfred Schneider, Norbert Bolz, Raimar Zons, Georg-Christoph Tholen, Jochen Hörisch, Wolfgang Hagen, Avital Ronell (and maybe also my own) was never able to give itself an appropriate name. It definitely wasn't 'media theory.'" Wolfgang Hagen's chapter in this volume, however, offers a view of TV history influenced by *Medientheorie*, yet also drawing on Luhmann's theory of evolution, and thus without Kittler's blind spot.
5. This turn of phrase occurs in Kittler 1996.
6. Winkler (1999) has formulated this criticism of Kittler as a form of *Sprachvergessenheit* or blindness to language.
7. This is Winthrop-Young's conclusion (2011: 143–46). Interestingly, the same has been said of Foucault (Burchell, Gordon, and Miller 1991).
8. This elision of the Real was already evident in Fredric Jameson's influential essay "Imaginary and Symbolic in Lacan: Marxism, Psychoanalytic Criticism, and the Problem of the Subject" (1977).
9. The key analysis is in Lacan 1981.
10. See the bibliography in Lindelof 2007.
11. In Lacan 1981, these two aspects are overtly linked in the form of a "discours" that the individual must internalize in order to become a subject.
12. Here is where an approach informed by *Kulturtechnik* could correct Zielinski, through closer attention to just these domains of production and distribution.
13. The criticism was made early on by Habermas in his contribution to Habermas and Luhmann 1971.
14. See in particular the curious passage in chapter 1 (11) where it is asserted that mass media's mechanical "Verbreitungstechnologie" has the same function [sic!] in aiding the differentiation of the mass media's system as the medium of money does for the economic system. This is, however, a confusion of different senses of the term medium: technological invention cannot be a symbolic medium of communication like money.
15. This role of *Vorstellungen* could be compared with that of the "third image" in Wolfgang Hagen's chapter in this collection.

16. See also Esposito (2002: 272): mass media have no symbolic medium.
17. Dienst 1994. On the relations of German and American media theories, see also Peters 2008.
18. Adorno 1997b 10:2: 507.

PART II

GDR TELEVISION

Chapter 3

"Just Like in the West, Except Different"

Television and Its Relationship to Film
in the Context of 1950s GDR Development

Thomas Beutelschmidt

"Just Like in the West, Except Different" is the title of Stefan Zahlmann's recent anthology about media in the GDR. Although this may seem a paradoxical title at first glance, it points appropriately to the "asymmetrically intertwined and contrastive history" in which both German states were firmly implicated (Zahlmann 2010: 190).[1] The collection of analyses, positioning, and remembrances by twenty-four authors proves that even twenty years after unification, the debate about the legacy of the GDR is still relevant. Yet the critical perspective is no longer dedicated solely to an understanding of "totalitarianism" one-sidedly aimed at an attempted *Durchherrschung* (thorough domination, in Jürgen Kocka's term) and including complete control of the media and public sphere as well. Instead, what is now foregrounded are "reciprocally successful or failed negotiations by media producers and receivers" under the governing conditions of GDR culture, as well as various program- or genre-driven and comparative approaches (Zahlmann 2010: 32). On the whole, GDR film and television history is now understood as an integral part of German-German cultural history in a common communicative universe. Nevertheless, cultural studies and communications disciplines have until now only touched upon the institutional and aesthetic complexities linking the DEFA studios and GDR broadcasting. They have concentrated more strongly on the inner logic of the respective *dispositifs* of cinema or television and thereby neglected intermedial processes of transformation or mutual dependences. Therefore, in the historical media overview that follows, the introduction of television will be treated not only as a singular "media historical blip" (Henning Wrage), but rather coordinated with DEFA and the larger cultural development of the GDR as well.

The relationship between the facilities in Babelsberg and Adlershof were ambivalent from the start, influenced both by competitive attitudes and also by attempts at cooperation (for a more thorough analysis, see Beutelschmidt 2009). On the one hand, one can observe certain convergences at the level of ideological requirements and shared personnel. On the other hand, the two media differentiate themselves at the level of their operative scope, content conceptualization, and aesthetic intentions, as well as in their target audiences, and their distinctive effects in the private sphere versus a public, collective cinematic experience. For that reason, despite appeals for cooperation, film and television pursued their own interests. This expressed itself not only in the competition for constantly scarce resources and qualified personnel, but also in their separate pursuit of known authors, popular stories, or public favor.

For all these distinctions, GDR television and DEFA can hardly be considered autonomous communicators. Despite the specific dynamics of their particular media and certain independent characteristics, they were always understood as *equal* sectors of the "socialist media landscape" and therefore both subject to a single central authority and cultural policy and dependent upon a common state plan. Television's implementation was expected to bring a diversification of cultural offerings and, thus, not a restriction but rather an expansion of the arts of film and radio, as well as theatre and literature—even if *Deutscher Fernsehfunk* (DFF) eroded over the long term DEFA's market share, influence, and narrative traditions.

In a *Festschrift* for the fifth anniversary of the founding of DEFA in 1951, film was celebrated "as the greatest form of mass art."(Ackermann 1951: 11) One could point confidently to postwar films that enjoyed success beyond the borders of the GDR, such as *The Murderers Are Among Us* (Wolfgang Staudte, 1946), *Marriage in the Shadows* (Kurt Maetzig, 1947), *Rotation* (Wolfgang Staudte, 1949) and *The Subject* (Wolfgang Staudte, 1951), all of which count as classics of German cinema as a whole. That initial euphoria was followed, however, by production cutbacks and massive intervention on the part of the party. To be sure, the film industry remained conscientious about its duties. It delivered, by Klaus Finke's account, approximately forty productions focused on socialist work, the work place, or the topic of world peace (Finke 2007).

Despite this evidence of subservience, DEFA was seen as a potentially unreliable force lacking in both party loyalty and the drive toward continued agitprop work.

The basis for this suspicion lay in the historical genesis of the film industry. Even if an SED conformist attitude was required, the ideological alignment of DEFA's political covenant of anti-fascist-democratic renewal was similar to that of the Kulturbund founded in July 1945. This was bound to popular front sentiments against National Socialism and simultaneously tied to bourgeois-liberal forces. At the same time, DEFA's aesthetic conception was not yet unilaterally fixated on the construct of socialist realism, that Stalinist cultural politics from the mid-1930s onward that drew upon heavy stereotyping and pathos. This foundational consensus led to conflicts, especially when the SED began to emphasize popular solidarity and partisanship. The DEFA leadership was accused of abuse of privileges and "ideological ambiguity," and top officials even suggested that it "failed to deeply appreciate such notions as perspective, power relations, the socialist camp, the taming of German militarism, and the development of socialism in the GDR" (Protokoll 52 1961: 5).

Certainly these experiences of crisis in the 1950s and the concomitant mistrust also played an important role in the gradual shifting of perspectives from film to television. It appears thus logical that functionaries sought to avoid any "birth defects" in the introduction of the new medium and assured their complete influence on the "Instrument of the Worker and Peasant State:" "The Television Center is a state political institution ... With these new propagandistic and agitprop possibilities the program must convince the workers of the truth of the policies of the Party and government and must mobilize and inspire them to meet the challenges of the party line."(Nehmzow 1954: 1)

Since 1949 the Politbüro made considerable investment development funds available to television. The new facilities, with their new *Generalintendanz Fernsehen* (television general director), fell under the direct authority of radio and thus created an administrative centralization of the broadcast media. With the start of the trial program on Stalin's seventieth birthday, December 21, 1952, the GDR joined the Soviet Union and Poland as the first Eastern European countries with regular broadcasting operations. With that the East German state could exercise its option in the international distribution and certification of television frequencies. At the same time it was reacting to the television activities in the Federal Republic and, more importantly, West Berlin, where the northern German station, Nordwestdeutsche Rundfunk

(NWDR) was already broadcasting programs. With support from the Radio Company of America the NWDR put on a convincing display of the new medium at the 1951 industrial exhibition. At first neither side reached an audience worth mentioning with their territorially limited signals. Until individual reception became available in the mid-1950s, viewing in the GDR remained limited to partially public television sets in cultural houses, workplaces, or so-called education premises of the National Front; this early form of "public viewing" was hardly enjoyable. Throughout the trial period lasting until 1955, the first domestically produced sets from the Rafena plant in Radeberg had only 30cm screens.

Due to a widespread lack of sets and weak signals, television enjoyed very little public resonance at first. Even the party apparatus had difficulty judging this new form of "collective organization" according to an expansion of Lenin's notion of the press (Lenin 1959: 309). Thus the Fourth Party Convention of the SED in 1954 saw no reason either to concern itself with or intervene in the development of television. Nevertheless, the industry's various branches found themselves in the same confrontation with obligatory cultural policies as did the DEFA facilities, radio, and the theater. The party line was still driven by rigid campaigns unmistakably waged against decadent or bourgeois reactionary performance techniques and discrediting Western-influenced formalism and cosmopolitanism: "Two forces wrestle bitterly with one another in the artistic realm: the representatives of humanistic culture struggle against the powers of barbarism, distortion, and destruction of our culture in the service of American and German Imperialism. Our German Democratic Republic is called to a task of true historical importance in this decisive battle for the humanistic legacy and the continued and exalted development of German culture ... All of Germany must witness our artistic achievements and it should also see whom they serve. For here we implement Lenin's maxim: 'Art Belongs to the People'" (Ulbricht 1954: 979).

Because the GDR's TV studios with their faulty equipment were little more than a laboratory, their initial trial program could not, either technically or aesthetically, live up to these lofty claims, nor could they offer an alternative to the cinema. The still rudimentary programs concentrated on news services, talk programs, and feature programs with film trailers supplemented by children's hours, music and dance, variety clips, and game shows. They liked to experiment occasionally with short chamber play-like scenes. In general a spectrum between indoctrination and entertainment emerged, one that hardly differentiated itself either dramaturgically or in aesthetic form from the mixed offerings of National Socialist television from 1935 to 1944.

The majority of television pioneers had been educated in publishing, journalism, theater, or radio and had experience in writing, editing, dramaturgy, directing, and acting. Thus they had strongly concentrated on the word and specialized in staging. Few had any familiarity with the art of finding visual equivalents for words, much less with montage or unusual shot composition. Thus early, primarily live broadcast productions stuck to linear narration with few temporal leaps, tractable conflict situations with minimal characters, unspectacular mise en scène, and strict shot/countershot set-ups, medium close-up shots, minimal camera movement, and infrequent cuts. Nevertheless, as in the West, those involved were determined to legitimate their work as an autonomous art form (Eckert 1953). They wanted their stylistically simple staging to be seen as defining a completely new form of expression situated between film and radio. "Wherever they follow their own laws in competing for the greatest aesthetic impact, TV and film will attain entirely different production methods. Even when television draws upon filmic resources, from an artistic point of view, it will still result in a made-for-television film and not a feature. The word film here implies only a word for the same technical medium" (Fehlig 1955: 2,7).

DEFA still retained the last word on fantasy production. Because no one had yet given thought to television's need for fresh talent, graduates of the film academy, which was founded in 1954, were not at Adlershof's disposal. Therefore the broadcasting executives made an effort to recruit experienced personnel in the film studios for their trial productions. The studio board agreed to a partial support deal and thus contributed to the success of the television project.

Those vocations that were primarily technical found in the new television center an interesting work environment, while intellectual and artistic circles remained at a distance from a new medium they viewed as profane, with its tendency to trivialize educated bourgeois values. Most importantly, prominent directors feared for their reputation and resisted television work despite lucrative offers. In their eyes, only feature films offered the promise of renown and the attention of film festivals, which, according to Horst E. Brandt, led to "good directors going to Babelsberg."[2] Only later did representatives of DEFA such as Egon Günther, Ralf Kirsten, or Horst Seemann come to appreciate the opportunity for development that television offered—such as the chance to treat different topics, to test the narrative possibilities of miniseries, or the ability to try out new production methods.

In another way, film again contributed decisively to television's establishment and consolidation, and to its initial ability to satisfy the demand for fictional productions. Since the new institution naturally had no archival productions in stock, it was dependent from the very start on the film market and had to cooperate both with the state-run distributors Progress Film-Vertrieb and those in Russia, Sovexport. Right from the beginning, recent and archived films were broadcast in awareness of the new network's own shortage of programming and in an attempt to raise its quality. Many prime slots in the weekly schedule were reserved for documentary and feature films.

This practice met with controversy in the filmmakers' fraction within the state cultural production. Thus although the new medium was given regular broadcasting rights, it was never granted any general influence on the productions themselves. One example of this ongoing differentiation of film from TV was the banished anti-NATO political thriller *Captain Loy's Dream* (*Der Traum des Hauptmann Loys*). Because its widescreen format made it ill-suited for television, it remained a cinema exclusive, a fact that was expressly advertised on its film poster: "This DEFA-film in TOTALVISION will not appear in the television program." The central distributors, who were also concerned about the combination of the constant presence of films on the small screen and declining attendance in the movie theaters, thereby attempted to support the film industry. From 1953 to 1957 cinema attendance rose to a high of over 3 million per year before sinking in 1960 to barely 2.5 million. Television viewing, by contrast, rose annually. With over 1 million registered sets in 1960, television reached an audience of 2.5 million viewers and broadcast 3,000 hours of programming.

By January 1956, its own self-definition and development had reached a point where the DFF could commence regular programming. The increasingly popular medium took up its system-stabilizing function as propagandist, educational institution, mediator of art, and entertainment provider. The Politburo and the responsible agitprop department of the Central Committee appeared to be satisfied. For at the subsequent (third) SED party conference only DEFA appeared to be ideologically on trial. What was seen to be lacking there was "the close connection of art and life" — a solution to which was provided during the decisive First Bitterfeld Conference (of authors) three years later (Ulbricht 1956: 188).

Although film production had recovered from the depths of the early 1950s, both quantitatively and qualitatively, pressure was again increased on the studios after the brief thawing period and de-Stalinization in the wake of the Tenth Party Congress of the Communist Party of the Soviet Union. With an eye to the reform movement in Hungary, the studios were accused of "irresponsibility and liberalism" as well as having taken the "false path of ideological coexistence" in the existing "struggle of the new with the old." (Brandis 1957: 7, 2).

Party functionaries acted quite consequentially during this crisis period in exploiting the advantages of television over film. They saw in the direct accessibility of various audiences and the medium's greater relevance and flexibility an operational advantage for their popular pedagogical mission of strengthening socialist consciousness and patriotic identification with the *Homeland GDR.*

TV programming experienced a qualitative boost at the end of 1955 in the form of newly available transmission technology. Television was finally mobile throughout the republic and could thus live up to expectations of unmediated participation. From here on out, images from political occasions and sporting events, as well as opera and theater performances, could be delivered directly into the home.

Standards for made-for-television films were also established during this period. An interest in valuable film copies for reruns and second-run cinema distribution, as well as those for international export or participation in festivals, was obvious. Likewise, pressure increased for historical material as well as realist depictions of everyday life with atmospheric location shots and multilayered narrative styles. The growing demand for opulent imagery, compelling backdrops, as well as a wealth of action was sated primarily via contracts with DEFA and co-productions.

1956 saw implementation of the first coproduction, *Damals in Paris (At that Time in Paris)*, an antifascist drama about the Parisian resistance directed by Carl Balhaus. That was followed upon in 1959 by the first commissioned productions that ranged from detective comedy, *Spuk in Villa Sonnenschein (The Ghost in the Sunshine Villa)*, to the Russian comedies such as *Wie die Wilden (Like the Savages)* to antifascist material such as the psychological portrait, *Die Dame und der Blinde (The Lady and the Blind Man)*, a story about the unsatisfactory treatment of the Nazi past in the Federal Republic.

DEFA thus supported the filmic development of fictional television production. The dramatic arts liberated themselves from the corset of the chamber play and increasingly oriented themselves toward cinematic standards. Its images were no longer subordinate to the ideational import of rational concepts. The dominance "of a verbal orientation, of the conceptual, or the non-iconic," could finally be in part overcome.[3]

Even if the choice of particular ideologically loaded general topics and patterns of argumentation was also typical of feature films, television was often quicker and more insistent than DEFA in responding to the challenges of the systematic construction of socialism. The programming staff saw itself particularly called to the task of justifying the implementation of forced social conversion such as rural collectivization or the nationalization of industry, and to stimulating economic growth. Collective behavioral norms and increased productive readiness, as well as more efficient work methods and state-of-the-art scientific and technical progress, were propagated through personalized case studies.

The high representative value of contemporary partisan television dramas is made apparent through two titles that served as role models for DEFA and from which the latter were forced to produce remakes for the cinema. A film with a view toward domestic politics, *Die grüne Mappe* (*The Green Folder*, 1959) was a spy story typical of the era, with a party secretary as a positive hero. It was then adapted in 1962 as a widescreen cinematic film, *Wenn Du zu mir hältst* (*If You Stand by Me*). Likewise, a 1959 film aimed at foreign policy, the pacifist television drama *Weißes Blut* (White Blood), which took aim at atomic armament in the West, was subjected to an even more elaborate cinematic adaptation in that same year.

Thus was television able to represent both the self-image and worldview of the all-powerful unity party perhaps more visibly than was DEFA. Its *Zeitstücke* (topical plays), dramatically expanded commentaries, and other half-artistic, half-journalistic mixed genres were grounded firmly in party doctrine. These preachy programs with limited realist detail often boiled down to "the emulation of an idea, the ideological *a priori* of Marxism-Leninism"(Wuss 1988: 75–76). A culture of real public debate was (intentionally) rendered impossible with such avowals of belief, a structural weakness to which Peter Hoff frequently called attention: "No one intended an expansion of the existing forms of the public sphere; rather what was ultimately a pre-bourgeois representational public sphere was established in which individual citizens could not participate autonomously" (Finke 2007: 43).

The "Television Pace-Setter" (Günter Herit) should not, however, be unilaterally reduced to its role as repressive instrument of manipulation. Even an early white paper from 1955 emphasized that the station "had not only to fulfill the agitprop and political assignments," since it is also "an expressive and unifying medium in the cultural and aesthetic arena that must satisfy the workers' needs for entertainment and relaxation" (Beutelschmidt 2008). It was especially television drama in this dual function that was called upon to sharpen its profile, performing a constant split between the indoctrination of class struggle and humanist enlightenment, as well as between the imperative to educate and giving shape to free time. Thus these dramas presented a broad palette of serious and light-hearted dramas or serious literary adaptations alongside more programmatic contemporary pieces.

Until 1960 alone one can find approximately 300 literary-based productions, in-studio guest presentations, and live transmissions of theater performances. Models of internationally recognized classics were regarded as "cultural heritage" inasmuch as they stemmed from a (purportedly) progressive tradition. Literary adaptations shaped from the very beginning the palette of offerings and played a not insignificant role in the latter's acceptance. They soon functioned as a trademark with high representational value and later as an export good of considerable economic value.

Growing diversification of programming, extended broadcast times, and increased coverage throughout the GDR contributed to television's ability to establish itself by the beginning of 1960s as a truly mass medium. It was not only an equal partner to the film industry, but also at the same time a worthy opponent. Thus in 1959 the third Social Unity Party press conference spoke of television as the "new weapon whose effects could possibly in the not too distant future exceed those of radio and other means of mass agitprop" (Norden 1959: 54). Even the cultural conference of the following year dedicated considerable space to the DFF. It was crowned "the most important instrument for influencing millions of people," one that would not only "stimulate and enrich the theater and film studios," but also "make a valuable cultural and didactic contribution on the road to an educated nation" (*Grundsätze* 1960: 431f).

Additionally, television garnered further recognition and higher appraisal through the consciously forced distinction of its achievements in programming. In particular, *Dramatische Kunst* was ennobled and raised to the same level as the high culture of literature and film. Between 1959 and 1962 multiple television shows were awarded national literary or art prizes, whereas DEFA went away empty-handed in the same period. Even film magazines such as the serious *Deutsche Filmkunst* reacted to the new medium and reviewed the newest TV shows or reported at great length on commissioned productions.

Thus GDR television achieved its breakthrough on all levels. Internally the upward trend continued with improved quality standards, popular detective series, ready-made family and adventure series, as well as numerous television magazine formats and ambitious miniseries, some of which eventually ended up on the big screen. Television's first venture in 1961 into the cinema, the uncomplicated comedy *Papas neue Freundin* (*Daddy's New Girlfriend*) became a great hit, reaching approximately 1.5 million viewers, thereby outperforming the two DEFA hits of the same year, *Die Glatzkopfbande* (Skinhead Band) or *For Eyes Only*.

Last but not least, DFF played a vital role in the Eastern European umbrella organization, INTERVISION, that served as an international program exchange for the Warsaw Pact countries and their Western partner, Finland. DFF is one of the success stories of television, even if the Adlershof broadcaster would, upon its ten-year anniversary in 1962, soon sink into deep political crisis. But that would be material for another chapter with the potential title: "1960–1970, Cultures under Modernization."

Thomas Beutelschmidt has published seven books and numerous essays on film and media, including *Kooperation oder Konkurrenz? Das Verhältnis zwischen Film u. Fernsehen in der DDR* (Berlin 2009); '*Audiovisuelle Literatur.' Datenbank der Adaptionen epischer u. dramatischer Vorlagen im DDR-Fernsehen* (Leipzig 2008); *Das literarische Fernsehen. Beiträge zur deutsch-deutschen Medienkultur* (Frankfurt/Main 2007), *Das Buch zum Film—der Film zum Buch. Annäherungen an den literarischen Kanon im DDR-Fernsehen* (Leipzig 2004); and *Sozialistische Audiovision. Zur Geschichte der Medienkultur in der DDR* (Verlag für Berlin u. Brandenburg, Potsdam 1995). He has also curated many exhibits and made films and videos.

Notes

1. Steinle (2010: 190) referring to the work of, among others, Christoph Kleßmann.
2. Author's conversation with Horst E. Brandt in Berlin on 3 May 2005.
3. The data bank on the DEFA-Stiftung website offers an overview: see Beutelschmidt 2010.

Chapter 4

ADVENTURES IN STAGNATION

Gottfried Kolditz's Unfilmed Project *Zimtpiraten*

Evan Torner

Dr. Gottfried Kolditz, one of East Germany's well-established genre filmmakers, left two films-in-progress behind when he suddenly died of an aneurysm on 15 June 1982, while location scouting in Dubrovnik, Yugoslavia.[1] One of these films was the DEFA *Indianerfilm*[2] *Der Scout* (*The Scout,* 1983), a GDR-Mongolian co-production, which was to begin principal photography in Mongolia in two weeks. This picture would instead be directed by Konrad Petzold. The other project was an ambitious DEFA pirate adventure *Zimtpiraten* (*Cinnamon Pirates,* slated for 1983) that was conceived in the late 1970s as a GDR-FRG co-production for West German television and East German cinemas. This picture would be placed on indefinite hold. *Zimtpiraten* tells the story of three seventeenth-century pirate captains and their mad-dash race from Amsterdam to be the first to colonize a newly discovered cinnamon island in the Indian Ocean. Thanks to mutually underhanded tactics that the pirate figures deploy from the beginning, two of the pirate captains—Don Fernandez and Mijnheer van Waalen—find themselves in a protracted, zero-sum battle over the course of their journey and, as a result, wind up the losers of the competition to the third pirate, English captain McIntosh. Treachery, witty banter, explosions, and the successive downgrading of the pirates' vessels throughout the story mark the main points of attraction for the film script, which appears to many degrees quite commercial in its form and function. Divided Germany appears to be the obvious allegory underwriting the narrative, but the pirates' skullduggery in the film does not otherwise correspond with the overwhelming media-political consensus between the two Germanies that let this pirate co-production get as far as it did.

Kolditz built his directing portfolio on DEFA genre cinema, with musicals, *Indianerfilme*, science-fiction films, and fairy-tales (for a full biography of the director, see Torner 2013a). His work marked an era following the 1965–66 crackdown of the 11th Plenum when the studio refocused its resources away from films dealing with present-day problems toward light, colorful entertainment cinema that would draw disaffected GDR audiences back into the cinemas. Yet with his death, his more or less idealistic vision for GDR cinema, in which "satisfied" viewers entertained by "cheerful" DEFA films would then (at least in theory) later return to the cinema and see a more serious film about present-day problems, also passed away with him (Kolditz 1970: 11). Kolditz had thus envisioned a cinematic subjectivity characterized not so much by East German socialist national interests but rather by the shared guilty pleasures of the middle and working classes; a kind of "normalized" media experience as part of Europe in the 1970s fitting the overall "normality" of the GDR depicted by Mary Fulbrook (2009)[3] In addition, this "normalized" experience would have in theory helped overcome the profound ambivalence between the DEFA film industry at Babelsberg and the GDR state television (DFF) as it existed in the early 1980s.[4] What this unfilmed pirate script suggests is exactly to what degree GDR cultural officials actually *agreed* with Kolditz's idealism about the purpose of entertainment in socialism and strove to overcome major economic and political barriers for the sake of trivial, homegrown genre fiction that would be potentially marketable abroad.

Kolditz's *Zimtpiraten* thus highlights both the opportunities and crises facing East and West German media at the beginning of the 1980s. These specific crises illustrate larger stakes on the stage of the Cold War—namely, media market saturation and divided German television's perceived drain on cinema revenues—which then achieve symptomatic expression in an all-too-allegorical pirate tale intended for the prospective pan-German TV audience. Rather than seeing the proposed colorful pirate adventure as a mere product of Kolditz's imagination or even of a specific "socialist" film tradition, I analyze it as a crisis product operating within overlapping transnational power networks[5] and utilize an interpretive apparatus that incorporates "ideology" as merely one discursive marker among many (Rodríguez 1999).[6] Since the lavish and cliché-ridden script itself had been green-lighted with few political or economic problems, speculation on "what if Kolditz had made the film?" proves actually less interesting than the intersecting conditions that enabled the production-never-to-be to come as far as it did.

In light of the situation at DEFA in the early 1980s, *Zimtpiraten* thus might be considered a *crisis product*. Crises in media history are so prevalent as to be banal. When they develop, they prompt shifts in subjectivities and media logics, though a system may be in crisis even as it entrenches itself in older modes of cultural production. Michael Wedel notes that "in historical writing, the turn toward a crisis metaphor as a reaction to observations of current processes of change [is] an all too familiar reflex"(Wedel 2010: 10). In an East German context, the DEFA was indeed in the middle of a "crisis" of creativity and material. The promise of cultural liberalization offered by Erich Honecker in the early 1970s had not been fulfilled; instead, the deportation of popular singer Wolf Biermann in 1976 led to a subsequent exodus of many popular stars (including Manfred Krug and Jutta Hoffmann), and the youngest generation of DEFA directors, including Dietmar Hochmuth and Jörg Föth, found themselves stymied at the beginning of their careers by delayed production and censorship. Money had receded from the film studios in such a fashion as to make the DEFA studios increasingly dependent on DFF projects,[7] and competition among East and West German broadcasters alike had intensified after the introduction of private television stations into the West. As Knut Hickethier describes the situation in the 1980s:

> The crisis of television was, on the one hand, that it had become taken for granted and could no longer be omitted from the everyday lives of the viewers. Indeed, it had appeared to be as common "as running water and electrical current." But on the other hand, it had to advance societal communication by trying to "raise awareness" of topics, such that it had to constantly offer something new and special. (Hickthier and Hoff 1998: 382)

Television had surpassed film in becoming exceedingly quotidian, such that films could now be employed as "eventized" content to interrupt the everydayness of television. In the West, the made-for-TV movie targeted the "middle-aged" demographic (14 to 49) (Davis 2000: 28), and sought to, as Sam Davis put it, "arouse enough interest that they might compete with soccer broadcasts" (2000: 30). But only those DEFA films that had proven to be *massenwirksam* ("effective for the masses") could truly create a television event that would attract sufficient viewer interest to justify the film's costs, regardless of what was playing on the other channels (Raundalen 2009). This crisis thus placed high Socialist

Unity Party (SED) cultural officials in a position to at least entertain the idea of creating blockbuster productions that would enjoy a televisual afterlife. And thus the odd alliance behind *Zimtpiraten* came into being: between Gottfried Kolditz (as director and scriptwriter), Gerd Gericke (as dramaturg and political advisor), the DEFA (as studio service provider and future distributor), the DFF (as co-financier), and the West German private TV production company Telepool (as co-financier and future distributor).

This low-brow pirate film property might be best seen as an artifact of a specific historical moment, one that refracts the socio-material forces of the time through the seemingly whimsical strokes of a screenwriter's typewriter. A sense of history must incorporate not only the facts of its given era, but also the cultural fantasies and political unconscious[8] arising from the minutiae of its fiction. People dream and—as it turns out—so do institutions. Vivian Sobchak sees productive scholarship emerging from such local and microhistories of not only films themselves, but also of what might have been films, and situates such an approach within a new film history that "recognizes history as inherently discursive, rhetorical, figural, tropological—'turning' both on itself and its being in time and language, veering off in strange directions from the straight and narrow, constituting itself in narratives and allegories" (Sobchak 2002). The film historian's duty within the twenty-first century is to untangle these threads long enough to tell a coherent story that reveals this very entanglement, before letting that story's re-mediation through discourse lift it toward uncertain horizons. Cast adrift in a zero-sum competition over their future livelihoods as Kolditz's pirates are, our own interpretations of the fragmentary, contradictory objects of our study must integrate them into transnational film history in a way that acknowledges the obscurity of these film objects while underscoring their importance precisely *as* fragments. In other words, an unfilmed DEFA pirate script reveals processes and perceived possibilities—the limits of both narrative and institutional imagination—that might very well prove more compelling than a formal film analysis of one of the DEFA studio's "classics" like, for example, *Jakob der Lügner* (*Jacob the Liar*, 1975) or *Der Fall Gleiwitz* (*The Gleiwitz Case*, 1960).

This essay interprets *Zimtpiraten*'s script and preproduction documents in terms of the Cold War media politics of the early 1980s, exploring the opportunities and crises that East and West German television faced at that time through the content and context of this unfilmed swashbuckler screenplay. These specific crises were allegorically converted into a pirate tale for a prospective pan-German TV audience. To properly frame the GDR ca. 1979–1982—the period in which the script was written, circulated, and contemplated—I first discuss notions of stagnation, crisis, labor power, and transnational leverage between the two Germanies and their respective histories. The aborted production history of the film constitutes a vacillation within the DEFA administration between hubristic casting/production decisions made in view of imagined *Massenwirksamkeit* and stark fear of economic loss, specifically of foreign currency, on the project. Lastly, I deal with the screenplay itself as a culturally and systemically overdetermined genre text, illuminating the theoretical issues raised in the first part with textual examples. At the end of the day, the script itself captures its fear of its own insignificance, a feeling of being left behind, of the stagnation produced by pointless competition, in telling generic forms and propositions.

Stagnation, Crisis, Labor

Social systems, including economic models, function, stagnate, and then experience crisis. Labor, whether creative or destructive, is applied to address these crises, and is itself then valorized or denigrated through the revised system's operations. Cultural representations of labor can serve as a barometer of this process. In European and American mass media fiction from the eighteenth century onward, valorized labor was that performed by the middle class in opposition to injustices committed by the aristocracy, church, and industrial capitalists, creating what John E. Davidson calls a "discourse of work as an indicator of middle-classness and belonging that supposedly unites us all, a value that erases (working-) class realities beneath a veneer of (bourgeois) individuality and meaning" (2012: 881). Like entertainment, which was, as earlier noted, one of the shared guilty pleasures of the middle and working classes, labor was thus a value that served as social glue, whether in socialist or capitalist countries. But the strategies of working against—and even the means of perceiving—so-called crises are often embedded within the structures of power that produced the crisis in the first place: labor as value can be as much a part of the problem as its solution. What I would like to suggest here is that the GDR's particular discourse of work is at least partially to blame for perceptions of stagnation and crisis, but that such discourse nevertheless serves as a useful heuristic category for media historians.

To say that GDR media occasionally experienced periods of "stagnation" or "crisis," or that their productions signify or perform "labor" to counteract these periods, is to use potentially overdetermined or ideological terminology. For example, let us define the word "stagnation," a word used to describe not only the GDR, but also the entire Eastern Bloc during the Brezhnev period (1964–1982). It can mean "to be settled," as in the desultory arrangement of particles of sediment on the bottom of a pond. Stagnation may characterize a period waiting for a crisis to jolt it out of its complacency.[9]

However, there are certain periods of stagnation that are intensely productive, and others less so. Stagnation in the political domain can go hand in hand with aesthetic innovation, as happened in the late nineteenth century or the 1950s in West Germany, when Adenauer's politics coexisted with Darmstadt musical modernism. Productive periods are those when sensed lack of movement becomes so palpable as to propel thinking into the distant past or the far future rather than towards immediate goals. A not-so-productive stagnation means the shutting down of the capacity to imagine outside stagnant conditions or to feel the decisive rift between expectation and reality, and/or lacking political capacity to seek out alternatives.

According to Michael Wedel, crises are a mode of perceiving and portraying a moment of stagnation in such a way as to enable a breakthrough. Such moments can be the primary locus of forms of art that, as Steven Shaviro interprets via Kant, "[throw] all norms and values into question, or into crisis" (Shaviro 2009: 1). Crises in film production have to do with any number of factors: major technology shifts, new demographic realities, the withdrawal of key supporters, or censorship. In fact, film history is nothing *but* perpetual crises, exemplified by the introduction of sound, competition from television, or the advent of the digital era.

Responding to earlier thoughts on the topic of crisis by Rick Altman (2004: 15–23) Wedel advises the media historian to look for crises in the epistemological intersection of objects of analysis with verifiable historical processes (Wedel 2010: 15–16). Privatization of television can constitute a crisis for public television structures, but only so long as one keeps in mind its long-term impact (i.e., decline of funding for public television worldwide combined with increase of subsidies for private stations). Crises have to decisively shift the society or means of production, and their resolutions do not always constitute "revolutions," but often rather a return to "normalcy." Thus it is also imperative, Wedel notes, to look at the continuities that persist throughout a crisis.

How do institutions respond to stagnation and crises? Until their dissolution or demise, institutions mobilize the power of representation to work against them both. Public relations and advertising budgets are deployed specifically to portray institutions as meeting challenges posed by crises without changing beyond recognition. Institutional processes moreover leave their traces within the film itself. It is here that I turn to Paul Willemen (2010) for his concept of "fantasies of labor power," or the fantasmic expression of the interrelationship between labor, capital, and the body through the semantic registers of film. Any given representational regime within a film reveals "an intricate patchwork of interest-positions" that correspond with interpenetrated modernizing and archaizing forces corresponding to pragmatic institutional (state-level/studio-level) goals. Individual filmmakers working within a specific system maneuver their texts through the financial, ideological, and representational possibilities of their production as they create them. In other words: individual film productions—or even the institutional plans for said productions—reveal idealized projections of and about specific institutions, connecting institutionalized subjectivity with institutionalized topoi with relationships to objects within those topoi.[10] We may illustrate this with concrete examples. In a western, life, like labor, is cheap on the frontier. In a pirate film such as *Zimtpiraten*, labor performed corresponds with primitive capital accumulation (i.e., theft) and a radically progressive means of organizing society (i.e., autocracy/democracy without aristocracy). In the case of *Zimtpiraten*, the work the pirate story is specifically intended to perform is to unite the East and West Germans as television and cinema consumer audiences via a genre cinema event, relying on the values, shared across classes, of labor and entertainment. The "fantasy of labor" we may see at work in *Zimtpiraten* is one of an institutional struggle against stagnation, and also of a film industry in crisis.

GDR Media and the 1980s

The concepts of crisis and stagnation provide a good heuristic basis for describing the situation in GDR television and film in the 1980s. Historians such as Charles Maier (1997) and Jeffrey Kopstein (1997) have long advanced the argument that the unsustainable East German economic base and the political inability to revitalize it were the core reasons for the nation-state's gradual state of overall decline. The 1979 Soviet invasion of Afghanistan and second oil crisis pushed all GDR dreams of economic independence out of the question. By that point, the GDR had already been financing its national imports for nearly a decade primarily through debt-funded investment from West Germany, eroding the country's fiscal security and forcing it into various slap-dash funding schemes to attract foreign currency (the watchword was *Devisenrentabilität* [profit via foreign currency]) (Madarász 2009: 56) Laura McGee calls the economy and cultural politics of the 1980s GDR a "desperate situation," and—drawing on the work of Dagmar Schittly on the topic—describes an internal unwillingness in the SED to even acknowledge the full scope of their problems at the time (McGee 2003: 446–48).[11] Stagnation of the East German economy thus became the unspoken structuring element of GDR culture, as one notices in the laconic writings of Ulrich Plenzdorf, the sarcastic ballads of Wolf Biermann, or controversial films such as Rainer Simon's *Jadup und Boel* (1980/1988). Not even the most trivial of genre productions could avoid the confluence of the feelings and facts of decline and, indeed, German-German co-production experiments such as *Zimtpiraten* were specifically leveraged as a bulwark against its effects.

The development of cultural-political "alternatives" during this time of stagnation was prompted by numerous media crises.[12] Privatization of television in the West, for example, opened up a host of new channels competing for the attention of audiences in both Germanies. This exacerbated the extant "content exhaustion" that both countries' publicly subsidized television stations already faced, and pushed these stations into the arena of what Simon During (2005: 111) calls "competitive novelty." Television would have to find a way to supplement its monopoly on simultaneity with, as William Uricchio (1998b: 123) writes, "cinema's necessary rupture of time." East and West Germany had used their public television stations and cinemas to broadcast what they perceived as their respective German heritages. Now both countries had to draw whatever viewer attention they could manage away from the narcissistic American-style programming of MTV and RTL or their own national soccer matches. Accompanying the new generation of competing channels was a marked reduction of East German cinema attendance. Movie viewing in Europe and the United States had already deteriorated since the 1960s with the introduction of color television, and East Germany was no exception. But by the 1980s, the only economically viable national cinema model worldwide appeared to be that of the blockbuster alongside ancillary merchandising à la Steven Spielberg (*Jaws*, 1975) or George Lucas (*Star Wars*, 1977). Maintaining and subsidizing cinema audiences had become an end of itself for the SED, which is why East Germany eventually turned to imports of Western science-fiction blockbusters such as Spielberg's *Close Encounters of the Third Kind* (1977, GDR release: 1985) to ensure box-office flow (Stott 2002: 91). Yet despite its considerable production infrastructure, the DEFA Studios at Potsdam-Babelsberg found themselves in no position to even conceive of such blockbusters, especially when some fifteen to twenty low-budget DFF television productions were instead utilizing its studio space in any given year, and creative genre reevaluations were not forthcoming from the third and fourth generation DEFA directors for structural reasons (Schenk 2012).[13] Thomas Beutelschmidt has gone so far as to assert that the DEFA and DFF "were hardly autonomous communicators, but could be understood as two dependent variables in the overall structure of the 'socialist media landscape'" (Beutelschmidt 2013). The final crisis of note concerned the upcoming fourth generation of DEFA directors and their viability as new artistic voices in the technocratic gerontocracy of the late GDR. As McGee argues, the youngest generation of film directors working between 1980 and 1989 faced many obstacles besides just the economy of scarcity (*Mangelwirtschaft*) between them and their first feature film (McGee 2003: 448). Directors such as Jörg Foth, Michael Kann, and Dietmar Hochmuth found themselves working on children's films, on international co-productions, and as assistant directors for most of their early careers before being permitted to work on a feature film. The third generation before them—consisting of Rainer Simon, Lothar Warneke, among others—were now shooting historical films after being disciplined for earlier aesthetic experiments verging on social critique in the 1970s. Neither generation had the leverage or political stamina to generate content that would credibly compete with the new private television offerings, nor could any DEFA director avoid the indirect treatment of this stagnation itself as a film topos. As a second-generation director with a potential blockbuster and (perhaps more importantly) a German-German finance strategy in hand, Gottfried Kolditz was positioning himself to address these precise crises with the *Zimtpiraten* project.

Nevertheless, the exigencies of German television history outside of a crisis perspective also assist in understanding the environment that produced the *Zimtpiraten* script. There are, in fact, few moments of East German television history *not* already inscribed with complicated German-German relations. For example, independent GDR television was only possible thanks to GDR radio director Hans Mahle's strategic recruitment of West German engineer Walter Bruch. But Mahle was then fired and replaced by SED functionaries in 1952 precisely for his association with instrumental border-crossers such as Bruch (Hickethier and Hoff 1998: 97–98). The cheap technical quality of GDR television compared with that of the FRG could be attributed to the West's successful embargo of television equipment during the crucial years of the medium at the end of the 1950s (Hickethier and Hoff 1998: 185). The DFF station in the 1960s was also subjected to pressures similar to the West German public stations, namely the pursuit of better ratings with low-brow television coupled with the production of high-brow, "quality" programming that would reinforce German cultural values but few would watch (During 2005: 113). While networks such as ARD and ZDF more or less financed the New German Cinema of R.W. Fassbinder, Werner Herzog, and Wim Wenders, the DFF produced weighty antifascist dramas such as *Gewissen in Aufruhr* (Conscience in Turmoil, 1961), *Dr. Schlüter* (1965) and *Wege übers Land* (Ways Across the Country, 1968) that also dealt with the shared Nazi past via provocative televisual language. Avant-garde cinema and television were the palpable result of increased television subsidy in the 1960s and 1970s, but viewer quotas for those programs fell drastically with the rise of professionalized sports and game shows (Hickethier and Hoff 1998: 354).[14] Both Germanies sought solutions to this disturbing new trend, despite the political divides of the Cold War, but shared solutions were rare. The 1976 expatriation of Wolf Biermann from the East to the West brought about a crackdown on quality productions at the DFF such as *Das Versteck* (*The Hiding Place*, 1977) or *Ursula* (1978), forcing the DFF's active search for actors and directors who would toe the party line (Hickethier and Hoff 1998: 404). The DFF would then be eclipsed on the "quality television" front by the 1979 West German broadcast of the Hollywood miniseries *Holocaust* (1978). With the advent of first color television and later digital television, the DFF found itself in the strange position of going further into debt to the FRG so that it could continue to broadcast combative messages against West Germany, despite the station having little new content to offer itself (Hickethier and Hoff 1998: 383).[15] In addition, the so-called alternative program structure of 1983 saw the near disappearance of critical films about the present (*Gegenwartsfilme*), historical or literary adaptations (except for disasters like *Sachsens Glanz und Preußens Gloria*, 1985–1987), and experimental programming of any kind in favor of more entertainment programming such as sports or Western feature films that nevertheless could not win back GDR viewers' attention (Hickethier and Hoff 1998: 405). The DFF continuously found itself at the mercy of the FRG, and yet was conversely propping up the DEFA studios with its own productions.

    DEFA was by no means insulated from the commercializing and ossifying trends affecting the DFF. When newly appointed DEFA studio director Hans Dieter Mäde was summoned to Erich Honecker's office in May 1977, Mäde's superior demanded films from him "that directly supported class struggle against West German imperialism" (Schenk 2009). Yet less than two years later, Mäde's office memos indicated movement toward the exact opposite pole, namely, increased entertainment programming and collaborations with West Germany. German-German co-productions were by no means a foreign concept to the DEFA, even in the Cold War: FRG filmmakers needed studio space, and the GDR needed foreign currency. Despite the initial failed attempt to co-produce and co-direct Thomas Mann's *Die Buddenbrooks* (1955) shortly after the author's death, both Germanies nevertheless managed to implement several East-West co-productions at DEFA: *Fräulein von Scuderi* (*Mademoiselle de Scudéri*, 1955), *Die Schönste* (*The Prettiest One*, 1959), *Die Heiden von Kummerow* (*The Heathens of Kummerow*, 1966), *Frühlingssinfonie* (*Spring Symphony*, 1983), and *Die Grünstein-Variante* (*The Grünstein Variant*, 1985). Each of the above productions had a West German film director employing the DEFA studios as a service provider, and the screen rights were ultimately kept by the private companies in the West. East German directors such as Wolfgang Staudte and Arthur Maria Rabenalt also worked in the West, a practice that ceased with the 1961 construction of the Berlin Wall.

What Mäde encountered in the 1980s GDR, however, was the devilish double standard for filmmakers to make films that addressed all the perniciousness of the West (as dictated by the party) and at the same time would be exportable abroad as some form of "entertainment." In the 17 November 1981 issue of *Neues Deutschland*, an infamous forged letter from Hubert Vater, an electrician in Erfurt, publicly demanded that DEFA films valorize the GDR's accomplishments rather than tell stories about figures on the margins (Vater 1981: 2). His call for more "militant" media content that accused Western capitalists for their crimes harkened back to the era of *Die Mörder sind unter uns* (*The Murderers Are Among Us*, 1946), and was taken seriously by DEFA filmmakers at the time, since he represented a presumably "average viewer" from their GDR audience (McGee 2003: 446). Yet this party-incited "everyman" criticism of film and television proved both stifling to the coming generation as well as unrealistic for the established filmmakers with regard to the increasing need for genre productions that would easily reach international markets. Dieter Wiedemann and Hans Lohmann derided this period of DEFA production as one of "strangling critique while at the same time simulating 'tolerance' and 'communication'" (1991: 43). Filmmakers and television producers alike found themselves on the receiving end of what Manfred Jäger calls the "chaotic cultural politics without strategic concept" of the GDR in the 1980s, evidence of a media crisis between resources and ideals (1994: 167).

Possibilities, Probabilities, and Production

To summarize the above, the state-funded DEFA studios experienced a period of structural stagnation in terms of creative output, financing, and audience interest. As both Benita Blessing (2009) and Ralf Schenk (2012) have argued elsewhere, the DEFA studios were already caught in a kind of prisoner's dilemma with regard to their aesthetic output, and the consequences were apparent to all at the time. Much like CEOs of today's multinational Hollywood, the studios had to deliver on precise targets set by stakeholders with regard to film cost and ticket revenues. A DEFA film had to be interesting enough to attract at least a small audience, but if it proved too attractive—like for example Heiner Carow's *The Legend of Paul and Paula* (1973)—then suspicions of subversive content would necessarily prompt official disapproval. Though they received a steady wage as state employees almost regardless of their output, DEFA filmmakers had to nevertheless manage the sociopolitical expectations about their films, maneuvering them through up to eight stages of screenplay development before possibly watching them become shelved anyway for reasons beyond their control. When coupled with the fact that most of the studio's directors by the late 1970s were white East German men over the age of forty (Kolditz included), one sees how an aesthetically uniform, risk-averse style developed as a bulwark to preserve careers and compromised a more nuanced vision of either the cinema or its audience.

This section discusses the script development of *Zimtpiraten* from its conception to its demise in the GDR context. Despite Jill Nelmes's assertion that the screenplay is a generally neglected art form with regard to film studies (2011: 1), DEFA memoirs and reference books have long dwelt on the restive potential of unfilmed scripts that might have been made in the GDR (Agde 2001; Wolf 2000). Many scripts were fully developed at DEFA, only to be turned down due to various political sensitivities. Jurek Becker's *Deutschland unter Brüdern* (*Germany among Brothers*, 1965) is one such script, martyred during the 11th Plenum crackdown. Another was Regine Kühn's *Schwarzweiß und Farbe* (*Black, White and Color*, 1981), a story about a lone fisherman's hut standing in the way of a new GDR power plant at Lubmin that was shelved due to the planned construction of a different GDR atomic power operation. But fully developed scripts were also rejected on the basis of being too entertaining. The adaptation of Lion Feuchtwanger's *Der falsche Nero* (*The Pretender*, 1973) could not come into being thanks to the script's exoticism and semblance to Italian *peplum* films of the 1960s (Wolf 2000: 31), and the musical adaptation of *A Connecticut Yankee in King Arthur's Court* (1964) was turned down on similar grounds. It is important to recognize that Kolditz's script was a rare DEFA script in that, despite its overtly commercial appeal, its abandonment after the multiyear screenwriting process had everything to do with Kolditz's inability to spearhead the project, and little to do with its ideological content.

Kolditz was the director best positioned at the time to meet the odd requirements of a "new" East-West German entertainment cinema to emerge from the media crisis. He had proven himself politically reliable through early work with the *Stacheltier* unit in the 1950s, then became known both for putting a socialist spin on Hollywood genres such as the musical with *Revue um Mitternacht* (*Midnight Review*, 1962) or the western with *Spur des Falken* (*Falcon's Trail*, 1968). He implemented those experiments off GDR soil, such as with his Mongolian fairytale *Die goldene Jurte* (*The Golden Yurt*, 1960) and Romania in *Im Staub der Sterne* (*In the Dust of the Stars*, 1976). His eagerness to experiment with the tricks of Hollywood spectacle, including the extensive use of stunt riders for the westerns and zero gravity harnesses for science-fiction, came with the counterweight of careful avoidance of all major political controversy: taboo topics, youth issues, and West German flirtations. Part of Kolditz's job appeared to be careful management of his political position, so he could tell the kinds of good vs. evil stories that were his wont. His films exhibited a straightforward, professional quality, and his narratives contained the kind of "humanism *sans* excess" that the Ministry of Culture used as a hazy criterium to judge Hollywood film imports (Stott 2002: 97). In a 2002 interview, dramaturg Gerd Gericke of the DEFA Gruppe Johannisthal commented that Kolditz was perceived as a "pleasant person with whom to work" and someone who consistently carried out seemingly expensive projects under budget (*Zeitzeugengespräch: Gerd Gericke* 2002). He had also been toying with the idea of making at least one of his *Indianerfilm* cycles—*Apachen* (*Apaches*, 1973) and *Ulzana* (1974)—as a television miniseries to offset studio costs. In other words, Kolditz was a low-risk, proven director from DEFA's second generation who would not require much oversight and who would breathe life into a new DEFA genre, much as he had done with the studio's *Indianerfilme*.

Zimtpiraten was selected in July 1978 by Gericke over two other Kolditz treatments: his sealab adventure *Eine Handvoll Dunkelheit* (*A Fistful of Darkness*) and the sci-fi mystery *Wer stiehlt schon Unterschenkel?* (*Who's Stealing Lower-Legs?*).[16] Gericke selected it on behalf of the pirate script's "plastic characters that make it possible to bring to the silver screen the political-historical background as well as our present-day perspectives in a visually pleasing form."[17] It also had a broad-based potential for screening at both the outdoor *Sommerfilmtage*—the outdoor screenings where the *Indianerfilme* reigned as blockbusters—as well as the evening DFF television "classics" block, which tended toward old UFA films as family-friendly light entertainment. With the proper cast, *Zimtpiraten* was also presumed uniquely capable of reaching West German and international audiences. This potential for apolitical internationalization prompted an English-language version of the script to be produced by October 1978 for DEFA to shop around to foreign investors. The cast Kolditz had in mind contained famous GDR character actors: Winfried Glatzeder as Spanish captain Don Fernandez, Milan Beli as Dutch captain Mijnheer van Waalen, Fred Delmare and Rolf Hoppe in side comedic roles, and Isabella—the contested love interest—played by none other than Angelika Domröse. The most interesting choice, however, was to cast ready-and-willing West German actor Gert Fröbe, famous for playing Goldfinger in the eponymous 1963 James Bond film, as the English captain McIntosh, who eventually wins the race in the film's story.

How did DEFA manage access to Fröbe, a minor Hollywood star? Since the production also required footage of three-mast pirate ships that DEFA simply did not possess, Kolditz was put in contact with a TV production company that did: the West German Telepool München. A three-day business meeting in Munich suddenly placed Kolditz and Gericke in negotiations with Telepool producer Friedrich Magold over a possible co-production between DEFA, Telepool, and the Yugoslav firm Jadran-Film. The co-production would have had DEFA front DM 3 million for studio shots, actor salaries, staff, and postproduction while Telepool would have put up DM 1.5 million for the exterior shots, film material, development costs, the big-name actor Fröbe, and a DM 500,000 security deposit with DEFA-Außenhandel. Telepool would retain the television rights, DEFA the cinema distribution rights. A second Munich meeting in April 1982 secured Fröbe's interest in the project. In end effect, GDR cultural functionaries proved quite willing to co-finance a pirate movie that would wind up as Eastern Bloc cinema and also as West German commercial television, then broadcast back over the border into most East German homes.

Another question remains: why choose the pirate genre for this border-crossing film? Historically, pirate films experienced their heyday during Hollywood's golden era (1930s–1950s), with *Captain Blood* (1935) and *Treasure Island* (1950) leading in box-office returns. But after Lewis Milestone's *Mutiny on the Bounty* (1962),[18] not a single attempted pirate film in global film history made its money invested back until the release of *Pirates of the Caribbean* in 2003 (Almereyda 2003). DEFA itself had made two ship-oriented films in the 1960s—*Die schwarze Galeere* (*The Black Galleon*, 1961) and *Der fliegende Holländer* (*The Flying Dutchman*, 1964)—but then abandoned the genre in favor of the *Indianerfilme*. How was the DEFA going to beget the ideal media object that Rüdiger Steinmetz and Reinholf Viehoff describe as "'a feature film effective with the masses,' seen as an attack against the West and the flight of GDR citizens" (Steinmetz and Viehoff 2008: 304), when they had experienced so little success earlier?

The productive stagnation articulated earlier serves as one explanation for using pirates. In a crisis situation, expensive experiments performed by reliable people become more readily explainable. Filmmakers from both Germanies suddenly found common ground in the will to entertain a wider conceived target market, and a product that would be seen as specifically "new" would help revitalize a cinema and television environment not yet structured to deal with heightened competitive novelty.[19] In his annotation to the *Zimtpiraten* script, Kolditz expresses confidence in the visual appeal of not only the historic milieu but also of the main characters having to use smaller and smaller ships over the course of the film. In other words, universal and nonpolitical humor underlying the actions of the characters would serve to bundle audience attention into some sort of aggregate box-office return.

Another explanation lies in the set of values inherently expressed through the pirate genre. Pirate films tend to concern interstitial transit between nations and myths of national authority (Rediker 2004: 10), an appropriate topic for a German-German film, as well as homelessness interpreted in a positive light (Suchsland and Alvarez 2003: 9). Rüdiger Suchsland and Constantine Alvarez (2003: 8–9) see pirates as operating in an "economy of wastefulness" with regard to liquor and other resources, and their social interactions in such films often contain a homosexual subtext. The romanticized Hollywood pirate is free to roam, free to settle his/her debts according to the pirate code, and free to reconfigure the social order on the high seas. "There is no other similar genre," Sabine Horst (2006: 25) writes, "that homes in on the right for free development and fulfilment of one's needs, or at least on a vanishing point somewhere on the horizon, in such a self-evident fashion." Pirates might have offered a finely balanced cocktail of fantasies for West and East Germany: hedonism and cunning on the one hand, the dissolution of hierarchies and the timeless space of the high seas on the other. Anxieties about supernations—the United States and the USSR—overtaking national issues with their dilemmas and problems could suddenly be resolved by watching the two Germanies figuratively bond as two squabbling pirate captains whose struggle ultimately comes to naught.

The Race to the Cinnamon Island

Zimtpiraten's plot typifies an action comedy, albeit one intent on demonstrating the fundamental interchangeability of the two protagonists. In 1725, news of a cinnamon island reaches Europe, and the Portuguese and Dutch empires each send a privateer to reach it first. After having his death by firing squad faked for him, Portuguese captain Fernandez receives the mission just as Captain Van Waalen is—through a sound bridge—informed of the cinnamon island in Amsterdam. The two captains, old friends and rivals, meet in a harbor tavern on the Isle of Ushant near Brest. As they compete for prestige at knife-throwing and the eye of the barmaid Isabella, each of their men sabotage each other's three-mast ship, only to find themselves in cannon exchanges with a third vessel piloted by Englishman Captain McIntosh. McIntosh finds out about the cinnamon island and sets off to beat both men at their own game. Fernandez and Van Waalen immediately turn their guns on each other when convenient, and during the battle they discover the now-stowaway Isabella, who is obsessed with Fernandez, disguised as a man.[20] Their joint voyage takes them to Nana Kru on the West African coast, where they call an armistice, which amounts to the two captains switching from throwing knives to dice. It is at Nana Kru that the viewer gets to see the horrors of the slave trade, as large black men load and unload boats under the eyes of the overseers. Two ships arrive and, through skullduggery, both captains manage to steal or win one apiece. In the hold of Fernandez's brigantine, he finds a host of women on their way from Le Havre to the convict isle of Mayotte to join their recently pardoned husbands. Some of the pirates suggest throwing them overboard, but they choose instead to make them jump overboard and swim to Mayotte when they came close. Isabella, who has been taken aboard Van Waalen's vessel, tries to seduce and kill her captor, but winds up helping rescue the crew of the brigantine (including Fernandez and a female stowaway Zouzou) after their boat is destroyed in a sudden storm. Determined to reach the island first, the captains each build themselves sloops, destroy them in mutual gunfire, and lash them together to form one raft. In the fog, Fernandez and Van Waalen have a heart-to-heart conversation and forgive each other. Then the fog lifts, the cinnamon island is revealed, the race is on again, and they swim out with their respective flags to try to be the first to colonize it. Sharks eat their flags, leaving the two captains at each other's throats on the beach. McIntosh suddenly emerges from the island, the English flag already flying over its soil, and the film ends with the captains' mutual failure.

Divided Germany's role in the Cold War could not be the more obvious as the allusion here. Each captain serves a specific nation (Portugal, the Netherlands—standing in for East and West Germany), but the conflict between them is ultimately quite personal, wasteful and silly. In the end, superpower England (analogous to the United States, the USSR, privatized television, or what have you) wins due to the captains' bickering. Kolditz depicts the captains and their crews as cut from the same cloth, but also bitter enemies. In his early treatment, Kolditz specifically defends the peculiar mix of humorous antics and brutal colonial violence in the film as its fundamental tension: "The turbulent, adventure-filled race sprinkled with many gags will take place against the backdrop of the brutal battle for colonies of the rising forces of European capitalism." But wider anxieties about media crises of the 1980s and East German postindustrial existence within a competitive and declining global cinema market also come to the fore.

Turning back to the notion of the script as a crisis product, one finds in *Zimtpiraten* ambivalence toward the slash-and-burn tactics of both capitalism and state-led socialism. One recalls Erich Honecker's decades-long deficit spending via the West German debt, which was ostensibly for the purpose of "the ever improving fulfillment of the growing material and cultural needs of the working people" (quoted in Hickethier and Hoff1998: 384). Throughout the film, Fernandez and Van Waalen's mutual destruction and theft of each other's vessels, the pirates' means of production in a Marxist sense, demonstrate the effects of cannibalizing one's own resources. The two captains are indeed willing to expend all their resources for their mission, and accept Pyrrhic victories that jeopardize their crew as victories all the same. From a national perspective, their reckless power over their ships and crews is vested in their prospective claims on the cinnamon island—a nameless future colony to be resource-extracted—in the name of Portugal and the Netherlands respectively. The pirates are not the individualist freebooters as they appear, but constitute quasi-national agents working in the service of early state colonialism out of greed, jealousy, and a will to survive. It is for these petty motives that they are presumably punished in the end. At this point, the Wild West of Kolditz's *Indianerfilme* should come to mind here with its scheming capitalist cowboys and noble, socialist Indians. But those earlier Manichean categories are discarded here for a cynical, picaresque narrative that satirizes its protagonists alongside the many colorful characters they meet on their journey.

Aspects of *Zimtpiraten* that could be discussed in terms of Willemen's schema of labor power include the odd gendered and classed roles found in the script. The female figures of the story serve as barmaids or stowaways, with their agency reduced to performance of maleness (i.e., the cross-dressing) or the laying claim on various male characters. The script makes repeated mention to the "bad luck" Isabella causes both captains. She plays the part of the femme fatale, fighting for the hand of Fernandez against the interloper woman Zouzou: again, a zero-sum conflict enacted in microcosm. The numerous jokes made about this large, segregated group of women being "disposable cargo," easily spooked, and "prizes" for the pirates to humorously pursue correspond with a somewhat reactionary gender-political stance compared with the admirable DEFA dramas of the 1970s such as *Der Dritte* (*Her Third*, 1972). Meanwhile, the male captains are caught in the trap of Cold War–style game theory, in which each of them by necessity must correctly guess the move of the other in order to maintain equilibrium. This results in a chaotic logistical nightmare that complicates their voyage, much in the way that GDR cultural politics proceeded as "chaotic" and "without a concept" during the 1980s. As the captains compete in the *symbolic* sphere—with knife-throwing or dice—they neglect or ignore the *material* sphere, causing them to consistently lose vessels to unruly elements in their midst. They fail as both moral and pragmatic leaders, and are thus equally punished for their oversights in the end (along with their crews). Whereas the early DEFA *Aufbaufilme* of the 1950s were about the rebuilding of German society following its destruction under the Third Reich, this genre film co-production would have enacted ritualistic destruction of smaller and smaller sets of resources, fed into the engine of unreachable economic goals and international strife taken to the personal level. Hubert Vater's 1981 critique could thus apply to the fluff genre entertainment of the GDR as well: the struggle of the workers cannot be found here either. The captains prove better drinkers and fighters than sailors, corresponding with the idea that Cold War had conditioned certain skill sets and class expectations in each populace that may not have been the most productive in reaching some shared social goal.

The racial dimensions of the script also prove somewhat disconcerting. For example, Yugoslavian shooting locations were to stand in for Liberia, Mayotte, and the Indian Ocean; i.e., half the world was to be found in a country a thousand kilometers southeast of Germany.[21] It thus inherits the aesthetics of race and landscape of European adventure films since the 1930s: exoticizing the Other for decorative purposes happened under socialism as often as under capitalism. The Nana Kru sequence at the height of the African slave trade recalls the antebellum South imagery of Konrad Petzold's *Indianerfilm Osceola* (1971), and it seems Kolditz's socialist duty to voyeuristically remind one of the brutality of this centuries-long industry. In one scene description, it reads: "At the pier, negroes as strong as a horse are balancing on tottering thick planks and carrying heavy bales from the hold of the ship ashore. They are brutally prompted."[22] Kolditz's story quite clearly depicts colonialism, slavery, and sexism as part of this zero-sum, selfish game of capitalist endeavor. Yet the frame of the film privileges the white male characters over the backdrop of oppressive exploitation in which they play their freelancing role (i.e., by taking the cinnamon island). The Germanies are still seen as *above* the politics of white superiority and the postcolonial exploitation of Global South resources, rather than thoroughly *imbricated* in them as a member of the Global North.

If the script proposes the ultimate unproductivity of zero-sum conflict, then its status as an expensive solution to a content crisis gives it access to a vivid societal subconscious. This film was to air on West German television, so naturally there would have been attractive women baring flesh (i.e., Isabella, Zouzou) and plenty of explosions. But the film had to fulfill the requirements of youth cinema for the DEFA *Sommerfilmtage,* which meant an easily legible moral about cooperation and solidarity. Kolditz's script presumes social inequalities of the colonial era to be objects of our voyeuristic sympathy, while the serious business of navigating the seas and violent exchanges are opportunities for slapstick and hilarity. Commercializing tensions render both the gags and the moments of seriousness to be utterly superficial, casting doubts as to the overall effectiveness of this movie gambit, had it been made.

Afterthoughts

The resultant *Zimtpiraten* film may very well have been mediocre, a bit of expensive pan-German pirate kitsch by a second-tier director screened for East Germans and then televised for both Germanies. In 1982, the DFF eventually put on a low-budget swashbuckling production entitled "Rächer, Ritter, und Rapiere" ("Avengers, Knights, and Rapiers") to address the problem of entertainment fiction, and the brief stock pirate ship footage used in Jürgen Brauer's children's film *Das Herz des Piraten* (*The Heart of the Pirate*, 1988) stemmed from the original Telepool agreement. A later film, Lothar Warneke's *Einer trage des anderen Last* (*Bear Ye One Another's Burdens*, 1987), specifically treats the topic of irreconcilable ideological conflict—between a Catholic and a socialist—in a light-hearted fashion reminiscent of Fernandez and Van Waalen's bickering. Its minimal legacy aside, however, *Zimtpiraten* helps illustrate several aspects of DEFA genre cinema in general. First, that the introduction of a new socialist genre at the DEFA studios more hinged on dependable individual agents like Kolditz seizing upon state-level uncertainty about overall media strategies than it did on the originality or entertainment value of what was on offer. The project lived and died, quite pragmatically, with Kolditz. Second, FRG-GDR co-productions could emerge with little political fanfare or fuss, and they presented opportunities to overcome a media environment drastically shifted in favor of private stations and the Hollywood blockbuster (Zimmer 1998: 2).[23] Finally, *Zimtpiraten* attempts to confer a sense of superiority over its squabbling protagonists, but thereby subsumes anxieties about women, nonwhite people, and the danger to which a country's elite exposes its citizens in the text. Kolditz's never-realized, potentially expensive German-German co-production was intended to depict the ridiculousness of zero-sum conflict and the importance of telling stories together as a collective.

I wish to conclude with this storytelling moment, the penultimate sequence of the DEFA film that never was. Mijnheer and Fernandez, by now archrivals, find themselves adrift on a raft in the Indian Ocean before they see the cinnamon island. As if adhering to the very definition of "stagnation" put forth at the beginning, the two captains appear to have stopped moving entirely, have ceased in their production, or have at least reached a moment of quiet within the cyclical crises that have spurred on their antics for the entire script. They have settled onto their raft, their mutually destructive sabotage leading to the unforeseen consequence of being quite literally stuck in the same boat. What transpires? They recollect and restitute, as they recognize the need for storytelling itself to maintain good-neighbor relations when neither can directly act to further their self-interest. They revel in shared history, as one might fantasize about the two Germanies if all political and economic conflicts could be set aside for a night; a Christmas Truce of 1725, if you will. Once the cinnamon island appears on the horizon and the frontier of wealth via colonial resource extraction presents itself, however, reflective stagnation transforms back into crisis and both captains deploy all their remaining resources to win an apparently zero-sum conflict. When they discover that it was their stagnation itself—and not their ambitious actions—that spurred truly humanistic and generative activity, they signal to the viewer the very elusive nature of any kind of "success" after a protracted conflict. Kolditz's script thereby signals a kind of threefold longing: for the methods and money of GDR television to help finance the future of DEFA feature films, for West Germany and East Germany to tell stories together once again, and for both the United States and the USSR to recognize the tremendous waste of their so-called Cold War. Reconceived in terms of continuous "crises" and both productive and nonproductive periods of stagnation, the Cold War imaginary I propose here appears less a neatly conceived historical epoch from 1946 to 1989, and more the sediment of long-standing discourses, desires, and disasters that now lies beneath our new period of unparalleled development alongside equally unparalleled stagnation.

Evan Torner is Assistant Professor of German Studies at the University of Cincinnati. In 2013, he defended his dissertation on race representation in East German genre cinema at the University of Massachusetts Amherst, and spent 2013–2014 at Grinnell College as an Andrew W. Mellon Postdoctoral Fellow. He has published several articles pertaining to East Germany, critical race theory, science fiction, transnational genre cinema, and game studies. His three major projects underway include the *Handbook of East German Cinema: The DEFA Legacy*, co-edited with Henning Wrage and under contract with Walter De Gruyter; a monograph based on his dissertation entitled *Solidarity? Race in East German Cinema*; and the monograph *A Century and Beyond: Critical Readings of German Science-Fiction Cinema*.

Notes

1. I would like to thank Stefan Kolditz, Michael Wedel, Birgit Scholz, Renate Goethe, and the Fulbright Commission for their help in various capacities in drafting this article. Also to Larson Powell and Robert Shandley for their patience for my own period of stagnation.
2. DEFA stands for Deutsche Film-Aktiengesellschaft or German Film Company. It was the state-funded East German film studio for feature, documentary, and animated

films from 1946 to 1992. The *Indianerfilm* was a film genre one could also call the "DEFA western," which involved depictions of Native American resistance against capitalist cowboys.
3. For more on the theory that the GDR was an entertainment-seeking, postindustrial white society like any other during its latter decades, see Classen 2010: 399.
4. See Thomas Beutelschmidt. "'Just Like in the West, Except Different' Television and Its Relationship to Film in the Context of 1950s GDR Development" in this volume.
5. See Halle 2008; Jahn-Sudmann 2009; Hjort 2010.
6. This approach is also utilized in Cooke 2005.
7. See Beutelschmidt 2013 regarding the early contortions of the film studio to the demands of television already in the 1950s.
8. The reference to Frederic Jameson's eponymous book, *The Political Unconscious* (1981), is anything but coincidental. His proposition of the measuring and evaluation of previous fantasies within frameworks of ideology appears to grow increasingly important in our excavations of trivial fiction from the recent and remote past.
9. In a more neoliberal vein—anything stagnant *is* by nature in crisis—as in, for example, the creative destruction thesis of economist Joseph Schumpeter.
10. For more on institutions such as cultural ministries or film studios as authors, see Christensen 2012: 2–3.
11. The text to which McGee extensively refers is Schittly 2002: 215–16.
12. For an overview of the trends discussed in this paragraph, see Dittmar and Vollberg 2004.
13. On the DFF being the primary financier of DEFA productions, Steinmetz and Viethoff 2008: 78.
14. Television subsidies drove (and drive) German cinema to such a degree that by the mid-1970s, one could no longer speak of a cinema vs. television divide, since television was the direct financing engine for most of cinema in either Germany.
15. See also Steinmetz and Viehoff 2008: 392.
16. Most of the material cited in this section is available in Gottfried Kolditz's *Nachlass* at the Filmmuseum Potsdam, courtesy of Birgit Scholz.
17. Production notes to *Zimtpiraten* found in the Kolditz *Nachlass*.
18. Milestone's film was incidentally one of the major early rerun successes on broadcast television during the 1960s and 1970s.
19. It is also interesting to note the pirate genre's serious literary popularity under the Third Reich, specifically the bestsellers *Der Schiffsjunge des Piraten* by Fritz Mücke, *Jörge, der Leichtmatrose* by Otfrid von Hanstein, and *Das Wrack des Piraten* by Friedrich Gerstäcker.
20. Her reveal is somewhat astonishing for an East German film, as a grapnel accidentally tears off her clothes during the fight, revealing her curves underneath.
21. This metonymy with regard to nonwhites and exotic locales is discussed at greater length in my dissertation (Torner 2013b).
22. This recalls the treatment of slaves in the Indianerfilm *Osceola* (1971), which was filmed with Cuban sugarcane workers and a slave driver with a whip in the background.
23. The trend would only accelerate after the Wende, with the stations RTL, Sat.1, and Pro Sieben dominating the German television (and European) market with their TV-movie productions by 1996.

PART III

TELEVISION IN THE FEDERAL REPUBLIC: AUTEURIST TV

Chapter 5

"A CHALLENGE, MAYBE THE GREATEST FOR A FILMMAKER"

Televisual Perspectives on
Rainer Werner Fassbinder's *Martha* (1974)

Brad Prager

Writer-director Rainer Werner Fassbinder's attitude about television changed and evolved, especially during the time he worked on his numerous made-for-television productions over the course of the 1970s. He shifted between various positions concerning the political prospects of television, particularly from 1971, when working for television seemed to offer an alternative to the infighting that had beset some of his stage productions, through to 1980, when he completed his mammoth fifteen-hour television adaptation of Alexander Döblin's novel *Berlin Alexanderplatz*. Initially Fassbinder had been optimistic about working in the television industry, which, thanks to Germany's publicly funded stations such as ARD and ZDF, had offered him and the other emerging auteurs of the New German Cinema generous financial support. In 1971 he lamented that his theater productions had not been reaching working-class audiences and drew the conclusion: "Only with television are things different: you find a truly diverse audience there. And I think television is, at the moment, the best way to communicate something to people" (Gröhler 1971).[1] A few years later, however, he had lost some of his utopianism and his confidence began to wane. Three years after the premiere of *Martha* (1974) Fassbinder commented retrospectively:

> Certainly I'll continue to work for WDR, but I'll go so far as to say that even today I couldn't make a television movie like *Martha* anymore. At the time, I made the movie to show a marriage as clearly as possible as a sadomasochistic relationship, because the more crassly you show that, the more married people have a chance to identify with your characters. At the time that wasn't a problem. If I approached them [television stations] with something like that today, alarms would go off. The thinking would be: This is an attack on existing social institutions. The television producer would wonder whether this wasn't one of those borderline situations where he'd have to cover himself. (Töteberg and Lensing 1992: 141)[2]

Despite his reservations Fassbinder worked on television productions throughout those years. Even after having withstood numerous controversies he made the television films *Bolwieser* (*The Stationmaster's Wife*, 1977) and, later, *Berlin Alexanderplatz*, drawing in both cases on the support of public broadcasting. He experienced frustrations and profound skepticism, but he neither gave up hope nor did he forsake the medium. In that same 1977 interview Fassbinder was also asked about *Acht Stunden sind kein Tag* (*Eight Hours are Not a Day*, 1972–1973), a television series he wrote and directed, which centered on the routine, job-related concerns of a working-class family in Cologne. The series took its protagonists' problems seriously, but also presented their daily life in a positive, even rosy, light, which became a source of controversy. He worked on the project in 1972 and 1973, and subsequently observed: "We'd never be able to make that nowadays. At most [we could make] one of those depressing realistic movies about workers" (Töteberg and Lensing 1992: 141). Although his perspectives on making television films seemed to shift relative to the fortunes of whichever project he was working on, the struggle to keep *Eight Hours* in production decisively jaded his overall outlook. He had hoped that television would influence public debate about the mind-set of the working class, but his experience with the industry disheartened him.

The director's disappointment stemmed in part from his inability to transform the middle class's understanding of working-class problems and the roots of class conflict, but it also stemmed from his frustration in dealing with television executives. Fassbinder had filmed five episodes of *Eight Hours* in 1972, and the series premiered on the station ARD over five nights between October 1972 and March 1973. In spring 1973 WDR, the station that had supported the series, announced that *Eight Hours* was being discontinued even though Fassbinder had already planned for and written three future episodes. He voiced publicly his irritation with his production company and asserted that Günter Rohrbach, who was then the head of WDR's television division, had made his decisions autocratically (Michael 1973).[3] Rohrbach was prominent among the leading television producers in Germany at the time and was known for tackling difficult themes. In an effort to compete with cinema audiences, Rohrbach declared that, from the producer's perspective, television and film productions should be treated as one and the same.[4] He pushed the limits in his willingness to tackle controversial themes and to use television in way that was intended to parallel the potentials of cinema, yet Fassbinder's work pushed too far even for Rohrbach. For his part, Fassbinder felt thwarted. His aim with *Eight Hours* had been to present television audiences with a working world that was not as "gloomy, wretched and inane" as had generally been portrayed ("Schön populär" 1972). He wanted to provoke viewers by depicting the working class differently, without the gloom and depression, and he intended for the characters in his series to be entitled both to their dreams and to the energy to realize them. He sought to present their situation as one with promise, and to empower his television audience by reminding them that, "as a group there exist possibilities that an individual doesn't have. That's a good thing, and it can lead to something" (Röhl 1973: 17). By 1974, however, Fassbinder grew concerned about whether he had hoped for too much, asserting that although *Eight Hours* led to a number of discussions with workers and union members, it "wasn't understood at all by the people I thought would certainly understand what was right and good about it" (Töteberg and Lensing 1992: 158).

During the period that followed—after he found himself disillusioned by his head-to-head encounter with Rohrbach—Fassbinder made *Martha*. The made-for-television marital drama was widely recognized as challenging and provocative, but for vastly different reasons than *Eight Hours*. Not long after the film's premiere in May 1974, *Spiegel* editor Hellmuth Karasek wrote that the film, which he described as one of the "most vexing" (*bedrängendsten*) in the mass medium of television, was tailored to push its performers, Margit Carstensen and Karlheinz Böhm, both to their limits and to the limits of the viewers' expectations (Karasek 1974: 120). Writing for the *Kölner Stadt Anzeiger*, Armin Halstenberg pointed out with relief that Fassbinder's newest work was "not an agitation-film" (*kein Agitationsfilm*), which may have been a swipe at *Eight Hours* (Halstenberg 1974). In terms of Fassbinder's aspirations for television, *Martha* represented a change of pace; rather than attempting to reach the wide working-class audience many television producers had been seeking, his new film was an experimental and sometimes disquieting confrontation with the institution of marriage. It deliberately borrowed its imagery and themes from cinema—from filmmakers such as Alfred Hitchcock and Claude Chabrol, and in some cases it interacted critically with those directors' best-known works, as will be shown later in detail. Fassbinder used *Martha* to challenge both the conventions of television and the concept of marriage. He went about it in a purposefully cinematic way, both exploring the boundaries of television as a realm of creative freedom, and using the medium to compete with and respond to cinema.

The production of *Martha* took place during what is generally depicted as a compulsory pause in the making of Fassbinder's theatrical film *Fontane Effi Briest* (1974). In September 1972 in northern Germany (in Schleswig-Holstein), Fassbinder began filming his adaptation of Theodor Fontane's 1894 novel, but in October the actor Wolfgang Schenk, who was playing Baron von Innstetten, fell ill. Filming ground to a halt and was only resumed a year later. In that time Fassbinder took up other projects at a feverish pace, starting with *Welt am Draht* (*World on a Wire*), a two-part adaptation of a science fiction novel by Daniel Galouye, which he filmed for WDR in early 1973.[5] In May Fassbinder recorded his Bremen production of Ibsen's *Nora* (*A Doll's House*), which aired as *Nora Helmer* in February 1974 on ARD, and in only fifteen days at the end of September he made *Angst essen Seele auf* (*Ali: Fear Eats the Soul*, 1974), which later competed at Cannes and was ultimately regarded as one of his most important feature films.[6] During that same interval, in the summer of 1973, he also completed *Martha*, which was a contemporary critique of the institution of marriage. Key thematic elements from his adaptation of Fontane inundated Fassbinder's modern-day narrative, and he explained to Christian Braad Thomsen, "if you want to tell this story, you do not have to adapt Fontane's novel. You can just as well invent a new story, and *Martha* is my personal version of this story" (Fischer 2004: 302).[7] The film's gender politics mirror those of *Effi Briest*, particularly that film's depiction of the relationship between Effi and her husband Innstetten, which has often been described as a portrait of a woman who willfully submits to her husband's condescension and cruelty.

Effi Briest is hardly straightforward in its gender politics, and when it came to Fontane's writing, Fassbinder spoke of admiring the author's subtle juxtapositions. He remarked that Fontane's language "describes things and situations so precisely and for that reason is never unambiguous." He continues: "[Fontane's prose] always describes a thing from two sides; even when he says a thing is this way, he says in the next sentence, Yes, but you can see it another way. Fontane never pins himself down. He says—let me put it very crudely—Effi is very happy, though you could also think that maybe she isn't. That goes all the way through the book" (Töteberg and Lensing 1992: 157). Fassbinder filmed his adaptation in black and white in order to bring into relief the shades of gray in Fontane's text; the writer gives with one hand what he takes away with the other, and Fassbinder sought to capture that on film. *Effi*, and by the same token *Martha*, presents itself as ambiguous and ambivalent in ways that Fassbinder's overtly political "agitation film" *Eight Hours* did not (Elsaesser 1996: 281–82).[8]

One should avoid relying too much on comparisons between *Effi Briest* and *Martha*. Although there are similarities, the latter is definitely not an adaptation of Fontane's novel. It deals with a grown woman who dotes on her father and is keeping company with him on vacation in Rome when he suddenly collapses and dies. Following his death, she returns to her home in Konstanz where she marries a man with whom she had coincidentally crossed paths at almost precisely the moment of her father's death. From the very beginning Martha's prosperous suitor acts as though he is alternately educating a child and a boor, making her feel worthless and berating her that she stinks. Fassbinder made clear that he thought education (*Erziehung*), specifically that of a wife by her husband, can also be termed subordination or suppression (*Unterdrückung*). These terms were often repeated in the criticism, and they guided many interpretations of the film.[9] At each stage Martha's husband treats her sadistically; he prevents her from having a life of her own, chooses what music she listens to, and controls her every move. In her struggle to flee from him she ultimately injures herself in such a way that she exacerbates her captivity, and the film ends on a grim note.

Only in a general sense can Fassbinder's tale, which borders on horror, be linked to or described as a modernization of Fontane's work. In terms of its narrative details it is more closely related to "For the Rest of Her Life," a short story by Cornell Woolrich. Fassbinder thus created a hybrid between a nineteenth-century German literary classic and twentieth-century American hard-boiled fiction. Woolrich's work was often adapted: Hitchcock's *Rear Window* (1954) was based on his 1942 short story, "It Had to be Murder," and François Truffaut made *The Bride Wore Black* (1968) based on Woolrich's 1940 novel of the same name. As a stylized melodrama *Martha* deliberately works both with and against the films of famous Woolrich adapters. Woolrich's story appeared in *Ellery Queen's Mystery Magazine* in 1968, but when *Martha* first aired on 28 May 1974 on the public television station ARD, Woolrich was not named as a source.[10] The second time the film aired the words "Based on motifs in a story by Cornell Woolrich" (Nach Motiven einer Erzählung von Cornell Woolrich) appeared on screen at the end (Berling 1992: 243). At the time WDR and Fassbinder did not negotiate for the rights to the theatrical release, and, owing to these issues, the film remained undistributed for nearly twenty years. Cinematographer Michael Ballhaus, the Filmverlag der Autoren, and the Fassbinder Foundation finally restored the film in 1993, and it had a theatrical re-release the following year.[11]

Fassbinder Under the Influence

How is it that Fassbinder came to overlook his own screenplay's debt to Woolrich? Based on the director's statements he suffered from what can be described as a paradigmatic case of cryptomnesia. The term is generally said to have originated with Carl Jung, who, in retroactively rescuing Friedrich Nietzsche from accusations of plagiarism, described a phenomenon whereby an author forgets the source of an idea and inadvertently claims it as his or her own. The ostensibly new idea is a memory that does not recognize itself as such. Cryptomnesia is generally said to affect those under an especially heavy workload, and at the time Fassbinder was publicly celebrated for being a workaholic. One 1974 headline quoted him saying, "Industriousness is my genius" (*Fleiß ist mein Genie*), to which he added, "when I read the paper in the morning I come across at least ten things I think could be written about" (Schrumpf 1974: 14).[12] Fassbinder maintained he had not read Woolrich's story, but ultimately, when he was confronted with the overwhelming evidence, he was unable to rule out the possibility that he had read and disremembered it (Thomsen 2004: 164).[13] He explained: "I have tried to talk myself into the notion that at some point I possibly could have read that story. On the other hand, it is a story that could have occurred to me as well" (es [ist] eine Geschichte, die mir auch hätte einfallen können) (Fischer 2004: 542).[14]

The word Fassbinder uses, *einfallen*, generally means, "to occur, as an idea," and Jung highlights that same word in his 1905 essay on cryptomnesia.[15] Jung describes cryptomnesia as a phenomenon by which a notion enters conscious thought indirectly as something like a "chance idea," and according to him, *Einfall* "clearly expresses the apparently fortuitous and groundless nature of the phenomenon" (Jung 1970: 96).

The term conveniently eliminates an author's plagiaristic intentionality from the act. From that perspective Fassbinder's assertion that the story "could have occurred to him as well" simply repeats the idea that it might have indeed entered into his consciousness, not that he would or could have invented it from whole cloth. Jung attributes floods of ideas that have detached from their sources—so-called "mass[es] of memories"—to geniuses or especially productive individuals, and such a description surely would have applied to Fassbinder in the 1970s (Jung 1970: 100). Therefore Nietzsche, when he drew without citation from Justinus Kerner's *Blätter aus Prevorst* (1831–1839), was not being deceptive, but was, according to Jung, simply doing the labor of aggregation for which geniuses are known. Jung elaborates: "The work of genius ... fetches up ... distant fragments in order to build them into a new and meaningful structure" (Jung 1970: 105).

From this standpoint Fassbinder was not deliberately taking what was not his, but was rather building others' ideas into "a new and meaningful structure." What, however, would have been his motivation for concealing the truth? Elsewhere he had unabashedly adapted works of world literature (by Fontane and Ibsen) and of popular genre literature, such as Galouye's *Simulacron-3* (1964). Whether or not one is troubled by Fassbinder's explanation, Jung's terms provide the means by which to understand the varied textual sources—if not Fassbinder's motivations—of the director's hybrid television film. The film is certainly an aggregate. Although the screenplay at times hews closely to the short story, Woolrich's presence can be seen as a single thread within a complex fabric. Given the role Woolrich had already played in cinema, and the cachet of cinematic intertexts he carried with him, it is difficult to imagine that Fassbinder consciously wanted to avoid admitting having borrowed from Woolrich. Perhaps Fassbinder should have more clearly avowed the influence, yet it may be accurately said that between Fontane and Woolrich, between Hitchcock and Truffaut, and between German novels, American noir, and French cinema, Fassbinder's television film was derived from a number of sources. It cuts against the grain of its medium through its many extratextual references, and, symptomatic of one of the crises facing West German television in the 1970s, specifically its struggle to compete with and dedifferentiate itself from cinema—it is a television film that disputes its exclusively televisual character. In 1975 Fassbinder explained: "[*Martha* is] not a TV film. It was financed and produced by TV, but it can be shown in theaters. It was made as though it were to be shown in theaters, even though it was only going to be shown on TV" ("A New Realism" 1975: 17).

The most evident similarities between Woolrich's story and Fassbinder's film concern their shared view of marriage. Fassbinder's perspective was that a wedded couple's bondage—whether one speaks of the late nineteenth century, as depicted in *Effi Briest*, or of the 1970s—is connected to violence. On this point the two share common ground. More specific similarities, however, are striking. The encounters at the beginning of both the television film and Woolrich's short story are set in Rome. Woolrich describes the couple's initial meeting: "Their eyes met in Rome. On a street in Rome—the Via Piemonte. He was coming down it, coming along toward her, when she first saw him. She didn't know it but he was also coming into her life, into her destiny—bringing what was meant to be." (Woolrich 2001: 288) Woolrich then repeats one particular sentence. He writes, "As their eyes met, they held. For just a heartbeat." Then, twelve lines later, he adds, "Their eyes met—and held. For just a heartbeat" (Woolrich 2001: 288). In Woolrich's prose the encounter brings time to a standstill, and he writes what is practically the same line twice, the second time adding an em dash, with which he accentuates that this meeting of eyes disrupts the course of his protagonist's life. In both authors' terms the story is about an impressionable woman whose life is derailed when she meets and marries a powerful man who turns out to be a sadist. Both use the relationship and all the abuses with which the pathological husband burdens his wife, acting as though they were customary elements of the marriage contract, to shed light on that institution's fundamentally sadistic nature.

Subsequent to the protagonists' initial meeting the two narratives diverge: in Woolrich's case we are taken to New York and in Fassbinder's to Konstanz. Despite these different settings, however, there are a number of points of intersection, and Fassbinder's story concludes with the same ghastly twist as Woolrich's: the wife, who has had an awful accident after momentarily escaping her husband's grip, finds herself in a wheelchair and becomes more than ever his prisoner. In Woolrich's case the title phrase appears at this point in the story as a haunting echo of the couple's marriage vow: "for the rest of her life." With his title Woolrich may have been toying with the resonance of the word "rest," meaning not only "that which remains," but also as a synonym for "repose." Just as one speaks about being in for "the ride of one's life," Linda, the wife in Woolrich's story, now finds herself in a wheelchair. The ride is over, and the real "rest" can begin insofar as she now surrenders and no longer struggles against the bond she sought and into which she willingly entered. Fassbinder's ending, however, leaves the viewer with questions: Is Martha supposed to be happy? Did she indeed get what she wanted? To his assertion that Margit Carstensen, who plays Martha, looks prettier than ever in the film's final moments, Fassbinder adds, "at the end of the film, when Martha can no longer take care of herself, she has finally gotten what she wanted all along" (Rentschler 1988: 168). If this is what he means to depict, however, he does it ambiguously. When the door on the narrow, steely elevator closes on Martha, locking her in with her husband Helmut, it seems to seal an unfortunate fate; it is as though the two are entombed together. The film's resolution, especially insofar as it concerns the wife's culpability for the violence in her sadomasochistic marriage, is anything but clear.

Fassbinder's film begins with a scene of ambiguity that underscores Martha's complex accountability for her own ensuing troubles: the concierge at the hotel in Rome where she and her father are staying states with confidence that Martha had winked at him, indicating her desire to have a male escort sent up to her room. Martha protests that she did not, but the suspicion lingers that she signaled and then conveniently disremembered doing so. The sudden appearance of an escort at her door is one of the film's first images. Played by the Moroccan actor El Hedi ben Salem and referred to by the concierge as "the Libyan," he stands behind her, silent as a mirage. The two stare at one another, but only after his gestures turn explicitly sexual—when he begins to lower the zipper on his pants—does she insist he leave the room. This moment of hesitation foreshadows Martha's behavior throughout the remainder of the film. She does not know whether she wants him there or not, and her own motivations appear to be even less comprehensible to her than they are to others.

This initial scene turns on desires that can be termed not only sexual but also Oedipal—or, to think again with Jung, her motivations can be tied to the Electra complex.[16] The Libyan appears in a white suit that makes him resemble a ghost, yet his ensemble also clearly evokes Martha's father's comparable outfit. She is an adoring daughter, and the brief glimpse into her father's behavior with which we are provided suggests that her desire for his affirmation is likely fueled by his cruel manners. When Martha offers to help him ascend the Spanish steps to the Trinità dei Monti, for example, he responds abrasively, asking why she is always trying to touch him. Steps are a recurring image in the film, and in tandem with Martha's evidently inhibited sexuality, their appearance evokes Freud's often quoted observation that "steep inclines, ladders and stairs, and going up or down them, are symbolic representations of the sexual act" (Freud 2010: 230).[17] After being ejected from her room the Libyan follows Martha down the hotel's grand flight of steps, and the threat of sexuality there reverberates through the large bust of a lion that roars from the end of the staircase's balustrade. These hotel steps foreshadow not only the Spanish steps in the following sequence, where Martha's father collapses, but also the steps that appear as a fixture in later scenes in Martha and Helmut's marital home, from the top of which Helmut beckons to his wife, occasionally wearing a telltale white suit.

At this point in the film, when Martha's father dies, the Libyan is again present. He first follows her down the steps of the hotel and then up the Spanish steps, which are at least an additional taxicab ride away.[18] He looms near the two of them but does not hide. If his presence is literal, then its narrative significance is unclear. One has to ask whether Fassbinder is asserting that the two of them are indeed in a sexual relationship. Perhaps it is a relationship that that the film's narrative will not explicitly avow; that is, we cannot see what Martha herself is unwilling to recall. In either scenario, as an image of unleashed male sexuality—a particularly threatening one owing to Italy's postcolonial connection to Libya following their ouster as a result of their defeat in World War II—the Libyan has symbolic meaning; he functions much like a portentous hand in one of Salvador Dali's dreamscapes. In this way the film's early sequences rely on a proliferation of symbols. The steps are suggestive, and Martha's purse takes on a similarly important role. Her father collapses on the steps, a mob gathers around, presumably to assist him, yet it looks almost as though this sexually liberated swarm of students is consuming him and thereby violently emancipating themselves from a prior generation's paternal authority. Fassbinder then cuts to an image of a hand reaching for Martha's unattended purse, which indicates that someone is stealing it. The hand does not look like the Libyan's, but we do not see to whom it is attached. Fassbinder shows us only a white sleeve, and a hand that wears what appears to be a wedding band. The wedding band may be taken to suggest that Helmut, Martha's future husband, is, at the moment of her father's death, taking possession of her sexuality. Christian Braad Thomsen makes a similar observation, noting: "The bag is a vagina symbol and the fact that it is stolen at the very moment her father dies signals that Martha's sexuality is now being stolen or confiscated forever" (Thomsen 2004: 157).

Such associations are particularly pronounced when viewed in light of this television film's major cinematic intertext, Hitchcock's *Marnie* (1964). The two films, *Marnie* and *Martha*, which center on cruel mar-

"A Challenge, Maybe the Greatest for a Filmmaker"   97

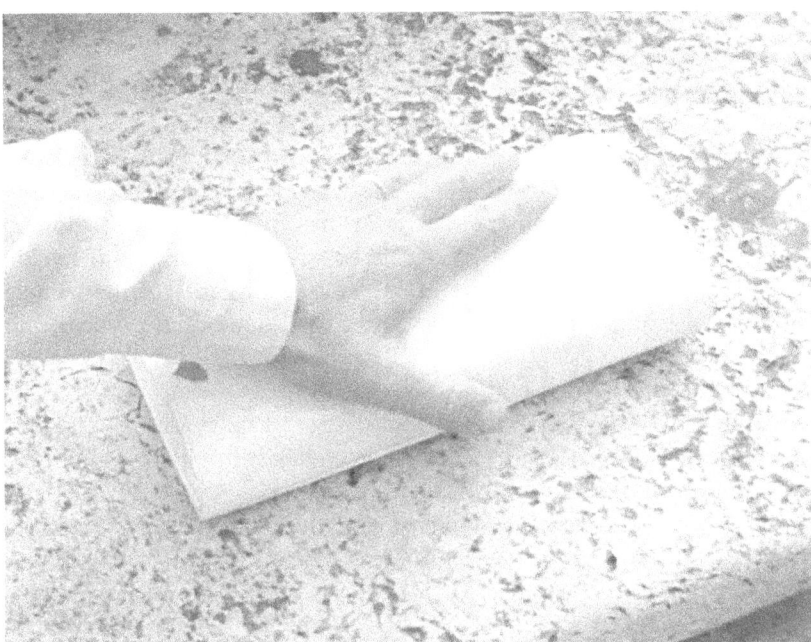

Figure 5.1. Above: A hand reaches for an unattended purse in *Martha*. Directed by Rainer Werner Fassbinder and produced by Westdeutscher Rundfunk (WDR) in 1974. Below: A purse beneath Tippi Hedren's arm in the opening moments of *Marnie*. Directed by Alfred Hitchcock and produced by Alfred J. Hitchcock Productions in 1964.

riage partners and even, in their titles, share a similarly *mar*riage-related phoneme, have a good deal in common. Hitchcock's feature film opens with a purse: the very first shot, immediately following the opening credits, is an image of an exceptionally vulval purse clutched beneath the actress Tippi Hedren's arm.[19] *Marnie* also more than once incorporates sequences in which children on the street can be heard singing—in tones that resonate eerily with the children at the beginning of Fritz Lang's *M* (1931)—a purse-related schoolyard rhyme. The children sing: "Call for the doctor / call for the nurse / call for the woman with the alligator purse." Marnie, who clutches her own purse firmly, is, as explained by Sean Connery's character, Mark, looking elsewhere for the love she wasn't getting at home, and for that reason she embraces her handbag protectively. At numerous points *Martha* explicitly cites *Marnie*, and the works' themes are related; in Hitchcock's film a powerful man blackmails a woman into marrying him, and their lopsided relationship becomes increasingly difficult for even the viewer to endure. Marnie, because she has been caught thieving, becomes Mark's captive. He tries to train her to act better by working through the traumatic childhood causes of her criminal actions. In Hitchcock's film her education is oppressive (put in Fassbinder's terms: *Erziehung* is *Unterdrückung*) in that Marnie spends all but the very first minutes of the film under her instructor's thumb. Fassbinder had seen *Marnie* and objected to the fact that Hitchcock provided his audience with clear psychological explanations. Fassbinder says: "I could simply not tell a story like *Marnie*, as *Marnie* is told, because I don't have the courage to be so naïve. Simply to narrate a film like this, and then at the end to give an explanation [as Hitchcock does]—I wouldn't have the courage. Maybe I'll have that one day, and then I'll be very Hollywood-like [*ganz wie Hollywood*]" (Fischer 2004: 296–97). Ambiguity is here put forward as an aesthetic principle. Fassbinder's film is in dialogue with *Marnie*, yet it was made for television, and rather than agitating for a class-based social transformation, Fassbinder now uses the opportunity to critique prevailing tendencies in the form of the melodrama, specifically to bring out the violence of what comes across merely as Mark's well-intentioned eccentricity in *Marnie*.

Even the name of Fassbinder's central character was chosen to reflect an intertextual cinematic connection. The name, Martha Heyer, recalls Martha Hyer, the actress who starred in Douglas Sirk's *Battle Hymn* (1957). Fassbinder had a well-documented fascination with Sirk's films, and in *Martha* his protagonist explains that she was born and now lives on Douglas Sirk Street in Konstanz. Hyer had more recently starred in

Picture Mommy Dead (1966), a curious, low-budget horror film that in Germany went by the title *Das Kabinett der blutigen Hände,* and which premiered there in 1970. That film is set in a house where a murder had taken place, as is the case with the house eventually occupied by Martha and Helmut in *Martha.* Moreover, the first sequence of *Picture Mommy Dead,* in which a father and daughter walk together down a staircase shadowed by a nun, establishes the film's terms and anticipates *Martha's* numerous flights of stairs. Not only is *Martha* an engagement with Hitchcock's cinematic motifs, but it also seeks to undermine the self-seriousness of his highbrow horror by deliberately underscoring its intimations of B-movie fantasies.

Zooming In

Perhaps more distinct among Fassbinder's stylistic choices was his engagement with French cinema: *Martha* was also made with an eye to the films of Claude Chabrol. Fassbinder had commented on Chabrol not long after he made *Martha* in 1975, and he even supplied the introductory essay for a collection of writings about Chabrol (Jansen and Schütte 1975: 7–16). He admired the French director's films but also commented critically on his depiction of marriage, which Fassbinder viewed as too redemptive (Jansen and Schütte 1975: 10). He notes:

> Chabrol is indubitably a proponent of marriage, as his later films prove. And marriage is primarily an institution that sustains the state. But Chabrol is opposed to hypocrisy in marriage, opposed to possessiveness, instead of being against marriage. It's all so cheap, the feelings and the needs, too. [There is] no indication that the needs people consider their very own are actually only the needs they're told to have. (Töteberg and Lensing 1992: 92)

Fassbinder uses a critique of Chabrol as a springboard to articulate his own views, yet the two were not so far apart in their stances on the violence implicit in the marriage contract. Films such as Chabrol's *La Femme Infidèle* (1969) and *Le Boucher* (1970) indicated as much. The possessiveness performed in those films was a symptom of the expectations of fidelity and in some measure servitude that come hand-in-hand with the marriage contract. Fassbinder's deeper criticism of Chabrol, however, was formal: it centered on the director's technique. Fassbinder noted, first of all, that when the opportunity came to work in television, Chabrol failed to acknowledge that this is the greatest challenge for a filmmaker. Fassbinder writes: "Chabrol's disdain for his audience becomes very clear in his four television movies. You just can't work as mindlessly and heedlessly for so many people as Chabrol does here. Instead of recognizing television as a challenge, maybe the greatest for a filmmaker, he sees it as a nuisance" (Töteberg and Lensing 1992: 95–96). Fassbinder's principal critique concerned Chabrol's reliance on the zoom. For Fassbinder the zoom was synonymous with television aesthetics. Although zooming was growing more and more customary for television, Fassbinder found it ham-handed, and he declared the zoom a specifically televisual technology, noting that it can be "truly disruptive" (*recht störend*) when seen on movie screens (Fischer 2004: 260).[20] He notes: "Sometimes you think Chabrol has just discovered the zoom, the most pathetic of all film techniques. In every film one or two incredibly beautiful traveling shots; otherwise, nothing doing—flat, slick images with no attention to the lighting or to the colors" (Töteberg and Lensing 1992: 16).

Throughout the 1960s and 1970s television relied more and more on zooms for daytime dramas, game shows, and talk shows (Butler 2010: 19). According to Jeremy G. Butler the zoom was employed as a straightforward means to underscore moments of emotional impact in soap operas, and Butler compares its use with that of the dolly, which was more expensive, but seemed subtler and therefore more cinematic (Butler 2010: 44). Fassbinder had worked in the theater, and for that reason may have been especially sensitive to manipulations associated with zoom lenses. He avoided televisual zooms in *Martha*, and Michael Ballhaus, his cinematographer on the film, recalled: "Fassbinder wanted me to photograph the entire film with one lens, without zoom. We maintained this principle with a few exceptions, and this was after we had just exploited the full range of technical possibilities doing [the television film] *World on a Wire*. This restriction led to new ways of thinking about things and fresh experiments" (Kardish 1997: 55). The absence of the zoom can be understood in contrast with the celebrated 720-degree pan Michael Ballhaus used in *Martha*. The shot, in front of the German Embassy in Rome, depicts the first encounter between Martha and Helmut. It is the film's visual centerpiece, and is perhaps well known because both Fassbinder and Ballhaus frequently spoke of it in terms of how it was distinguished from television style. The circular pan, which required a sweeping camera motion, is, regardless of Fassbinder's apparent cryptomnesia, a visualization of the couple's initial encounter as Woolrich describes it. Time seems to stop. The swirling camera seals Helmut and Martha together and foreshadows their ultimate entombment at the film's end. The sequence featuring the circular pan is deeply stylized. The sweep of the camera is an ostentatious gesture, and the actors stand strangely motionless at the center of the shot. Moreover, the Libyan, who would have required yet another taxicab ride to trail Martha to this third location, is once again inexplicably present.

Owing to its stylization, as well as to the peculiar presence of the Libyan in the frame, the circular shot reads as theatrical, yet these stylizations and cinematic affectations were precisely what made *Martha* challenging for television. In a similarly stylized and artificial sequence at a wedding party Martha and Helmut meet again for the first time subsequent to their encounter in Rome. Everyone seated at the long table faces outward, toward the center of the room (and toward the camera), despite the fact that there is no evidence of other guests. The dramaturgical irreality seems to indicate that we may again be inhabiting the phantasmatic space of Martha's imaginary. Helmut's brother, Hans, is getting married, and behind the long guest table are copious mirrors. Candelabras and flowers are everywhere, and although the setting is contemporary, the atmosphere is anachronistic; the décor and the dialogue could have been lifted from the pages of *Effi Briest*. Even in a private romantic moment between Helmut and Martha, when the two of them step outside for air, Martha's mother looms in the background much as the Libyan had loomed in the background the first time she and Helmut met. She is clearly discernable yet quite improbably goes unnoticed.

Fassbinder's *Martha* has come to be most widely known for its "sunburn scene." While the newlyweds, Helmut and Martha, are on their honeymoon in Italy, the two take in the sun. Helmut remains fully dressed and Martha sunbathes in her bikini. He knowingly encourages her to not put on sunscreen, explaining that he wants to see her get tan as soon as possible. The viewer watches Helmut take note that Martha has fallen asleep in the sun, and if he or she had at that point any doubts as to whether Helmut were being deliberately sadistic, all misgivings are quickly resolved. He fully recognizes that Martha will turn as red as a lobster. In the next shot she lies on their hotel bed in pain, and Fassbinder communicates her intense discomfort. The redness of her burned skin makes the image excruciating. Helmut blames her for falling asleep in the sun, because, as he didactically explains, when we sleep the body puts up no resistance. He then begins to touch her abdomen. The camera lingers on his hand, and the image is similar to the earlier one of a hand grabbing Martha's purse; it again indicates that

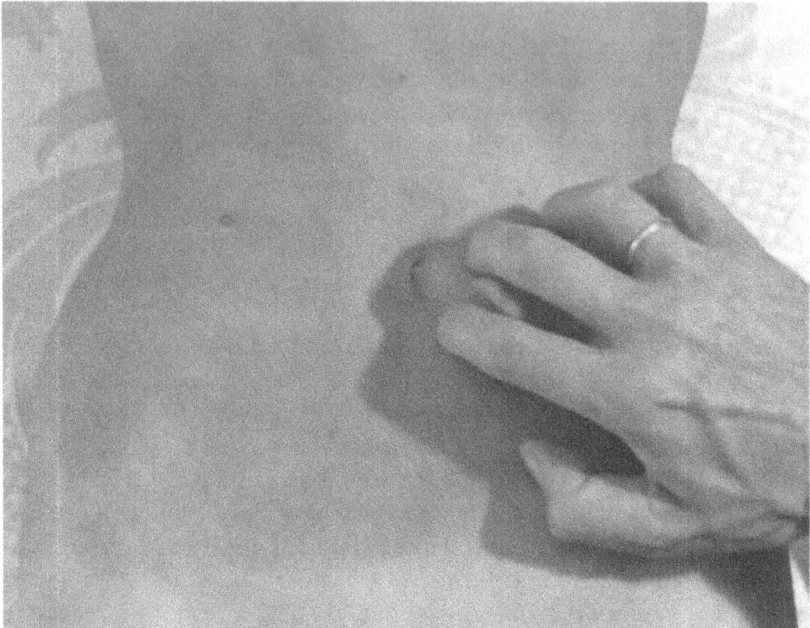

Figure 5.2. Helmut touches Martha's sunburned abdomen in R. W. Fassbinder's *Martha* (1974).

someone else is in control over her sexuality. After first touching her, he throws his body on hers, and rather than further depicting her pain the camera pans across to the bars that constitute the patio railing, and which provide a view of the broad Mediterranean horizon.

The sequence makes entirely clear how sadistic Helmut is. It is also, at the same time, an explicit reference to Hitchcock's *Marnie*. The first scene of physical intimacy between Marnie and her husband is also not directly displayed; here too, the camera looks away. Hitchcock's film more or less directly asserts that Marnie, who suffers from frigidity as a result of a childhood trauma, has finally surrendered to Mark's advances. What we see of their encounter resembles a rape. It is, however, only obliquely marked as sexual violence in Hitchcock's film, and Fassbinder, to offer contrast, highlights the extent of his protagonist's pain. In *Marnie,* the newlyweds are on their honeymoon—just as in *Martha*—but in this case the two are on a cruise to the South Seas. Marnie is forced to lie down on the bed, almost completely immobilized by fear and psychic pain owing to her violent reaction to being touched. We can detect the influence of Jung—or Jung via Freud, whom Hitchcock certainly read—in the director's rendering of the scene. Here and throughout the film Marnie's reactions are what Jung would depict as hysterical responses to resurfaced memories. Jung happens to describe these hysterical reactions in detail as part of his cryptomnesia essay, because childhood traumas are also memories that cannot be recognized as such.[21] Significantly, insofar as an examination of the influence of

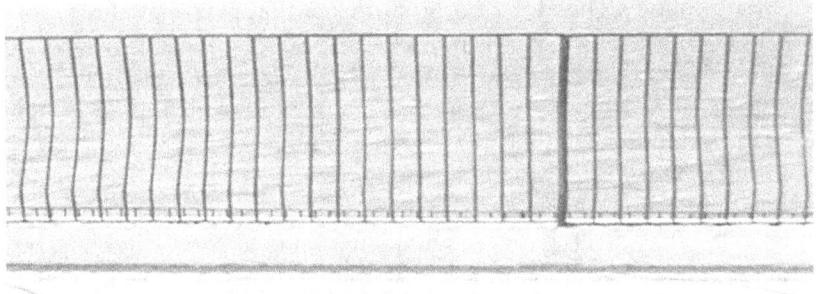

Figure 5.3. Above: The patio railing and the horizon in R. W. Fassbinder's *Martha* (1974). Below: A closed window, looking out at the horizon in Alfred Hitchcock's *Marnie* (1964).

Marnie on *Martha* is concerned, at the very moment when it seems that Marnie has finally surrendered to Mark the camera pans to the left, off to the horizon, toward the portal window and onto the wide sea. The similarity between the two directors' choices—between Fassbinder and Hitchcock's use of imagery—is quickly recognizable.[22]

At the onset of the sequence, as Helmut had set to sunbathing, he is depicted reading Hans Kilian's *Das enteignete Bewußtsein* (*The Expropriated Consciousness*, 1971). It may seem bewildering that this character has chosen a book of this sort. The study is an attempt at a dialectical sociology, one that aims to go beyond Freud and Marx. Kilian's critique of Freud follows Theodor Adorno's concept that psychoanalysis is ultimately bourgeois insofar as it is an effort to bring the subject around to a harmonious status quo (Kilian 1971: 213–15). His critique of Marx is that he is too absorbed in objectively defined relationships, that is, in material conditions (Kilian 1971: 52–54). Both are thus treated as "system immanent," and Kilian chides the two for being not adequately social thinkers. His liberating discourse with respect to his theme rings similar to that of Herbert Marcuse: time and history—the basis for Kilian's sociology—give humanity a "fourth dimension." Kilian introduces his argument:

> We stand at the end of the age when power structures class divisions, and we are on the threshold of a new culture, one that this book understands as the arrival of "four-dimensional man." The system characteristics of the new culture must take other life conditions into account, through which humanity as a whole, as well as the individual, is forced to recognize its existence as a four-dimensional process of progressive change and to regulate or—in other words—steer its history and evolution itself. (Kilian 1971: 20–21)

Kilian calls for a dialectical sociology that would push past Marx and Freud, but why does Fassbinder put this book in Helmut's hands? Helmut is an unlikely reader of Kilian insofar as he is, to all appearances, a bourgeois and socially conservative engineer who specializes in the structural statics of retaining dams. The choice may have to do with irony and ambiguity, but more likely this constitutes a tongue-in-cheek reference to *Marnie*: in that film Sean Connery's Mark recommends—at a moment when Marnie is nearly catatonic as a result of her awakened childhood traumas—reading none other than Carl Jung's *The Undiscovered Self*, which deals with the relationship between the self and mass society. Jung's book was published in 1956 and in English translation in 1958. In Kilian's *The Expropriated Consciousness* Fassbinder found an analogue to Jung. Both Mark, in *Marnie*, and Helmut, in *Martha,* take a similarly didactic attitude toward their spouse, and in neither case is reading a contemporary academic text on individual and mass psychology a measure of progressive attitudes; it is instead a display of condescension.

Kilian's book calls for a revolutionary mode of social thinking, yet his vision is less practice oriented than that for which Fassbinder had implicitly agitated in *Eight Hours.* Moreover, it is unclear that *Martha,* despite the fact that it aimed to reach a broad television audience, was in any way about liberation. Martha can hardly be said to come to consciousness that she needs to get out from under Helmut, her oppressor. Shortly after the two become engaged, Martha meets Kaiser, a man who is introduced to her as a new colleague at the library where she works. He is the one to whom she later turns when she tries to make her escape. He has taken over the job from her former colleague, a woman, and, although he is kind, he is not what Martha is looking for in a man. With respect to Helmut he is feminized, and for this reason Martha turns to him as a potential ally. Fassbinder expresses her affinity with Kaiser by shooting the two in movement together; it is a counterpoint to the circular pan that initially bound her to Helmut. The two walk as one in the library, and a similar shot appears later, when their movements are tracked in the park. In the library sequence—in their initial encounter—they sing a child's song that was composed in 1967 by Josef Guggenmos: "What does the mouse think of on Thursday / ... The same he thinks on every day / ... If only I had a 'sausage-bread' / with lots of sausage and little bread!" (*Was denkt die Maus am Donnerstag / ... Dasselbe wie an jedem Tag / ... O hätte ich ein Wurstebrot / mit ganz viel Wurst und wenig Brot!*). Fassbinder has them sing the lyrics up to this point, but subsequent parts of the rhyme are omitted. He decided not to include the dream of a revolution on the part of the properly fed mouse. The song continues, alluding to an upheaval: "There'd be gusto, there'd be power / Soon I wouldn't be so small / I'd soon be big as an ox. / ... That would be splendid / that would be right / and as for the cat / ... he'd be doing badly." (*Das gäbe Saft, das gäbe Kraft! / Da wär ich bald nicht mehr mäuschenklein / da würd ich bald groß wie ein Ochse sein. / ... Das wäre herrlich / das wäre recht / und der Katze / ... ginge es schlecht!*). The new colleagues never reach the part that describes the cat's bad day. It is therefore all the more significant that Helmut at a later point murders Martha's cat Rubel. Martha, who falls to the floor crying about the dead cat, will know that there can be no powerful "animals" in the house but Helmut. Fassbinder's ending offers no hope for a revolution, and no optimistic impression that the oppressed have options that might lead to emancipation. Insofar as Martha is the mouse, she will never wrest power from the cat in charge.

Not only can one conclude that there is little hope, but Fassbinder also would like for us to conclude that Martha has had a hand in her own demise. He makes this point explicitly in his conversations with the actress Margit Carstensen, and it may have been via the misogyny expressed in that transcribed conversation—one in which he is being deliberately provocative—that he, with this film, expresses an affinity with Hitchcock, who was often accused of misogyny.[23] The 1973 conversation concludes with Carstensen telling Fassbinder that he's a wretched person for his perspective on Martha's degradation and then asking how she is supposed to pull herself together in the wake of their mortifying exchange (Rentschler 1988: 171). In the film itself Martha turns the wheel that drives the car off the road. She has intervened; Kaiser is driving, yet she causes the accident that leaves her paralyzed. The spinning wheels of their overturned car foreshadow the wheels of her wheelchair, and likewise recall the prison constructed by Ballhaus's circular shot at the moment she and Helmut first met. The spinning shot, the film's many circular picture frames, the wheels of the wheelchair, and even the couple's wedding rings are all figurations of the prison into which Martha has stepped. Max Bruch's "Violin Concerto in G-Minor" concludes the film. With its romantic motifs, it gestures ironically at closure and also hints that the sorts of romantic fantasies in which Martha indulged may have contributed to imprisoning her. Finally, in the elevator, she is in a box that more than anything else resembles a coffin. Christian Braad Thomsen writes,

> The conclusion is ambivalent. Helmut now has Martha where he wants her, but the terrible point is that, in fact, Martha is also where she—or at least part of her—would like to be: tied to a wheelchair for the rest of her life, at the mercy of Helmut and therefore without any responsibility of her own. All through the film Martha has felt most comfortable in the role of the child, made dependent first by her parents, then by her husband. (Thomsen 2004: 161)

Here one might disagree with Thomsen: the ending is more ambiguous. Interpretation is, of course, in the eye (and, perhaps, the ear) of the beholder, but Martha does not seem to be where she would like to be. She arguably looks more vacant and lifeless than content.

A final assessment of how Fassbinder saw the political and aesthetic possibilities of television can be found in Wim Wenders's film *Room*

666 (*Chambre 666,* 1982). For that film, a number of filmmakers, including Michelangelo Antonioni, Werner Herzog, Steven Spielberg, and Fassbinder, who were all in attendance at the Cannes Film Festival, answered questions about the fate of cinema relative to the looming shadow of television. It was May 1982 and television was very much the focus of Wenders's study. He left a television on in the background as a bit of mise-en-scène, perhaps as an indication of the extent to which television was cutting into the West German cinema market over the course of the 1960s and 1970s, and the various filmmakers were put in the position of talking past the monitor's steady stream of images. Fassbinder died weeks later, and this was among the last times he was captured on film. He seems impatient and responds tersely as to the difference between television and cinema, summarizing: "Today there is sensational cinema which is bombastic and spectacular. That's one side. But on the other hand there is very individual cinema, or the national cinema of individual filmmakers, which is more important today than that cinema which is no longer distinct from television." His assessment seems to bespeak the concern that cinema and television were threatening to merge. Television, as he saw it, had potential as an emancipatory medium. His work on *Eight Hours* had suggested as much. However, television also had potential as a place from which to critique cinema. Fassbinder used *Martha* as a platform to engage dominant voices such as Hitchcock and Chabrol, and to bring out what was unspoken in their work. His insistence on television's potential, as well as his hopes, however frequently they were dashed, can also be viewed as an insistence on television's distinctiveness as a revolutionary medium, exceeding cinema because it reaches a wider audience. That television would one day be "one and the same as" or "as good as" cinema was hardly desirable.

Brad Prager is Associate Professor of German at the University of Missouri, Columbia. He is the author of *After the Fact: The Holocaust in Twenty-First Century Documentary Film* (Bloomsbury, 2015), *The Cinema of Werner Herzog: Aesthetic Ecstasy and Truth* (Wallflower, 2007) and *Aesthetic Vision and German Romanticism: Writing Images* (Camden House, 2007). He is also co-editor both of *Visualizing the Holocaust: Documents, Aesthetics, Memory* (Camden House, 2008) and of *The Collapse of the Conventional: German Cinema and Its Politics at the Turn of the Twenty-First Century* (Wayne State University Press, 2010).

Notes

1. The German reads: "Einzig beim Fernsehen ist es anders: Da trifft man wirklich ein vielschichtigeres Publikum. Und ich find' das Fernsehen im Moment die beste Möglichkeit, andern Leuten was zu erzählen."
2. The original interview is "'Lieber Straßenkehrer in Mexiko sein ...': Spiegel-Gespräch mit Filmregisseur Rainer Werner Fassbinder über seinen Weggang aus Deutschland" *Der Spiegel* 29 (July 1977): 140–42. Cited text is on 141.
3. See also Gast and Kaiser, who explore Rohrbach's decision and his disappointment with the three upcoming scripts (1977: 110).
4. See Hickethier and Hoff 1998: 247–48. On the extent to which color television was cutting into cinema's audience, see Evan Torner's contribution to this volume.
5. For background on this television film, see Prager 2012: 245–66. According to Peter Berling, WDR gave Fassbinder the project as a consolation prize (*Trostbonbon*) for the problems with *Eight Hours* (1992: 202).
6. The chronology is provided in Kilb 1994.
7. The German reads: "wenn man diese Geschichte erzählen will, dann braucht man eigentlich nicht Fontanes Roman zu verfilmen. Dann kann man genauso gut eine neue Geschichte erfinden, und *Martha* ist meine persönliche Version dieser Geschichte." See "'Ich will, dass man diesen Film liest': Rainer Werner Fassbinder über *Fontane Effi Briest*, über Anarchisten und Terroristen und über seine Frauen Filme" in Fischer 2004: 302. The cited interview is with Christian Braad Thomsen and is from 1974.
8. Fassbinder makes the comparison himself in Töteberg and Lensing 1992: 158; The original German passage is in *Kino* (1974), 29. Thomas Elsaesser compares Fassbinder's Fontane adaptation with *Martha*, noting that both share a high degree of ambivalence, despite their vastly different negotiations of their respective narrative voices (1996: 281–82).
9. See Fassbinder as quoted in Roth 1983: 168, which reads: "Martha wird eigentlich nicht unterdrückt, sondern erzogen. Und diese Erziehung ist gleich Unterdrückung."
10. The story was translated into German in 1969 as "Für den Rest ihres Lebens." See Woolrich 1969: 11–32.
11. On the rerelease see Giesen 1994 and Körte 1994.
12. The German reads: "Wenn ich morgens die Zeitung lese, fallen mir mindestens zehn Stoffe ein, über die man schreiben könnte." See Schrumpf 1974: 14.
13. Thomsen writes, "Fassbinder declared that he had never read the short story. But when he was confronted with it, he had to admit that the resemblance was striking. He could not, therefore, exclude the possibility that he had once read the story and forgotten it again, but that a subconscious memory of it had remained" (2004: 164).
14. The German reads: "Ich habe versucht mich einzureden, das ich vielleicht die Geschichte irgendwann einmal gelesen haben könnte. Auf der anderen Seite ist es eine Geschichte, *die mir auch hätte einfallen können*" (Fischer 2004: 542). The interview originally took place in 1980. Italics added.
15. Jung attributes his knowledge of the phenomenon to the Swiss psychologist Théodore Flournoy. Jung's essay "Cryptomnesia" (1970: 95–106) was originally published in German in 1905. Reference to Flournoy appears on 101.
16. Jung first uses the term in 1913, and it was published two years later in his *Theory of Psychoanalysis* (1915: 69–70).
17. See Freud 2010: 230.

18. The Spanish steps are also coded as sexualized by virtue of the students who linger there. Martha's father, clearly of a generational difference from the students, complains about their behavior. They carry the trace of sexual liberation with them, particularly because those steps and the youth culture attracted to them feature prominently in Federico Fellini's feature film *Roma* (1972), which opened in October 1972 in West Germany.
19. See Modleski: "In Hitchcock's films, women's purses (and their jewelry) take on a vulgar Freudian significance relating to female sexuality and to men's attempts to investigate it" (1988: 78).
20. Responding in 1982 to the statement, "Godard once said that the zoom replaces 'work' on the set, because people no longer move their asses," Fassbinder replied: "That's right. After the discovery of the zoom, lots of people used it. They thought it was great because they thought they no longer needed to build rails. That's totally screwy, of course, because the artificiality of this camera movement is clearly communicated to the viewer. This type of camera movement—the zoom—is pretty much dead" (Fischer 2004: 607).
21. Marnie's responses nearly perfectly reflect reactions that Jung (1970) uses to illustrate cryptomnesia. He describes a certain kind of female hysteria as "nothing other than a caricature of normal psychological mechanisms" (98), and goes on to explain: "Recently I had to treat a hysterical young lady who become ill chiefly because she had been brutally beaten by her father. Once, when we were out for a walk, this lady dropped her cloak in the dust. I picked it up, and tried to get the dust off by beating it with my stick. The next moment the lady hurled herself upon me with violent defensive gestures and tore the cloak out of my hands. She said she couldn't stand the sight, it was quite unendurable to her. I at once guessed the connection and urged her to tell me the motives for her behavior. She was nonplussed, and could only say that it was extremely unpleasant for her to see her cloak cleaned like that. These symptomatic actions, as Sigmund Freud calls them, are very common among hysterics" (98).
22. Fassbinder was explicit about engaging in precisely this type of citation elsewhere: He explains to Wolfgang Limmer and Fritz Rumler in "'Alles Vernünftige interessiert mich nicht'" that he tried to re-create the closing shot of *Marnie*, in which Marnie suddenly recognizes where her sickness comes from, as a scene in his own *Despair* (1977), based on Nabokov's novel of the same name, but he couldn't pull it off for logistical reasons (Fischer 2004: 537).
23. See Modleski's (1988) discussion of the issues surrounding Hitchcock's treatment of women, esp. 1–15.

Chapter 6

Nah am Fern

Kluge TV

Stefanie Harris

In 2010, Alexander Kluge was awarded the Grimme-Prize for lifetime achievement, one of the highest honors in German television. In their adulation of Kluge, the Grimme Institut praised his long-standing career across multiple media platforms, commending in particular his twenty-plus years in television production, during which he created a "media cosmos" from his unique style of selective montage of stories, music, interviews, images, texts, and reflections (Alexander Kluge— Begründung des Stifters 2010).¹ Although citing Tom Tykwer who once called Kluge "a media antidote to the ratings-hysteria of the commercial television world," the Institut's *laudatio* could not help but remind its readers (twice!) of Kluge's more common depiction as a "ratings killer" by the former head of RTL, Helmut Thomas, who once dubbed the programming that Kluge's production company created for the commercial television network, "twelve-tone music in the circus" (Besondere Ehrung des DVV für Alexander Kluge 2010). Kluge is lauded both as the epitome of creative television production while simultaneously failing hopelessly at commercial success as measured in ratings. Tucked into the television schedule between late night broadcasts of American imports (*The Bachelor, The Mentalist, Hawaii Five-0*), shockumentaries on domestic violence, and second run feature films, Kluge's television productions challenge the viewer to experience television and to reflect on the representation of individual experience in a wholly different way.² Kluge's television productions function, in other words, as a performative television criticism within the medium of television, constructed both to reveal latent forms of the industrial organization of consciousness and to interrupt them, and this within and alongside familiar broadcast material and programming. One might interpret Kluge's lifetime achievement award as a sign of the conclusion of a project perhaps only partially fulfilled, and wishful thinking at least on the part of the executives of the private channels, if Kluge had not already long since moved on to new forms of digital distribution and broadcast, signaling the end not of his own relevance but of the model of commercial television itself.

If television studies and television criticism usually take one of two roads—an historical approach that compares the institutional development of television within different political, economic, cultural, and ideological contexts; and a media-theoretical approach that highlights the aesthetics of television as a specific medium and the intermedial relationships between television and other media—then the television work of Alexander Kluge demands that we do both. For to focus individually on technological development, individual programming, viewing patterns, or remediations is to examine how people watch television and what they watch without questioning the system that makes viewing or programming possible. Kluge's television broadcasts, beginning in the late 1980s, emerge from the specific media historical context of the introduction of private commercial broadcasting in West Germany, as well as from an articulated theoretical position on the public sphere and the mass media, and the distinctive though recognizable audio-textual-visual strategies Kluge had already worked out in prose and film. This essay examines three areas with regard to Kluge's television productions: the technological, industrial/economic, and political forces that shape the material conditions of production and distribution; the links between television and larger symbolic orders of social and political lives (or the public sphere); and the construction of meaning in traditional (and now Internet-based) television programming and production.

For those more familiar with German film history, Kluge is typically cited as one of the most prominent signators of the infamous Oberhausen Manifesto of 1962, in which a new generation of German filmmakers protested against a bankrupt film landscape and called for a "new German cinema" that would, among other things, take on Germany's recent past. Kluge's own cinematic practices serve as a second-order reflection not only on cinematic representation, but more specifically, on the sociopolitical and cultural implications of the role of material practices in the construction and transmission of personal and cultural memory. Kluge's films and prose narratives cross genres—combining documentary and fiction, text and image, impersonal and personal points of view, broad historical perspectives and the confusion of minute details—in order to mediate between personal experience and the public recording of and discourse on these events. Further, Kluge's text- and image-based work addresses the power and illusion of the image, both still and moving, and prompts us to recognize the way that film and television play an important role in the formation of a collective attitude toward the past, present, and future. Rather than a totalizing and ultimately foreclosed view of history and the present, rendered as an abstraction and reducible to cliché and thereby separated from the individual's lived sensory experience, Kluge's concern is with contributing to the creation of a productive public sphere, one that requires active participation on the part of the viewer and would permit the viewer to reclaim individual subjective experience through sensory and emotional registers.

In his writings on his film work, for example, Kluge has often discussed undoing the viewing habits (*Sehgewohnheiten*) of a domesticated, industrialized consciousness: "the perspectives of traditional realism construct an ideological mass, an apparent-reality, onto which habits crystallize. These habits are programmatically similar to the pedagogical training of the apparatus of consciousness, the official, domesticized consciousness, which plays a role in social development" (1975: 209). What Kluge means is that the apparatus of consciousness is trained and pre-scribed (literally, written in advance) by the economic and political forces of postcapitalist industrial society. Ideological abstraction organizes concrete material, thereby ruling how we will perceive and comprehend specific and individual events. In this context, Kluge elaborates two types of realism: the one is the superficial reproduction of outward reality that only confirms, and thereby affirms, the existence of what it shows and permits only passive reception; whereas the second, and the method favored by Kluge, is critical and subversive, seeking out the individual response that has been marginalized, obfuscated, or even censored by the deceptive order of things. As a result, his work intentionally speaks to the senses, to the emotions, and to the imagination, rather than preprogrammed logical facilities (the intellect) and learned behaviors and ideologies (the official apparatus of consciousness).

Directed against the cultural fictions that mythicize human experience, Kluge's work takes part in the debate about the media itself, and the preconditions and potential of art in capitalist society. Demonstrating, analyzing, and challenging conventional forms of perception and expression, his work across media platforms serves to stimulate viewer awareness, provoke, and question. In other words, it is an explicitly political practice that protests so-called official or legitimate cultural forms. The project is not a narrowly aesthetic one, however, but rather seeks to open up spaces for production of what Kluge has called counterpublic spheres, which could serve as forums for individual imagination and public debate in protest of increasing media concentration. The reader or viewer as producer is a critical concept, as differentiated from the passive consumption of media (in a frequently quoted statement, Kluge exhorted his film audience to create the film in their own head through their own processes of association and imagination). Kluge could have been speaking of any of the media he works in, when he asserts that his ultimate goal is to keep television (or film, prose narrative, and now, the Internet) open to that which takes place outside of television—to render visible what is screened off or screened out (Fast 3.000 Sendungen 2010–2015).

Windows

In their introduction to *European Television History*, Jonathan Bignell and Andreas Fickers remind us that a central part of the dramatic narrative of early television in Europe after World War II was the hope that television would be a strong agent of democratization, underscoring their point by quoting Adolf Grimme, the first director-general of public service television broadcasting in West Germany and namesake for the prize described earlier, who presented television in 1953 as the medial reincarnation of the classical idea of democracy: "Television takes the place of the agora, or meeting-place of the whole nation in which direct democracy can be realized" (2008: 41). That this new agora is the site of only one-way communication, however, already reveals the limitations of this new public sphere. Public-service television in postwar Europe is marked especially by its educational and pedagogical mission and its goal of producing national citizens (Collins 2004: 33–51). In Germany, for example, television was closely linked to the new state constitution, and it followed a federal public service model with independent broadcast authorities in each of the Länder, collaborating under the umbrella of a federal (but not state-controlled) agency. West German media policy was dictated by a "deep-rooted, historically determined and highly self-conscious concern to legally safeguard the free expression of opinion, information and culture against control or interference either by the state or by any dominant social or economic interest" (Humphreys 1990: 294). Advocates of the postwar media landscape repeatedly stressed key features that are enshrined in the institutional protocols, including: decentralization; free expression against control by the state or any other dominant social or economic interest; balance of opinion, information, and culture; and the manufacture of pluralism—tenets upheld consistently by the Federal Constitutional Court at Karlsruhe. For the first thirty years after the introduction of the first public broadcaster in 1952, television production in West Germany was largely restricted to public-service television: ARD, ZDF, and the so-called third channels. Influential commercial and political interests, along with advances in telecommunications and satellite technology, eventually contributed, however, to the emergence of a "dual" television landscape in Germany in the mid-1980s with the introduction of commercial television alongside public service broadcasting, and the rise to prominence of the new private channels. In 1984, the Federal Constitutional Court had already underscored the legal possibility of a dual broadcasting system. Critically, however, the court sought to secure the position of the public stations, maintaining that public-service television must be guaranteed the technical, structural, and financial means to fulfill its mission, and in order to remain competitive should be permitted more latitude to program in the broad entertainment category while still adhering to legal requirements of diversity and balance. Commercial broadcasters, who were granted significantly more leeway for popular programming in order to recover their start-up costs, were nonetheless required to provide regional "window programs" (*Fensterprogramme*) for the broadcast of local independent productions and productions from minority groups.

If this narrative (highly abbreviated here)[3] is often told in broad histories of German media as a shift from the status of television as a pluralistic forum and a productive component of the public sphere to its degeneration into the crass commercial interests of the monoculture (if not the decline of democratic ideals in the face of the modern corporate-industrial complex), Kluge's critique of television in *Public Sphere and Experience* (1972), co-authored with Oskar Negt, offers a very different perspective in which despite, if not because of, its institutional structure, public-service television was always an active part of the consensus-building apparatus of the bourgeois public sphere. Indeed Peter Humphreys shows convincingly in his study of media and media policy in West Germany that public television was never free of politics and powerful interest group influence in the precommercial era, resulting in the substantial diminishment of a so-called pluralistic system of internal regulation (1990: 155–292). Although Negt and Kluge do not provide a media history in their volume, nor take on individual instances of programming per se, they examine the technological, economic, and cultural contexts of a compromised institution that must force an overabundance of material through "the needle's eye of two networks and the 'mini-network,' Channel Three" (1993: 116). Compressed and condensed into compartmentalized time slots, the material offered to the viewers is rendered increasingly abstract in an attempt both to representatively reflect the entire world *and* to eliminate any information that disturbs this image of completeness. (I will return to this problem of compartmentalization, compression, and condensation.) As Negt and Kluge wrote: "The orientation of television toward the happy medium, middle-of-the-road public opinion, nonradicalization, the limitation of expression, program balance, toward the so-called lukewarm character, results from this organizational principle and could, under the social conditions in the Federal Republic, be changed only if other enormous disadvantages were also accepted" (1993: 112). Two things are important here. First, the *institutional construction* of pluralism and diversity of opinion, under the constraints of limited channels (and here I refer both to a television channel and the broader concept of a "channel" from communication theory), has a leveling effect in which differentiated views and ways of knowing become increasingly less pronounced. Second, in light of this problem, the authors appear already to advocate (some fifteen years before Kluge's own involvement in television) a dual television landscape because of the potential benefit that would accrue (despite other negative repercussions): "A full realization of the potential of television would certainly no longer lead to the monologue form of program television" (1993: 114).

Some of the earliest conceptions of television had indeed highlighted its potentiality as a reciprocal medium much like the telephone, functioning as a symmetric device for recording and transmitting. As a dialogic medium, television would resemble what Bertolt Brecht had demanded of two-way radio, to whose medial character, programming, and distribution structure early television more closely corresponded than it did to cinema (2000: 41–46). With "dialogic," I draw less on the terminology of Bakhtin than the media criticism of Vilém Flusser who likewise argued that the monologic structure of television as a programming system leads to "depoliticization." Instead of publicizing the private, it privatizes the public (Flusser 1997: 103). Flusser dismisses the bulk of television criticism for analyzing the medium outside of its social context, and thereby repressing the instrumental character of television. Drawing instead on communication theory, Flusser calls discursive or one-way communication "entropic," by which he means it reduces the amount of information available to the public. Dialogic communication, on the other hand, results in a greater sum of information at the end of the process than at its beginning. Because television provides us both a representation and a conception of the world, this increase of information is crucial to fostering diverse and autonomous thinking (Flusser 1997: 108).

The "negentropic" possibility of dialogic media is likewise at the heart of Kluge's project, which is rigorously (and exhaustively) cumulative even as it engages in repetition and variation, denying rigid compartmentalization and compression. In opposition to the consensus-building television of the public-service sector, we might say that his work is even "impolite"—in the original sense of the term, describing that which is not smoothed, polished, or burnished, neither clean, nor neat, nor orderly. In an apt self-description of the kinds of television programs he would later go on to produce, Negt and Kluge argued already in *Public Sphere and Experience*: "Expanding the capacity for perception seems to be a prerequisite for all real social transformation" (1993: 102).[4] Negt and Kluge take a decisive step beyond Flusser, however, in their assertion that one cannot expand the possibilities of television merely by writing about it. "A mode of production that is as self-sufficient as television can be critiqued only by an alternative form of production" (1993: 127). Kluge's television counterproductions (*Gegenproduktionen*) are therefore positioned as active and performative modes of television criticism, or what his production company calls "practical criticism."

Kluge's production company has been a major beneficiary of the new media laws that were written in the creation of private television broadcasting in the various German Länder in the 1980s. In the hopes of securing some form of public service broadcasting within commercial broadcasting, the issuance of licenses to private broadcasters was made contingent on the guarantee of specified amounts of airtime or independent broadcasting windows for local producers and minority groups. As Johannes Rau, then minister-president of North Rhine-Westphalia, maintained in 1987, "We cannot privilege developments that marginalize the small 'factories' of artistic creativity, because industrially produced units of programming will flood the market. That's why I'm in favor of cooperation between the small and the large producers, between mid-sized 'manufacturers' of 'imaginative programming' and the large-scale television broadcasters" (Uecker 2000: 58). These media laws are further tied to the Basic Law of the Federal Republic that restricts the sole proprietorship of a *Leitmedium* (key or defining medium) like television. Since 1987, the majority of Kluge's work in moving images has been through DCTP (Development Company for Television Program), which was granted the license to produce programming for the commercial stations Sat 1, RTL/RTL-plus, and later, VOX. As Kluge has argued, "the public sphere is common property and cannot be purchased outright" (2008a). Controlling shares in DCTP are held by four major parties: Alexander Kluge (37.5 percent), the Japanese advertising firm DENTSU (37.5 percent), Spiegel Verlag (12.5 percent), and Neue Zürcher Zeitung (12.5 percent). On its Internet banner, DCTP proudly calls itself an "independent producer in the midst of commercial-TV" and describes itself both as providing a valuable service to the commercial channels that require a certain amount of independent programming in order to maintain their broadcast license *and* as a subversive force as counterproductive to that same apparatus. If television has been described as "flow" at least since Raymond Williams's television studies of the 1970s, then Kluge's television strategy might be seen as an interruption, both in terms of "flow" as "an integral part of television as a commercial form, something planned by networks, stations, and programmers to maximize viewers, and therefore central to the commodity logic of the medium" and "flow" as the seamless integration of television into domestic space and daily life (White 2003: 96).

Kluge calls his programs *Kulturmagazine* (cultural magazines). His three main series—*10 vor 11, News & Stories,* and *Primetime/Spätausgabe*—have varying run-times of 15, 24, and 45 minutes each, and address topics from culture (with an emphasis on music, opera, and film), history, and politics. Although press materials from DCTP on any individual *Kulturmagazin* usually describe an evening's program with the tag line, "fascinating and informative," the network bosses have more frequently described them as "ratings killers" and claimed that they have nothing to do with television. If, however, as Knut Hickethier has argued, the magazine format of television is emblematic of the broader effects of compression and condensation in the television landscape as a whole, then Kluge's self-conscious appropriation of the format of the magazine is an attempt both to make explicit and to undo its standardization (2002: 195). For his are not the news and culture magazines with which we are abundantly familiar and that touch on current events in politics and society with a few limited and closed examples that serve to stand in for a whole and totalize experience; rather Kluge's programs remain deliberately open-ended, stochastic, and incomplete, combining (even recycling) image, sound, and text. Eschewing the rhythm of standard television program flows, Kluge plays with production length, privileging "robust brevity and radical length" (2008a). Whether a Music-Film Magazine, Minute Film Magazine, Street Ballad Magazine, Image Magazine, or even a Hardcore-Techno Magazine (all titles taken from Kluge's broadcasts), the viewer recognizes the format as one with which s/he is both already familiar and seeing for the first time.

Kluge's foray into television has sometimes been read as a strategic move into a new medium in order to remain relevant as distribution and funding for independent film became increasingly scarce in the early 1980s—an *Autorenfernsehen* that would find a home for *Autorenfilme*. And Kluge's emphasis on cinema, opera, and literature, especially in the early years of his television productions, has frequently been noted. Kluge himself, however, describes his shift as a necessary step in preserving an active stance in how media define and are defined by a culture.[5] (And as I will show at the end of this essay, his more recent moves to digital redistribution of the broadcasts and an Internet platform indicate a shift in media generations.) Calling film a *Gründermedium* (foundational medium) Kluge states that television plays (or, once played) the role of *Leitmedium,* and maintains: "It is not a matter of whether I personally like television or, under certain circumstances, find it appealing. We poets forgo a public application of the poetic if we don't produce autonomous texts for the dominant medium and cultivate that medium" (2003).

Rather than a close reading of a particular television broadcast, I will instead describe three major through lines that, although central to Kluge's larger artistic project, come in for unique treatment in the medium of television: the privileging of emotion, the interrogation of media, and the asymmetric relation of the individual to historical experience. My examples are drawn from some of the first broadcasts in 1988, and from some of the most recent programming. This will also allow me to discuss the shift in the media through which the "television" work is broadcast and received, namely, the migration of content onto DVD and its redistribution through Internet TV.

The first *Kulturmagazin* produced by DCTP, "Die Afrikanerin oder Liebe mit tödlichem Ausgang," aired on RTL in May 1988 and took the form of so-called *Minutenfilme*—short excerpts of operas whose scenarios all revolve around the tragic consequences of love.[6] This 24-minute broadcast is indicative of a strain of Kluge's programming that showcases the so-called traditional arts, including poetry, opera, and film. Less a high culture primer for low culture TV folks, though, opera is used to depict an emotional landscape that is endlessly figured.[7] Through a female announcer, the broadcast is called an "imaginary opera guide" but would perhaps be better titled, "scenes from the periphery," since many of the short clips highlight the prompters or *souffleurs* underneath the stage rather than the singers themselves. This idea of an imaginary opera program draws on Kluge's well-known ideas of a viewer who co-creates a film in her own head through the imaginary processes spurred by the flow of images in the visual event. The television-magazine includes ten opera clips, including *Othello, Carmen,* and *Aida,* but also clips from the 1918 Ernst Lubitsch film adaptation of *Carmen* starring Pola Negri, clips from Volker Schlöndorff and Margaretha von Trotta's film *Fangschuß* (1976), and an imagined opera of Stanislaw Lem's *Solaris* (Michael Obst's opera did not premiere until 1996), thus expanding the idea of what constitutes opera. The caption, "Opera Clip," is often a misnomer for images that do not show an opera; in other programs, the numbering of the clips themselves breaks down (skipping out of order or omitting numbers altogether), thus scuttling any ideas of ranking, progression, or other fixed organizational narrative. The program indeed exhibits many of the hallmarks that mark much of Kluge's programming, namely, the selection of a central theme that is worked out in a montage of image, text, and sound that crosses genres and formats. The choice of "love" is an exemplary topic in Kluge's oeuvre, however, and thus not surprisingly serves as the first program that aired inasmuch as it situates the work and his privileging of emotion in the context of the author's larger project of interrupting and offering an alternative to a dominant public discourse that totalizes human experience both at the level of the individual, and the broader context of historical understanding. If on the one hand, "love" serves to propel the storyline for a series of operatic and cinematic texts, we find that "love stories" are a frequent component of Kluge's work for their performance of an emotion that resists abstraction, classification, or thesis (as Kluge wrote in the forward to his volume of love stories, *Labyrinth der zärtlichen Kraft*).[8] "Love" reminds us that human experience is non-totalizable, both at the level of the individual and the broader context of social understanding.

    This is not to say that these, or any of the other broadcasts on love, are all feel good stories of love at first sight, harmony, and happily-ever-after—the broadcast's title has already alerted us to that. These human relationships include surprise, cunning, violence, failure, loss, desire, regret, revenge, deception, hope, protection; love in times of war, revolution and political collapse, usually with unerringly catastrophic results. And we view repeated constellations of the conflict and convergence of law and love, society and love, politics and love, economics and love, scientific knowledge and love, and so on. Kluge's interest in the love story can be read in part, then, as a privileging of emotional relationships as a way of reclaiming autonomous experience within and against a collective historical narrative and concomitant social, legal, and especially, economic orders. In various iterations of the theme since the first broadcast in 1988—whether word-images set to music, interviews with so-called theoreticians of human relations and analyses of depictions of love, short cinematic narratives adapted from Kluge's own stories and cut from his films, video recordings of opera and other theatrical performances, and montage sequences cut from other, primarily silent, films—the history of love is presented as a through line in the history of human civilization (ancient Babylon to the present), and one that cuts across and combines high and low culture (Hölderlin and D. W. Griffith, opera and the street ballad), the political and the intimate (Odysseus and Penelope, Princess Diana and Prince Charles, Bill Clinton and Monica Lewinsky). The broadcasts usually highlight the asymmetric connections established between everyday life and the abstract spheres of the law, politics, and industry, especially in order to highlight discord, contradiction, misunderstanding, and confusion. Thus, for example, courtroom scenes break down, insurance claims are not paid out, and congressional hearings devolve into chaos in their contact with the particularities of intimate life. Love stories, as such, are presented as functioning simultaneously as normative and subversive, prescriptive and obstinate, singular and universal, social and biological, learned and innate. Through these and other love stories, Kluge is able to show how the public sphere is unable to accommodate the individual, even as it alleges to represent the whole of society.

Islands

Although Kluge's broadcasts, and the cultural programming that otherwise appears on commercial television, are often called cultural "windows," perhaps a better word might be "islands," with all the positive and negative connotations such a metaphor implies. Kluge's critique of the television landscape is essentially one of differentiation and autonomy, whereby he stakes his modernist claims while acknowledging their relationship to the commercial sphere. In 2008, Kluge released a fourteen-DVD collection with over thirty hours of television broadcasts, titled *Seen sind für Fische Inseln*. Inside the accompanying prose album, in typical Kluge style and citing unnamed experts, the author writes that some of the most dynamic evolutionary processes can be found in the great lakes of Africa, where he claims that certain types of fish have spawned over 500 new varieties in less than 100,000 years. Archaeobiologists are said to say that "lakes are like islands for fish." Large land and sea masses (like all monocultures, superpowers, and corporate giants) repress variety, whereas islands (and, presumably, independent programming) house and nurture the possibility of evolutionary variety.

With this we come to the second important emphasis of Kluge's broadcasts (although I must stress that often the three elements that I appear to be isolating here appear simultaneously within a single broadcast), which is the foregrounding of their own processes of mediation. So, for example, interviews are carried out in noisy hotel restaurants or against the backdrop of a newsroom filmed at significantly higher speed. An interview with a non-German speaker may carry a cacophonous audio track in which one hears the participants in the interview speaking either German or English along with the simultaneous translation provided by a translator who often occupies the center of the frame. The reproduction of live performances of opera or other theatrical productions is cut with full-screen images of the set, the recording transfer on a video monitor, and the production room in which videotape rolls.

This self-consciousness of media practices and media production (not just a reflection on what is shown but explicit attention to how recordings are made and edited) is appreciated most vividly perhaps in the interviews from Kluge's so-called series of "Facts & Fakes" that construct a parallel universe of the interview process spun off from monologic standardization, and serve as metacritical moments wherein not only the subject under discussion but the presentation of the interview process itself is cast into relief.[9] These programs feature interview sequences with actors posing in the roles of experts and specialists. An important example from the first year of production of *10 vor 11* is "Antiquitäten der Reklame," first broadcast on RTL in November 1988 and described as: "Forgotten ads, lost objects, the commercial as art. A *Minutenfilm* Magazine. With lots of music." The 24-minute broadcast edits together a diverse collection of print and television ads, from the early twentieth century on, and even constructs its own advertisements, superimposing a pair of shoes over a film still of Brigitte Helm, for example, or intercutting advertising slogans and logos with documentary footage of what appear to be Hitler Youth performing gymnastics routines, thereby showing the relationship between entertainment, politics, and commerce, and their mutual reinforcement in the public sphere. The broadcast also includes a seven-minute interview with one Gert Mückert (played by Alfred Edel, a familiar actor from the New German Cinema, and one of Kluge's frequent collaborators), who presents himself as an advertising researcher (*Reklameforscher*) and expert on the fine distinction between *Reklame* (advertising) and *Werbung* (marketing). When asked by the interviewer, Kluge, to state the difference between *Reklame* and *Werbung*, Mückert claims that *Reklame* is spontaneous and built on ideas, but that *Werbung* is strategic and intensely rational. Marked by their high level of abstraction, marketing strategies are, Mückert says with a smirk, "ads for institutions." Mückert/Edel goes on to give three rules for marketing, which not coincidentally parallel Kluge's early critique of public-service television and "the ecological threat to the structures of consciousness" posed by industrial television programming (1988b: 99): the abbreviation of the message (condensation), the penetration or repetition of the message (compartmentalization), and the establishment of a promise but no more than one, for that may already be too much (compression). In this conception Mückert claims cheekily that it is incorrect to ask whether a marketing campaign is "successful," rather only the degree of its effectiveness. The discussion on *Reklame/Werbung* thus serves as a unsubtle critique of larger broadcast television practices in which corporate programming only serves as *Reklame* for the larger institutional structures that it supports. In this way, the conversation almost reads as a metaphor for the difference Kluge will attempt to establish between his own television broadcasts and those of industrial production—a difference between concrete visual fantasy (dialogic) and its dissolving into mere design or pictorial language (monologic).

If "Antiquitäten der Reklame," and other similar broadcasts, may have opened a window onto that which television screened out when it originally aired in 1988, the migration of the video onto DVD puts the broadcast in productive dialogue with the larger scope of Kluge's productions and permits a different temporal narrative to emerge. The synchronic mode of the daily television schedule is simultaneously embedded in a diachronic system of decades of visual productions. Further, the formatting of the fourteen discs constructs a different viewing scenario of the work, as individual programs are isolated from broadcasting flows, but for that gain in the creation of new constellations or *Magazine,* and are juxtaposed with supplementary printed and audio texts. So, for instance, an entire DVD is dedicated to the notion of work, and includes broadcasts dating from 1995 to 2007, that depict steel mills and steel construction; chaos and confusion and the four-day weekend; the auction value of currency from the concentration camps of the Third Reich; as well as interviews with Joseph Stiglitz on globalization and the economy, the author of a book on organization management, the head chef of the Berliner Ensemble, and Helge Schneider as Fred Peickert, in another "Facts and Fakes" interview, as an unemployed worker from the former East Germany. Kluge's broadcasts find here not only a new generation of viewers, but also a new way of looking at his work not possible under the restrictions of the television broadcast schedule. The scope of the set, especially in combination with the hours of programming organized and available on the website, dctp.tv; the growing number of DVD editions appearing in Suhrkamp's filmedition series (*Nachrichten aus der ideologischen Antike,* 2008; *Früchte des Vertrauens,* 2009; *Wer sich traut reißt die Kälte vom Pferd,* 2010; and *Theorie der Erzählung,* 2013); and the DVDs that accompany recently released books, such as *Labyrinth der zärtlichen Kraft* (2009), all lead one to the conclusion that Kluge's *Fernseharbeiten* have always been self-consciously part of a multimedia landscape, and one now in which television and the Internet merge.

Coral Reefs

In a recently released e-book, *Die Entsprechung einer Oase* (2013), Kluge seems to have moved on from traditional broadcast television and writes explicitly on the role of independent production and distribution networks in the digital age, thereby providing a methodological rationale for the migration of his own television productions to the Internet via DCTP's television portal, www.dctp.tv. Invoking a younger generation throughout the short essay, Kluge makes explicit that the generational shift after 1989 must not only be understood sociohistorically as the end of the postwar period, but especially as a commercial and technological history of new media.[10] Kluge's own Internet presence, secured some twenty years after DCTP's first television productions, also signals a generational shift in the identification of the prevailing *Leitmedium,* when broadcast television's claim to this title cedes to the digital info-tainment space of the Internet itself. Kluge thus shifts his own focus here from counterproductions in commercial television to the maintenance of a counterpublic sphere in the digital realm.[11] Kluge sees his digital enterprise as directly related to the project already initiated with *Public Sphere and Experience*:

> We are engaged in very collective work here; there are pieces from a lot of different filmmakers and authors. ... But everything that I've been doing for the last 21 years with dctp is just a continuation of a book that I once wrote with Oskar Negt, *Public Sphere and Experience* (1972). In it we provided an answer to what Habermas wrote in *The Structural Transformation of the Public Sphere*. We were interested in the concept of experience, how do people register things—this may be more or less objective, but the emotional responses of people are objective too. This is a theory of the public sphere that I'm still very attached to. Namely that there should be a public sphere, and precisely among those who are present. (2009c)

Even as the German *Mediengesetze* (media laws) of the 1980s show signs of irrelevance some three decades later, Kluge has moved into new networks of distribution, where he is no longer "dependent on ratings" (Kluge 2013). The Internet alters the calculus of distribution. More radically than the transfer of the television broadcasts to DVD, which opens possibilities for a different space and time of viewing practices but still remains tied to the distributional structure of commercial media, dctp.tv finally realizes the possibility of itself serving as a distribution network, no longer squeezed into a "window" or confined to an "island." A critical component of this endeavor is assisting in the growth and development of microproducers.

If the Internet is depicted as both a desert and a vast ocean of data, alternately emphasizing sameness and magnitude, Kluge claims to offer DCTP's website as an "oasis" in which the user can cultivate and grow their own personal interests, serving as a "rest stop" [*Ruhepunkt*] amidst the nondifferentiated flows of the so-called public sphere that limit and cripple experience:[12]

> No individual alone can cross an ocean of information; she would never arrive at the other shore. If you started out from Brittany, intending to swim across the Atlantic, you might get five kilometers out. At which point it would be good to have a boat. Here, a boat corresponds to an oasis, a fixed location. This dialectic between plenitude and a location where I am still myself, is a movement that leads to the development of a strong core. (2013)

The ideal website, in this view, is one that offers the possibility for subjective experience, and validates individual emotional and sensory registers. Further, Kluge underscores the links established among various "oases," constructing individuated "trade routes" (*Handelsstraßen*), in which information is exchanged, reconfigured, and recontextualized, and offering alternative pathways from the so-called superhighway and easy on-ramps constructed by the media conglomerates.

These small collectives, set in contrast to the Googles and Microsofts and Apples of the world (and not dissimilar from Rau's distinction in 1987 between smaller and larger television producers), form the basis of what Kluge depicts as a "coral reef" in the ocean of the Internet: "A classical public sphere prevails from these collectives—one might compare it to a coral reef in nutrient-poor waters, where diverse species sustain themselves by working together" (2013). Able to survive in a tough environment, the coral reef actually improves the overall quality of ocean life, functioning as diverse ecosystems that increase biodiversity and protect shorelines. Kluge's depiction of a digital countersphere thus serves as a manifesto some fifty years after Oberhausen not only to produce content—videos and songs, poetry and other texts, interviews, blogs, digital art, or any other creative work—but most importantly, vehicles or "receptacles for content" (*Gefäße für Substanz*) through which a "personal public sphere" is created.[13] Likewise the Oberhausen Manifesto was most importantly not simply a call for a new type of film (or *Substanz*) but a call for change in the material conditions of film financing, production, and distribution more generally (*Gefäße*), thereby reminding us that the media-historical narrative cannot be limited to technological developments but is always also a narrative of the sociopolitical and economic context of production, distribution, and reception. Clearly Kluge is not part of the generation Geert Lovink has decried for failing "to grasp the Internet and take it serious[ly] as an object of theory" (Strathausen 2009: 58).

dctp.tv serves as a platform for the remixing of content from *10 vor 11*, *News & Stories*, and other programs produced by the company and its partners, while also distributing new content created specifically for the site, and establishing links to a broader micronetwork of conferences, bloggers, independent content providers, and more.[14] The archivization and organization of the broadcasts on the dctp.tv website is again instructive. Video programs are managed in diverse and overlapping organizational strands under headings such as "Grosse Themen," "Gärten der Neugierde," "Nachrichten Werkstatt," and "Partner Personen & Events," which together form and re-form into thematic nodes, even more numerous thematic threads, and a constant stream of recent DCTP broadcasts. As with his DVDs, Internet television affords Kluge the luxury of intensifying the effects of individual programs themselves, namely, creating *magazines* of work that juxtapose various broadcasts alongside each other, sometimes in startling ways, that serve to provoke new ways of perceiving the world as it is conceptualized and represented.

This brings me to the third of the through-lines in Kluge's television broadcasts (and indeed, a vital component of his prose and film work as well), namely, their concern with the asymmetrical relationship of the individual to historical events—whether it be the invention of the guillotine (the subject of a broadcast in 1988)[15] or, more recently, the global economic collapse or the events of 9/11 and the attacks on the World Trade Center—and where multiple connections (associative, historical, emotional) across time and space serve us better in understanding the past, apprehending the present, and preparing for the future. So, for example, Kluge not only connects the global financial crisis with the crash of 1929, but also with other global catastrophes (including Chernobyl and the terror attacks of 9/11) (2009b). We see an example of this in one of the thematic loops on the dctp.tv website: "Der Anschlag auf die Twin Towers." The series consists, for now, of five videos: an interview with a Washington Post journalist (Anne Hull, well known for her Pulitzer Prize–winning series on Walter Reed Hospital in 2007) who had been on the scene in lower Manhattan, cut with early cell phone footage of the towers burning; an interview with an expert on cultural studies on the series of superheroes comics put out in reaction to 9/11; a video of time lapse photographs of the construction site at Ground Zero; a documentary on the construction of a steel housing that contains the ruins of the Chernobyl disaster (and had been originally proposed to cover the ruins at Ground Zero); and an "interview" with an attorney (played by Peter Berling) charged with sorting through the complex insurance claims in the wake of the collapse of the twin towers. If the journalist, Anne Hull, is depicted almost as a latter-day Gabi Teichert (one of Kluge's memorable cinematic heroines)—Kluge even calls her a "patriot of the public sphere" (*Patriotin der Öffentlichkeit*), with a nod to his film, *Die Patriotin*—all five of the videos go to the question: "How does one report on a catastrophe of this magnitude?" What material is relevant? What is omitted? What is accidental? What is forgotten? What is too small to be included? What is too complex for single expression? All questions that public and private television and Internet content either totalize or isolate, subsuming the event under an ideological narrative or segregating it from larger and differentiated histories of catastrophe.

"Ein Gehäuse aus Stahl für Tschernobyl" explores the link between the attacks on the World Trade Center and the nuclear catastrophe at

Chernobyl through an idiosyncratic link: the American engineering firm Bechtel, which bid for (and ultimately lost) the contract to oversee the cleanup at the World Trade Center site and later designed a 20,000-ton steel dome to enclose the toxic remains of Reactor 4. The six-minute video is a montage of photographs of the rubble of the Twin Towers, the concrete sarcophagus entombing Reactor 4, video of cleanup attempts at both sites, architectural renderings, and text-images narrating the link between the two events, all set to Stockhausen's "Helikopter-Quartett" (1992–1993). The video explores the story of one connection between catastrophes of an almost unimaginable magnitude to suggest that we as individuals can only grasp events of global scale through these multiple, interconnected narratives. Upon accepting the Adorno prize on 11 September 2009, Kluge argued: "We need them because realities like the financial crisis or asymmetrical war impact people's lives directly and cause injury, and yet at the same time they seem almost like fantastical fictions. In order to deal with these realities and to orient ourselves in these labyrinths, we can't limit ourselves to a single narrative, rather we need a radical variety of expression" (2009b). A collage image from the video in which the steel dome seems to enclose simultaneously the rubble of the Twin Towers and the Chernobyl reactor, the Statue of Liberty, a Manhattan street, and construction trucks, provides almost a visual shorthand for Kluge's method as a whole: the relationship of two catastrophes that is neither causal nor one of analogy but of a fortuitous link (the steel construction) through which the larger question of catastrophe can be explored; the role and construction of iconic images (the Statue of Liberty) and how quickly even the seemingly least constructed images (the cell phone footage of the disaster) are absorbed by the consciousness industry (the skeleton of the World Trade Center ruins); and finally the individual story: who is driving the truck that enters the scene at bottom left? It is an image montage that denies categorization, compression, condensation, but seeks to undo precisely what the steel dome has been constructed for: the burial of the catastrophe.

At the start of the dual-television landscape, Kluge warned, "The simple addition of media worlds produces repressive works of art. Real human and historical relations are *repressed*. This prospect is disastrous for the community, and very seductive to opportunists" (1988: 101; emphasis in the original). Kluge's own work—in television, video, and the Internet—seeks to deconstruct these myths of immediacy and completeness and instead to develop viewers' awareness of the production process, to unseat the viewer and to challenge her to ask, to engage, and to participate in reclaiming the "classical" public spheres. New media, Kluge suggests, may offer the possibility for both: richness and diversity, as well as universal access. Kluge's criticism in the 1980s of the univocity of both public and industrial media, supported by media laws, could apply just as well to our situation some thirty years later:

> Compare this with the riches of the classical public spheres, with ... what constituted music, theater, classical film, newspapers, the narrative arts, and a science that is more than popular broadcasts about stars and animals. Such riches had *one* flaw: not everyone had access to them. But it would be a criminal act of destruction to preserve the exclusivity of these *bountiful modes of expression* and simultaneously to discard the utopian possibility hidden in the classical public spheres: that it is possible for one individual or another, *and possibly even for everyone, against all probability* to know something, to be fully aware, etc. Anyone who destroys the classical public spheres commits a crime against history. (1988: 99; emphasis in the original)

Stefanie Harris is Associate Professor of German and Film Studies at Texas A&M University. Her work includes *Mediating Modernity: German Literature and the "New" Media, 1895–1930* (University Park: Penn State University Press, 2009) and articles on Herzog, Kluge, and Sebald, with other publications in *Gegenwartsliteratur, German Quarterly, Historical Journal of Film Radio and Television, Modern Austrian Literature, New German Critique, Translation Perspectives,* and elsewhere.

Notes

1. All translations in the text are my own, except where otherwise noted.
2. Titles taken from the television schedules for SAT1 and RTL during the week of 5 February 2012.
3. For a detailed presentation of the histories of West and East German television, see: Hickethier and Hoff 1998.
4. Likewise, Flusser will claim: "It is no exaggeration to say that we know and experience the world, and that we act in it, within the structures that are imposed on us by the codes that inform us. ... Our 'being-in-the-world' can be changed, if the structure of our codes is changed, and this is important not only for the understanding of our situation, but also for any effort to change it" (2004: 16).
5. In the so-called "Mainz Manifesto" (1983), for example, Kluge's immediate concern is not that the private channels will broadcast low-brow content, but rather that media producers will themselves control the distribution outlets. His counterexample is the individual news kiosk, which is not owned by the conglomerates that produce most newspapers (1988: 96–102).

6. For detailed listings of individual broadcasts of the three *Kulturmagazine* (*10 vor 11, News & Stories,* and *Primetime/Spätausgabe*), see: Schulte 2000: 401–38; Gruber and Schulte 2007.
7. Lest we are inclined to view opera as too high brow for television, one of Kluge's funniest broadcasts is an interview with Peter Berling in the role of the famous baritone Edouard de Scaramberg, called "Der Kunst weiht' ich mein Leben. Ein Bariton outet sich als Doper" (I Gave My Life to Art. A Baritone Outs Himself as a Dope-Fiend) (Premiere: 30. April 2007, DCTP auf RTL).
8. "No matter what one says about romantic relationships, it is immediately contradicted by their natural abundance of casuistry. Love is a millipede. Whenever one tells stories about it, comprehension, categorization, and theses are never a virtue" (2009a: 7).
9. Tim Grünewald (2005) has focused specifically on Kluge's interviews addressing Islam and terrorism after 2001 to show how Kluge not only gives air time to counterstatements that are generally absent from the mainstream media, but more importantly, subverts normalizing aesthetic conventions. The critique thus does not simply address content, but the circulation of discourse itself.
10. On the larger subject of media generations, see the essays in Hörisch 1997.
11. I offer that Kluge's ongoing project of intermediality is one variation of what Carsten Strathausen asserts as a project of "new media aesthetics," especially as Kluge's work never strays from the central question: "why media studies matter" (2009: 57).
12. "[Negt and Kluge] seek to widen the notion [of the public sphere] in such a way as to secure its constitutive relationship to the very possibility of social or individual experience in general. The structure of the 'public sphere' is now seen as what enables experience or, on the other hand, what limits and cripples it. This structure also determines that fundamental modern pathology whereby 'experience' itself is sundered, its unevenly divided halves assigned to stereotypical public expressions, on the one hand, and, on the other, to that zone of the personal and the private which seems to offer shelter from the public and the political at the same time that it is itself a social fact produced by the public and political" (Jameson 1988: 156–57).
13. Kluge's e-Book is the first in a series published by mikrotext, founded in 2013. In effect, it doubles as a manifesto for the publishers themselves, who plan to bring out micro works that are intended to be read and discussed as functional examples of this "personal public sphere" (note that Kluge's text is described in the promotional materials as "approximately 50 pages on a smart phone").
14. This emphasis on external linking is relatively new in the ongoing development of the website and may reflect Kluge's own evolving thoughts on the creation of productive digital counterpublic spheres. The dctp.tv website has undergone significant site revision in the past year. A programmatic statement on the website now reads: "The goal of this program is to present the PRINCIPLE OF INFORMATION in an exemplary fashion in moving images on a shared platform: in the midst of the online hustle and bustle, as a counterpart to TV, and in tune with the turbulence in which digital media are constantly mutating."
15. "Die Guillotine oder die Kategorie der Plötzlichkeit. Mit Karl-Heinz Bohrer" (Premiere: 26 December 1988, DCTP auf RTL).

PART IV

PRESENT AND FUTURE PERSPECTIVES

Chapter 7

TELEVISION HISTORY IN GERMANY

Media-Political and Media-Ethical Aspects

Rüdiger Steinmetz

Introduction

Media policy (*Medienpolitik*) includes the domain of political actions and decisions by state institutions and parties, as well as by their representatives in the domain of media. The term may also refer to the conditions of media and to specifics of program design. The extent of media-political planning (*Gestaltung*) differed in the BRD and DDR, and also varied over the course of television's development.

Since there are different ideas about the good life and right behavior (philosophical ethics), media ethics may be defined in several areas as an applied ethics. Media ethics may be applied above all to maxims of action and orientation for individuals such as journalists, program designers, and spectators (individual ethics); institutions and organizations (social ethics); or enterprises (business ethics) in the domain of media and their respective actions, conducted in accordance with a principle of responsibility.

Media-ethical norms of action are valid only for a specific time and are thus also to be classified relative to their respective social forms within this temporal frame. Media policy and media ethics are tangent to each other and may even be derived from each other to a certain extent, since in both areas it is a question of political, social, and medial value orientations. Both domains are above all normatively oriented, since it is a question in both of the setting of parameters, whether political or ethical.

After World War II, two distinct social systems developed in Germany. For the newly reestablished media of press, radio, and television, different consequences were drawn in East and West from the failed totalitarian media system of National Socialism. From this, two divergent definitions of media's tasks resulted.

German Media in "Contrastive Dialogue"

In order to understand television in both German states, we must elucidate their organizational conditions and their embedding in cultural and political history. The stamp set on media structures by the respective Allied powers in the Western occupation zones (United States, Great Britain, France) and the Eastern ones (Soviet Union) is essential to understand television in the GDR and the BRD. In the same way, we must consider the developments of the Cold War, as the ideological and technological competition of political systems was manifested more than anywhere else in Germany. The German-German border was not closed off, for despite the increasingly impenetrable boundaries (Berlin Wall, barbed wire, "death stretch" since 1961), close human and medial relations persisted, even if ex negativo. Between the two German states there extended across the border a "contrastive dialogue" in the domain of media. This term designates an interactive feedback loop of discussion, which was for a long time set up not for the purpose of mutual understanding, but for that of "contrast" and delimitation with the opponent.

Communications between the German states took place on three levels. First, there was exchange on the individual level—between individuals, families, and groups during visits, usually going from West to East; there was also contact via letters and sporadically via telephone.

Second, this took place on the political and economic level, in the form of official and partly also unofficial "official" contacts (for instance, concerning the regulation of agreements on permits allowing citizens of West Germany to visit East Berlin and the GDR, or in transit agreements regarding traffic between the BRD and West Berlin, or German-German trade and sport, but also agreements about artistic performances across the border, licensing for publishers, and so on). These contacts were not always publicly visible.

Third, contacts happened on the medial and public (program) level of broadcast media: due to the border-crossing nature of electronic media radio and TV, a contrastive dialogue happened above all between them. This had consequences especially in the GDR, because there the Western and Eastern offerings were used more intensively than in the

West, where GDR media were hardly noticed at all and citizens limited themselves to the offerings of their own media.

This dialogue was asymmetrical, due to the different constitutions and purposes or goals of the media in both states. GDR broadcast media were, as state media, mouthpieces and official announcers for state and party. A double media-political control structure—consisting of state committees and those of the socialist block parties under the rule of the SED—influenced both the medial structures (macro level) and the details of programming (micro level).

West German broadcast media were and are, in contrast, much more complexly organized. Public broadcasting (radio and TV) is constituted federally (ARD) and centrally (ZDF) and is by definition distinct from the state and noncommercial. Public programs do not necessarily correspond to the viewpoints of those in power or the parties, although quite a few West German politicians would have liked to have it that way and thus tried again and again since the 1950s to bring the media closer to the government and the parties, albeit without success. Since 1984, private and commercial programs have been added to this mix, but they too have refused to be only a mouthpiece of the state and the parties.

Thus there was a dialogue between the media systems of East and West, which used the same language and, on the surface, largely comparable medial forms of representation. Those responsible for TV in the East saw themselves, via this dialogue, in a constant struggle with the TV of the "class enemy" in the West, and thus in permanent competition with Western programs. They therefore constantly referred to these Western competitors in their own programming policy. For Western TV personnel, too, the GDR system always represented a point of reference (usually only structural) in the form of an imperative to delimit itself from socialism and its principles. This was, however, formulated less explicitly on the level of programming. There was thus never a "radio silence" (*Funkstille*) between the two media systems, not even in the frostiest periods of the Cold War (end of 1950s–beginning of 1960s, and beginning of the 1980s). Yet after the German unification in 1990, people in united Germany still had to find a common media language, even after the establishment of a unified media structure.

Media-Ethical Similarities and Differences

Media ethics must be viewed against the backdrop of opposing media policies. Media ethical problems resulted again and again in both media systems from the divergent evaluation and representation of the relation of individual and society in TV programs. While in the West, the individual with his or her initiative and productive force was in the foreground, and the postulate of freedom was meant to guarantee this individual development, the individual only counted in the East if it could integrate itself into the collective. The solution since the collectivization of agriculture in the beginning of the 1950s was, for example, "from I to we."

The different directions and emphases in specific program areas of television may be derived from this difference in fundamental attitudes. While in the West, positive or negative dramatizations of the individual were prominent—and sometimes tainted with sensationalism as well—the individual in the East served above all to become a positive example for others and for the collective.

Common to TV programming in both countries is, however, that they worked toward forms of individual behavior that were deemed appropriate to society and its demands. Although the individual was and remains prominent in Western programming, the modes of behavior propagated there still aim for social responsibility and respect for valid social norms. Even in private TV broadcasting, which thematize and diffuse private conflicts above all—as in the so-called court shows and the daily talk shows—the attitudes and virtues called for by the moderators were and are always conservative: dependability, a sense of responsibility, loyalty, and socially conscious action are termed good and even demanded. On the other hand, GDR TV never ceased to single out individual accomplishments and encourage the individual to more effort and to a more engaged action. It was not least the fictional programs that served in both media systems to demonstrate these individual achievements of conformity to social norms and make them sensually intuitive—if need be, also through the representation of "corrections" that became necessary if the individuals refused to grasp the problem, or through showing negative consequences.

Fundamental dramaturgical messages were and are much less prominent in media-ethical discussions; instead, what is important is the direct and intuitive mode of appearance of individual situations and behaviors. These debates intensified above all with the establishment of new formats in private programs in the 1990s.

At the center of these discussions were new entertainment formats that established themselves in the 1990s, such as daily talk shows, confrontainment-shows, and the like. They made the individual particularities, actions, problems, and fears of people available to a mass public. Everyday people were here displayed for fifteen minutes with their personal confessions and actions in extreme situations, and the exhibitionism of the actors and their medial presentation answered a demand of the viewers for sensationalistic presentations. The ethics discussion thematized the responsibility of individual editors and reporters—along with that of those responsible for programs, and finally that of the owners of media films—for their marketing of individuals. Among the questions publicly discussed were: is it legitimate to expose individual people if they voluntarily put themselves in such situations and apply to appear in programs known for exploiting private destinies in a manner that affects the public? Or can the individual, despite his or her passive experience with the media, not anticipate this medial marketing and must thus be, so to speak, protected from himself or herself?

These media-ethical questions of principle were asked less on the level of the media political difference of East and West. Here ideological oppositions were dominant, and set the terms in relatively simple fashion for media-ethical positions of principle. The discussions of television became more sensitive and volatile from the 1990s on, particularly in the question of differences between public and private TV.

If public television saw itself, in its obligation to program mandate and broadcasting laws, as bound to ethical norms that had long been consensually valued in society, then these norms and values seemed to be revoked by commercial providers, who saw that they could gain viewers through violating taboos in a tendentious manner. What was acceptable and possible in programming, and where were the limits to obtaining information, to the form of its presentation, the representation of certain themes and the mode of address to the viewer? Which information and presentations should not at all be presented? Who was responsible for overstepping boundaries, and how could they be fined for this?

Over and against individual freedom in social communication are the obligations of media providers to social acceptability and orientation toward the common good. Fundamental ethical notions (such as communitarian ethics), which concern universal ideas of value, human existence, and dignity, thus determined responsibility, duties, and virtues. Potential themes here include protection of youth and of users, authorial rights, freedom and diversity of opinion, questions of possible media manipulation, the endangerment of the individual's private sphere, the mixing of advertising and PR with editorials via surreptitious advertising, product placement, and other means.

It is above the churches that have here formulated media ethical principles, which may offer a framework even if it is still very general. According to them, media and communication should orient themselves to whether they serve man, opening possibilities of life, not limiting critical abilities and encouraging community life. Christian media ethics are oriented toward the dignity of man, which is closely linked to freedom and self-determination (Rat der Evangelischen Kirche Deutschlands 2008).

Fundamental works of media ethics call for values like protection of human dignity from commercialization and economic reductionism, protection from instrumentalizing people for entertainment purposes, and protection of victims in reporting on disasters. Nonetheless, converting media ethics into policy via the creation of laws is always difficult, since this requires public consciousness of the problem and compatibility of the laws with the German Constitution. Since media policy, as a policy pursued by the state chancelleries of the governments of the Länder, is also often interested in the economic potential of media industries (and seeks to have media enterprises based in their *Land*), and this economic potential lies above all in the commercial domain, such media enterprises are not subject to many restrictions.

Media Political Development of Television

One may divide the development of television in Germany after 1945 into the following phases, which were in both German states partly parallel, and partly divergent:

West	**East**
To 1952: phase of experimentation	To 1955: experimental phase
From 1953: set up phase	From 1956: set up phase
1960s: establishment as mass medium, consolidation of programs and organization	1960s: establishment as mass medium, consolidation of programs and organization structures
1970s: differentiation of programs and organization structures, innovation and diversification	1970s: differentiation of programs and organization structures, innovation and diversification
1980s (first half): transition to dual system, intensification of entertainment	1980s (first half): assimilation to the West, internationalization of program

1980s (second half): consolidation and differentiation of the dual system	1980s (second half): stagnation, contradictions, ambivalences
1990–91: extension of organization and programming of all TV channels toward the East	1990–91: new beginning, democratization, phase-out of DFF, systemic change

From 1 January 1992 onward: all-German, federal, democratic TV system: diversification and profitability of the first private-commercial programs; market leadership of commercial providers; establishment of 24-hour broadcasting; increased ethical problems with new formats; stronger orientation to consumerism and advertisement. Establishment of Pay TV (Premiere).

Second half of the 1990s: beginnings of digital TV, new niche programs; heightened entertainment orientation of programs and concentration on cost-effectiveness; shift from cultural to business-driven conception, at first in a national context; alternations in organizational and business structures.

From 2000 on: deployment of new popular formats.

2006: beginning of Internet TV. Heightened discussion of media policy and planning, regulation and oversight of contents, techniques, and business linkages.

Media Policy Developments in the 1950s

The development of broadcasting (radio and TV) in the years from 1945 to 1955 was essentially influenced by the Allies, who set their stamp on broadcasting systems. In the Western zones there arose a public TV system independent of the state, which was noncommercial and centralized (British and French zones) or federalized (American zone). In the Soviet occupation zone, TV was established as a state-run, centralized system. These broadcasting systems were set up even before the founding of the two German states BRD and DDR in 1949. The first broadcasting institution, founded in 1947–48 on the basis of broadcasting laws specific to the Land, was Northwest German Broadcasting (NWDR) in Hamburg; there followed Radio Bremen (RB), Hessian Broadcasting (Hessischer Rundfunk, HR in Frankfurt/M.), Southwest German Broadcasting (SWF in Baden-Baden), South German Broadcasting (SDR in Stuttgart), and Bavarian Broadcasting (BR in Munich). Broadcasting in the Soviet occupation zone (SBZ) was organized by the state from 1945 onward and answered to the directives of the Socialist Unity Party (SED).

Television arose both in West and East after the respective foundations of the two states and in the wake of the creation of the organizational structures of broadcasting (at first only radio). Political interest in TV as a new medium was little developed at first among politicians of East and West, since they were more concerned with the familiar media of the press, meaning radio and film. Only at the end of the 1950s and the beginning of the 1960s, with the establishment of TV as a mass medium (1.2 million viewers in the BRD in 1958, 1.03 million in the GDR in 1960) did politicians recognize the significance of this new medium for their purposes.

In the West, the independence of broadcasting from the state was set in the broadcasting laws of the Länder, and when TV programming began, this was then extended from radio to the new medium. The basis of all following broadcasting laws, still valid today, was Article 5 of the German Constitution: "Everyone has the right to express and diffuse his opinion in word, writing, and image and to be informed from generally accessible sources. Freedom of the press and freedom of reporting by radio and film are guaranteed. There can be no censorship."

This independence is supposed to be ensured up to now in public broadcasting institutions by three instances: the Administrative Council (Verwaltungsrat), the Broadcasting Council (Rundfunkrat; in the ZDF, the TV Council), and the intendant. In the supervisory committees, the Broadcasting and Administrative Councils, the caretakers of political interests had and have a considerable influence.

In the GDR, TV reported to the State Broadcasting Committee. State and party set clear parameters for cultural and educational contents. The "elevation of the educational level of our workers" through publicistic programs was in the foreground, and light entertainment was only a concession to "petty bourgeois" social needs. The program had to fulfill agitatory tasks and was "a means of expression and connection in the cultural-artistic domain, and (had to) answer the needs of workers for entertainment and relaxation," as it said in an internal study of the German TV Broadcasting (DFF) in 1955.

Due to the democratic constitution of the media, there were no such parameters in the West that would affect concrete programming, except for the obligation to respect the federal constitution. The principle of distance from the state (*Staatsferne*) had, however, first to be developed over the course of long political discussions. Thus, for the first chancellor of West Germany, Konrad Adenauer, the principle of broadcasting's independence from the state, which had been decreed by the Western Allies, along with its federative structure, were both a thorn in his side. He wanted to create a federal television controlled by the federal government. In 1961, however, he was stopped by the Federal Constitutional Court, which stipulated the public and nonstate character of broadcasting (not least due to the scarcity of TV frequencies).

Until 1972, the names of programs in East and West still made their claims to be representative of all of Germany. Since 1 November 1954, the ARD (Arbeitsgemeinschaft der öffentlich-rechtlichen Rundfunkanstalten der Bundesrepublik Deutschland) produced the collaborative program *German Television* (today called *First German Television*), and in the GDR, from 2 January 1956 to 11 February 1972, there existed the *German TV Broadcasting* (DFF). Later it was renamed *Television of the GDR*. This claim of both systems to represent all of Germany was, however, a matter of lip service.

Media Political Developments in the 1960s

In both German states, the 1960s were the decade of an intensively developing TV boom. After the phase of experimentation and construction, television consolidated itself in the 1960s in its organizational and program structures.

In the Federal Republic, Second German TV (ZDF) arose in 1963 from the remains of Konrad Adenauer's attempt to set up an additional broadcaster, which had been stopped by the Constitutional Court. It was established on the level of the Länder. The founding of a Third Program was then conceded to the institutions of the ARD and set up from 1964 on.

The "first TV ruling" of the Federal Constitutional Court in 1961 is called the Magna Carta of broadcasting in the Federal Republic. There followed in subsequent decades other principled court rulings, which cannot be discussed in detail here. (They would include the Court's 1971 ruling on VAT and the private radio ruling of the Federal Administrative Court; the FRAG-Free Radio Inc. ruling of 1981; Lower Saxony ruling in 1986; that for Baden-Württemberg in 1987; NRW ruling of 1991; HR-3, 1992; first radio tariff ruling, 1994; brief sport reporting, 1998; the basic legal capacity of private broadcasters, 1998; second radio tariff ruling, 2007; ruling on participation of political parties in private broadcasting, 2008.)

Media policy was and is directed in the Federal Republic by the Länder, and then regulated on a higher level by the Federal Constitutional Court. The broadcast rulings of the highest court thus constitute in a certain way a bridge between media policy and media ethics, for this adjudication is based on ethical maxims for the development of coexistence of individuals and society as a whole.

These fundamental judgments over almost five decades are not unalterable. After the court had determined the public character of broadcasting in 1961, it accepted, with the technical extension of TV broadcasting through satellite and cable, private program providers in 1981. The maxim remained unchanged that—according to Article 5, Par. 1, sentence 2 of the Constitution—the guarantee of broadcasting freedom is demanded, and with it a media order in which the "diversity of existing societal opinions should find its expression in broadcasting with the greatest possible breadth and completeness."

Rulings from the highest court are only made when medial and media-political changes have already been occurring for a longer period of time. Thus it may be that TV, as we have so far known it, has become so deeply changed and differentiated by the Internet, by globalization and the convergence of classical media, that there is nothing more to secure or regulate on the basic of the court's commandment to preserve diversity.

In the GDR, the 11th Plenum of the Central Committee of the SED in 1965 effected a considerable media-political and media-ethical caesura. If for a brief period after the building of the Berlin Wall in 1961, a climate of medial and artistic liberality had arisen, this plenum and its cultural-policy orientation led to a heightened censorship of programs and to personal suspensions of work. The Department of Agitation and Propaganda of the Central Committee of the SED strengthened its influence on television. At the end of 1965, the intendant, Heinz Adameck, received cultural-political directions almost every day from the Central Committee or the Politbüro, which he then transmitted to his co-workers, of whom the leaders and many others were members of the SED or its affiliated block parties. In long-term "perspective plans" and individual "yearly plans," "ideological guidelines" played a central role. They directed the development of themes and formats for series and individual broadcasts, all the way down to genres, specific statements, formal implementation, and casting. In daily news reports official formulations were handed down. There was a "hotline" between the "Aktuelle Kamera," the news report of GDR TV, and the Central Committee Secretary for Agitation and Propaganda. These clear parameters and the filtering by precensoring were complemented by a censorship after the fact.

On 3 October 1969 the DFF began broadcasting in color and, at the same time, a second channel. Western color broadcasting was inititated two years earlier, in 1967. Even this occasion would become a political event. Most importantly, the decision to employ two different color systems, PAL in the Federal Republic and SECAM in the GDR, was driven by political considerations, since these two systems were incompatible with one another. For this reason one could not, for a long time, view Western images in color and vice versa. The choice of SECAM was predetermined by the Soviet Union, and the contrasting color system fit into the GDR's "new course" that aimed for international recognition and a two-state German solution.

Direct or indirect political influence over time created media ethical problems in the East as well as in the West, albeit much less prevalent in the latter case. Media's influence on people was considered to be similarly large in both states. There were, for that reason, political interventions or attempted interventions in ARD and ZDF programming. They remained highly selective and rare and were not, as they were with DFF and Television of the GDR, anchored in the permanent organizational control structures as preliminary censorship. The broadcasting councils in the West could only admonish stations after the fact. But even at the more conservative-leaning Bayerische Rundfunk, this was put into practice only for occasional theatrical stagings (Fritz Kortner's "Lysistrata's Message"), made-for-TV productions (Rainer Erler's "The Drilling Hole, or Bavaria is not Texas," Rosa von Praunheim's "It Is Not the Homosexual Who Is Perverse, Rather the Society in Which He Lives," or Alexander Ziegler and Wolfgang Peterson's "The Consequence," 1977), and even the youth program "Zoom" from 1971.

Developments in the Media Politics of the 1970s

One (media) political turn in the GDR came about through the replacement of the party and state council chairman, Walter Ulbricht, by Erich Honecker. At the Eighth SED Party Convention in June 1971, Honecker formulated the foundations of new media policy, one that concentrated more on entertainment and placed higher societal demands on television. He challenged the DFF to "overcome a certain boredom" in both of its programs. Such formulations did not just represent some sort of nonbinding suggestions; rather they set parameters to be followed by the broadcasters and eventually leading to a larger reform of programming. According to one of the first reorientations toward entertainment at the beginning of the 1970s (the second followed in 1982–1983), ideological guidelines were henceforth not to be mediated directly, but rather through sentiments and moods.

The growing self-confidence of the GDR expressed itself in 1972 in the renaming of the DFF to "Television of the GDR" as well as in a forced ideological programming struggle against the West. In the 1970s there were no longer shows explicitly directed to Western viewers. Television was built up as a medium specifically for the GDR viewer. At the same time in the 1970s the first informal contacts with ARD and ZDF were developed into more intensive relationships.

National political developments such as the new "Ostpolitik" of the Federal Republic under Willy Brandt and Walter Scheel (Foundational Treaty FRG/GDR, 1972) and the Helsinki Accords on the Conference for Security and Cooperation in Europe also influenced both media politics and specific programs. Thus permanent correspondents were set up in the two capitals, Bonn and East Berlin, with Lothar Loewe (ARD) and Hans-Jürgen Wiesner (ZDF) in East Berlin and Heinz Grote (Fernsehen der DDR) in Bonn.

For several reasons the first half of the 1970s brought a period of openness to new forms and content. This was due, in the West, to democratization movements such as the student movement and the new "Ostpolitik" and, in the East, as a result of the change of direction initiated by Erich Honecker. The media politics influenced the climate in different ways in each of the German states.

In the East, the expatriation of the folksinger Wolf Bierman (1976) led to a drastic change in mood among artists and intellectuals. It also changed the attitude of the party toward television. The Politbüro determined a detailed annual program for the network and expanded down to the finest detail its control and censorship in the person of Eberhard Fensch and his colleagues. Longtime program director of GDR television, Heinz Adameck, referred to this period as "the worst time … self-censorship, the interference, the situation created by decisions from above, made it impossible to breathe." In the wake of reporting on the Biermann expatriation, or on the isolation of the dissident Robert Havemann, or the self-immolation of Pastor (Oskar) Brüsewitz, the ARD studio in East Berlin was faced with closure. In the end "only" the West German correspondent, Lothar Loewe, was expelled on Christmas 1976, due to his report for the ARD news program *Tagesschau,* in which he said: "Every child here in the GDR knows that the border patrol has the strict orders to shoot people like rabbits."

In the West a media political fight broke out between the partisan camps of the SPD and CDU regarding the future of media technology. A report from the government-appointed Commission for the Expansion of the Technical Communication System (KtK, 1975) became the premise for political conflicts. Technical and programmatic tests and pilot projects (which were in fact already the introduction of videotext, broadband cable, and satellite television) began to be discussed in 1978 and, from 1982 on, came to fruition. With the technical enabling of multiple television channels, the basis for the "frequency shortage" argument formulated in 1961 by the Federal Constitutional Court collapsed.

Development in Media Politics in the 1980s

With the possibility of new broadcasters due to further-developed satellite and cable technology through the 1981 decision of the Federal Constitutional Court, the way was cleared for new content providers and therefore for the commercialization of the broadcasting system. This began with the so-called *Urknall* (big bang) attributed to the Rhineland-Palatinate premier, Bernhard Vogel. The big bang marked the beginning of the cable television pilot project as a competing broadcasting system.

After the 1982 regime change from the Social Democratic and Free Democratic Schmidt/Genscher coalition to the conservative/Free Democratic Kohl/Genscher government, the media industry and publishing interests in the Federal Republic reached their long-held goal, namely, a private-commercial competitor to the public broadcasting system. Thus began the networks Sat.1/PKS (Programmgesellschaft für Kabel-und Satellitenrundfunk, 1 January 1984) and RTLplus (1 February 1984) as the first private, commercial competitive networks, ones in which newspaper and magazine publishers such as Bertelsmann, Gruner & Jahr, and Springer, as well as film distributor Leo Kirch were involved. Other networks were added in 1987. One result of the controversial commercialization was the strengthened emphasis by broadcasters, including ARD and ZDF, on entertainment.

Citizens' groups such as the BBU (Federal Citizens' Initiative for Environmental Protection), the BIKK (Citizens' Initiative Against Cable Commerce), and the "Klingenmeister Circle," as well as the Author's Guild fought against the "entertainmentization" of television. Arguments against the the flood of programming, "illiterization," destruction of the family unit (everyone has his own television), sexist and pornographic programming, disenfranchisement, and citizen surveillance all stood at the heart of their media ethical concerns.

This entertainmentization of television in the Federal Republic also had an effect on East German television. In the general—and above all economic—stagnation of the GDR of the 1980s, viewers fled GDR television, especially from their own productions, such as *Ein Kessel Buntes* and *Showkolade*. As a consequence, beginning in 1982–1983 a further GDR television reform was undertaken, one that would bring the networks in line with West German and international trends.

A contradictory situation arose in the mid-1980s due to the planned stationing of midrange Pershing missiles in the Federal Republic, one that cooled the German-German political climate. At the same time, however, a billion-Deutschmark credit for both the Martin Luther anniversary celebrations and those of the 750th birthday of the city of Berlin, as well as Erich Honecker's 1987 visit to the Federal Republic, all led to a number of closer ties. The cooperation agreement between ARD and ZDF on one hand, and one with Television of the GDR on the other, led to an intensification of content exchange and mutual production support. This was in line with the political zeitgeist of the late 1980s, the expressed intention of which was to "resolve any emerging points of contention." ARD became the most important customer of GDR television programming outside the Eastern Bloc.

After Honecker's visit, ARD/ZDF and GDR-Television went from media competitors to partial working partners. This working relationship between the television systems of East and West, which centered primarily on nonpolitical programming such as fiction television and entertainment, lasted until September 1989. Antagonisms grew in the latter part of the decade, however, at the level of topical reporting. West German correspondents cooperated with GDR dissidents and broadcast their footage on topics such as deforestation or environmental degradation in the GDR on news feature and political programs on ARD and ZDF. They also reported on demonstrations such as the Rosa Luxemburg protests in January 1988 and 1989.

Television of the GDR was quite slow to react in September 1989 to the wave of emigration through Hungary and Czechoslovakia and the growing protests among the population. The cause of their hesitation lay both in the parameters of their media politics, in their focus on the celebrations surrounding the fortieth anniversary of the founding of the GDR, and also in stubborn conservative habits within the television studios themselves. Changes came most hesitantly to the news program *Aktuelle Kamera*.

An extraordinary bit of media politics took place on the evening of 9 November 1989: Günter Schabowski, secretary for information of the

Central Committee of the Social Unity Party, held for the first time an international press conference, which was shown live on GDR-Television. Toward the end of the press conference, around 7 p.m., he announced the immediate opening of the Berlin Wall and the borders to the Federal Republic. He pulled a note from his files containing the just-passed version of new travel regulations and stated:

> The travel rules are not yet in effect, but are still a proposal. But they were passed today, as far as I know (*Schabowski looked to his right at the Politbüro member*). A recommendation of the Politbüro was taken up that one passage of the Travel Law should be applied, the one which, as one so nicely or unnicely puts it, regulates "permanent departure," that is to say, the leaving of the country. Because we find it an impossible situation that this movement [of mass emigration] is taking place through an allied country, which has not been easy for this country. For that reason we decided today to enact a regulation that will make it possible for every GDR citizen to leave the country through existing GDR border crossings. I have also been notified, comrades, that already today such an announcement has been passed around and should already be in your possession.[1]

Thus did one arbitrary act by a political actor, prematurely announced on live television, bring about the opening of the Berlin Wall and East German borders. Thousands upon thousands of people made their way to the gradually opened border crossings. Television not only broadcast the historical moment live; it also worked to put it on the political agenda.

All evidence indicates that this press conference had been prestaged. Günter Schabowski planned how it would proceed, as his handwritten notes prove: "TIME! Just before closing and end of debate, cite the account given by the Ministerial Council!!! No Politbüro document!!! Passed by the Ministerial Council!!! Read the new travel regulation." Schabowski was enough of a media professional to know that, if he had read the new travel regulations at the beginning of this first-ever press conference for the international press to be broadcast live on GDR television, this would have been the immediate end of the broadcast. Therefore he waited until the end when someone mentioned the key words "travel regulations." This role was taken by Riccardo Ehrmann, the Germany correspondent for the Italian news agency, ANSA, whom Schabowski chose over a British reporter, even after the latter had already begun his question. After the fact, Schabowski portrayed this scenario as a communication breakdown.

With the exception of the ARD channel, WDR, and SFB (Free Berlin Channel), television in both East and West was paralyzed by the news of the opening. The SFB questioned West Berlin's governing mayor about the announcement within twenty minutes of this news. ZDF and the commercial channels failed to grasp the opening of the borders on 9 November 1989. The GDR border patrols as well as the Ministry for Security were taken completely by surprise by what they viewed as a premature action. Even they followed the events on West German radio and television, which, beginning with the 8 p.m. evening news, switched over to a live broadcast.

Political control of the media in the GDR ceased on this date. In the winter and spring of 1990 round table fora on media policies, including old and new experts as well as members of citizens' movements, discussed the media perspectives of the GDR. For a while, GDR viewers accepted the unfamiliar, quite flexible broadcast plans, with new and occasionally investigative shows. For a few weeks they looked to their own, changing television networks for current information and discussions. Television in both East and West utilized its particular capability of live broadcast reports to portray a greater sense of topicality and authenticity. A brief period of new freedom, and a the same time one of great uncertainty, began in the GDR, one that gave to the new self-liberated GDR Television a certain psychotherapeutic function.

Developments in Media Politics in the 1990s

On 5 February 1990 the law granting unlimited freedom of information, opinions, and media was passed in the GDR. Thereafter, broadcasting and the press in general and especially television no longer fell under the control of government and the Socialist Unity Party, which had, in the meantime, renamed itself the Party of Democratic Socialism. Organizational survival strategies for the giant television apparatus (with approximately 14,000 employees), ones that would be both legally and economically viable, were sought at the Round Table discussion and in the boardrooms of GDR Television. But conditions changed rapidly. After the currency union with the Federal Republic on 1 July 1990 and unification of both German states under the provisions of the Federal Basic Law on 3 October 1990, GDR Television began its integration into the German federal television system. Decentralization and regionalization of television in the East began in the wake of the founding of the five new German federal states in October 1990. This transformation resulted in the removal of programming from GDR Television onto the frequency formerly used by the DFF-Länderkette (the GDR regional broadcasting whose signal did not reach across all parts of the East). ARD and ZDF occupied the frequencies formerly used by the two primary East German channels, which was perceived by many East German citizens as a form of media occupation by the West.

Rudolf Mühlfenzl, former director of programming for the Bavarian channel, Bayerischer Rundfunk, and then president of the State Center for New Media, was named the executive in charge of broadcasting in the newly created federal states. Between 15 October 1990 and 30 December 1991 Mühlfenzl transferred personnel, programming rights, and real estate held by the DFF to the newly founded state broadcasting systems MDR (Central German Broadcasting) and ORD (Eastern German Broadcasting of Brandenburg). The state of Mecklenburg-Vorpommern entered into the coalition of states that runs NDR (Northern German Broadcasting). The new broadcasting companies with headquarters in Potsdam and Dresden began programming at midnight on New Year's Eve, 1991.

German unification created for the public broadcasters a considerable expansion of viewership and diversification of their organizational structures. ARD expanded by two new members with concomitant structures. ZDF differentiated itself, as well, through the founding of new regional studios. Through the fall of the Wall and unification, the commercial channels also experienced an expansion of its audience in the form of ever greater market shares. Shortly thereafter, RTLplus and, eventually, Sat1 began operating in the black for the first time. RTL became the market leader in 1993. If the years 1990 through 1995 stood for the commercial broadcasters as a time of expansion and the consolidation of program and market shares, beginning in 1995 the pendulum swung back to the public broadcasters, especially the regional channels.

Nevertheless the commercial channels expanded their advertising revenues through conversion to twenty-four-hour formats and development of their own, economically produced and more attractive formats. By comparison, advertising revenues fell at the public broadcasting networks. The ensuing discussion about tying charged broadcasting fees to the rate of inflation became a kind of media political thumbscrew. This increase of DM 5 in the fee charged to television set owners to an annual fee of DM 28.25 led to a fundamental debate about media policy, one that forced politicians to extract from the public broadcasters considerable budgetary cutbacks. The broadcast fee (for both radio and television) had always been a political football. The initial fee instituted in the Federal Republic in 1954 was at first DM 5 and remained stable for sixteen years. In 1970 the basic fee was raised by 50 cents and the separate television by DM 1. Thereafter the fee was pegged to the inflation rate in four-year increments.

From the 1990s till today, debates about the financing of public broadcasting have become more heated. They pit ARD/ZDF on the one side and, on the other side, the minister presidents of the federal states, who are charged with their oversight because of their cultural policy mandate. An independent body of experts called the Commission on the Mediation of the Broadcast Institute Financing has advised the minister presidents since 1975. Since a 1997 decision by the German Constitutional Court, its decisions have been mostly binding, which has not hindered a few minister presidents from attempting downward corrections of its fee recommendations. On 1 January 2009 the mandatory broadcast fees were raised 95 cents to €17.98.

The tougher the competitive struggle between the public and the commercial broadcasters, (to which, from 2006 on, was added the competition between traditional broadcasting and the Internet), the more controversial the broadcast fees and public broadcasting expenditures have become. The VPRT (Association of Private Broadcasters and Telemedia), the lobbyist for the private broadcasters, charged that ARD and ZDF have used the fees, which are meant for their basic costs, for commercial ends, as for example for extensive online offerings and the acquisition of expensive sports broadcasting rights. The media politics of these accusations forced ARD and ZDF to reduce their online presence considerably. In 2009 the State Broadcasting Act for the Regulation and Control of Online and Web 2.0 Activities of Public Broadcasters were enacted.

Political intervention in the commercial broadcasting sector became necessary in the late 1990s. Despite the apparent expansion of programs, the market consolidated down to very few providers. The complicated system of cross-ownership, that is the mutual and multimedial proprietal system, was no longer manageable, so that the danger of a monopolizing media force arose. Therefore a new state broadcasting act came in force on 1 January 1997 that substitutes the limitation of programming influence through ownership through a limitation of viewer market share, that is to say, to a model that was oriented on audiences. A 30 percent market share quota served from that point on as an indicator of a "dominant opinion driver," which affected primarily large media conglomerates such as CLT/Ufa (Bertelsmann), the owners of, among others RTL, Vox, and N-TV, and the Kirch group, which held Sat1, ProSieben, Kabel 1, N 24, etc.

The 1990s also witnessed the introduction of pay TV, at first in the form of the analogue broadcaster, Premiere, which began its service on 28 February 1991. In 1997 the tridigital channels came online, the most dominant of which was DF 1, which introduced multiperspective coverage of a Formula 1 race from the Hockenheimring race track.

Pay-per-view television and its driving force, Leo Kirch, and television as a whole entered a new phase during the competition for exclusive media broadcasting rights. Current feature films and attractive sports such as soccer, Formula 1, and tennis guaranteed high ratings. As long as the reach of pay-per-view remained limited, as it was in the 1990s, the topic of "exclusivity" was of little media political interest. Broadcast rights for the Bundesliga (Federal Soccer League) remained in the hands of public broadcasters. But media politics came to the fore when Leo Kirch attempted to acquire exclusive broadcast rights for the 2002 and 2006 FIFA World Cup for pay-per-view in order to use this as a breakthrough event to assist in audience acceptance. The politicians insisted that media ethics viewed soccer as a basic need and that therefore important matches had to be broadcast on free television.

The 1990s became a decade of economizing in television, that is to say, cost-benefit analyses, target audiences, and success orientation took a front seat. A transformation took place from the view of television as a cultural object to one of TV as a market object. This change began in 1984 with the introduction of the dual system in the West and was continued in the East in 1990.

The Political Development of the Media since 2000 and the Debates on Media Ethics

Two format developments since the 1990s that led to intensified audience ties had a dimension of media ethics. These two formats took a form that has been called "affect TV" (Bente and Fromm 1997).

- Talk and confessional shows during afternoon programming, beginning with Hans Meiser and Ilona Christen (1992–1993 on RTL) and with *Arabella* (1994, ProSieben)
- New entertainment formats beginning with the 24-hour surveillance series *Big Brother* in 2000. More than anything else, this program, also referred to as a Container-Show, set off considerable ethical debates about the media. The display of privacy was widely criticized. Critics also viewed it as infringing on the participants'

human dignity, as the contestants were put under excessive psychological pressure and the constant observation to which they subject led to tremendous emotional strain.

Public debates centered on the breaking of taboos through the intimate confessions of talk show guests, or for that matter, the continual surveillance of people in precarious and constantly stressful situations with the help of multiple cameras. The ethical problem consisted not only of the personalization, the intimatization, and the emotionalization, but also in the authentic visual tickle and its attraction. Beginning in 2002 with *Germany Looks for a Superstar*, these affective elements were bound to two other economic ones, namely, the exploitation of the desire to become a star and the cross-media marketing made possible by the particular talents put on display in pursuit of this desire, i.e. singing, modeling, or dancing. Both the commercial and the public broadcasters countered this trend of ethically debatable affect television with two other developments: courtroom shows, beginning in 1999 with *Quarrel at 3* (ZDF) and *Judge Barbara Salesch* (Sat. 1), and quiz shows, beginning in 1999 with Günter Jauch's *Who Wants to Be a Millionare* and *Quiz with Jörg Pilawa* in 2001.

An intense ethical debate about the media escalated around the show *Get Me Out of Here, I'm a Star* (RTL, 2004). The series was decried as "disgust television," a violation of human dignity of participants. The Commission for the Protection of Youth from the Media (KJM) judged it, however, not to be an infraction of youth protection laws. In the cultural sections of newspapers, psychologists criticized the show's sadism. The Society for the Prevention of Cruelty to Animals protested the show. A state representative, Dietrich von Gumppenberg from the Liberal Democratic Party, even instituted a court injunction. It became clear from this that societal taboos still existed and that many viewers still drew moral boundaries.

Media political hopes accompanied the introduction of digital television in Germany on 24 October 1997. The state minister presidents, and somewhat later the federal government under Gerhard Schröder, fired off the starting gun on the digitalization of broadcasting. Their task was to disseminate digital broadcasting in radio as well as television by 31 December 2010 so that analogue transmission could be eliminated. This proved to be unrealistic and unachievable, due to, among other things, the media convergence that has since taken place. Media convergence means on one hand that broadcasting with its users and online communication via Internet and computer with its own separate users have become closer, and on the other hand, that the borders between individual and mass communication are disappearing. The notion of broadcasting under the conditions of digitalization must be redefined.

IP television exists in Germany since 2006, beginning with the offerings of T-Online, Arcor, and ZDF. Media experts predicted this to be the television of the future. IPTV is a part of the so-called triple play of the digital process, one that stems from the melding of Internet, broadcasting, and telephone communication. Therefore the political and legal framework considerations regarding the media are again up for discussion. Through the digitalization process, the prevalent distinctions between programming providers (broadcast institutions) and online providers (telecommunication) have been lifted. From a technical perspective, everyone can do everything. This has also made obsolete the distinction in mandates between the states and the federal government, the cultural mandate belonging to the states and the technical authority for transmitters and telecommunication to the Bund; the same dissolution holds true for international networking and globalization.

The separation of political duties in the broadcasting laws on the one hand and the telecommunication, media services, and data protection laws on the other, will be difficult, in the short term, to maintain. Moreover, from ethical and political points of view, the supervision and control of content will become even more difficult, especially as economic globalization leads to worldwide networking that itself cannot be controlled.

We must add to the mix the politics and financing of the public broadcasting system (broadcasting contribution = mandatory broadcast fee) in the face of the crisis of classic media through changing usage habits, global and national/regional media concerns in cut-throat competition, the notion of glocality, social media, and regional television. Contained in this diagnosis are at once political and ethical questions about the media, for both present and future. How can a society still be formed? How can critical questions still be heard in the cacophony of communications? How can we carry on discourse or find sustainable solutions to the problem of how humans are to lead their lives and act responsibly?

Rüdiger Steinmetz is University Professor of Medienwissenschaft and Medienkultur at the University of Leipzig. He has written or edited a dozen books on film and media, including (as editor): *Das digitale Dispositif Cinéma. Untersuchungen zur Veränderung des Kinos* (Leipziger Univ.-Verlag, Leipzig 2011); the textbooks with DVDs *Filme sehen lernen 1: Grundlagen* (Zweitausendeins, Frankfurt a.M. 2006), *Filme sehen lernen*

2: Licht, Farbe, Sound (Zweitausendeins, Frankfurt a.M. 2008), and *Filme sehen lernen 3: Filmmusik* (Zweitausendeins, Leipzig 2011), along with *Das Leipziger Dokfilm-Festival und sein Publikum II. Eine Nachfolge-Studie 2006 zu Image, Akzeptanz und Resonanz* (Leipziger Univ.-Verlag, Leipzig 2007) *Deutsches Fernsehen Ost. Eine Programmgeschichte des DDR-Fernsehens* (Verlag für Berlin-Brandenburg, Berlin 2008), and *Digitale Leuchtturmprojekte des lokalen und regionalen Hörfunks und Fernsehens. Social-Media-Programmfeedback in Deutschland, Großbritannien und den USA* (Berlin: Vistas 2014).

Notes

1. Editors' note: this speech can now be read online at: Guenter Schabowski, "Guenter Schabowski's Press Conference in the GDR International Press Center," *Making the History of 1989,* Item #449, https://chnm.gmu.edu/1989/items/show/449 (accessed 28 August 2015).

Chapter 8

GERMANY AS TV SHOW IMPORT MARKET

Lothar Mikos

In Germany, the first television program was broadcast on Christmas in 1952. Until 1989 there were two different kinds of broadcasting systems in the two states of Germany: a public service broadcasting system in West Germany and a state-controlled broadcasting system in East Germany, the former GDR (Hickethier and Hoff 1998; Steinmetz and Viehoff 2008). The broadcasting systems were typical for the countries in the Eastern and Western blocs. In the Eastern Bloc countries, state-controlled television was the rule. Most Western European countries established public television broadcasting systems, combined in some cases with private stations. This was also the preferred model in the United States and Latin America. Because television sets were quite expensive at first, the new medium spread only slowly among the population of each country. By the 1960s, however, television had reached the masses and become the primary medium.

The implementation of television as a mass medium in Germany was linked to popular cultural practices, as for instance football. The early years of public service broadcasting in the Federal Republic of Germany (FRG) saw two major live events: coronation of Queen Elizabeth II in 1953, and the Football World Championship in Switzerland in 1954. The sales of TV sets in the FRG increased rapidly during the championship and the month after the German team had won the World Cup. In January 1954 there were 11,658 TV sets, a lot of them in pubs. In December 1954 there were 84,278 TV sets, and a lot of them in private homes (Mikos 2002a). The industry had to work hard to satisfy the customers' demands for TV sets. The magazine *Der Spiegel* reported on 7 July that year that the exciting live screenings of the World Championship caused a big run on TV sets. The stocks of manufacturers like Telefunken, Saba, and Mende were sold out. Philips sold 1,000 TV sets in only fourteen days. An enormous number if we consider that there had been only 1,117 TV sets in the whole FRG a year before. The manufacturer Saba advertised its model Schauinsland W III with the words: "You can participate in this immediate event that is expected with great suspense!" (Mikos and Nutt 1997: 172). The supporter and prospective owner of a television was promised that he had not to worry about tickets or the weather. The wins of the German team had a beneficial effect on the sales of TV sets.

Pubs were the preferred place to watch the World Championship for most of its audience. Up to 150 viewers crowded into each pub during the live transmission of the games. They had to pay for tickets, but got a beer free. On average ten to twenty viewers watched TV sets in private homes at the same time and nearly sixty to seventy viewers in every pub or as "window shoppers" in front of the window of a TV set dealer. Even in the German Democratic Republic (GDR) were sold more TV sets than ever before. Mainly viewers in the regions where they could receive the public service broadcasting of the FRG were attracted by the football program of 1954. The broadcast of the World Championship was also the advent of the European Broadcasting Network, later known as the EBU (European Broadcasting Union).

The 1980s saw the deregulation of the television market in most of the West European countries. Private commercial television was introduced. New Year's Eve 1984 was the starting point of commercial television in West Germany, and there has been a permanent growth of the number of TV channels available since. The commercialization led to an increasing number of channels that was multiplied again by the digitalization of television in the 1990s. Meanwhile more than 400 channels seek to inform and entertain German audiences; around forty of them are free to air channels that could be received by cable, satellite, or DVB-T. All these channels are constantly looking for content, not only on the national German market, but also in other countries. With its nearly 82 million inhabitants and 36 million TV households, Germany is the biggest TV market in Europe, even more so if one adds Austria and Switzerland as partly German-speaking countries. This is one reason why German broadcasters were self-satisfied and were not looking to sell their programs to foreign markets, even if there were some exceptions like the crime series *Derrick*. But since the beginning of television, German program chiefs were looking for content that could be licensed or adapted in the United States and the

United Kingdom, both countries that were more experienced with television.

Although television as an institution was regulated by nation-states in individual countries, the creators of television programming looked to other countries for orientation. The American television researcher Timothy Havens (2006: 16) correctly stated, "The international exchange of television programs dates back as far as television broadcasting itself." Programs were copied, programs were bought from other countries, and joint live broadcasts were organized. The first major international events in European television were the coronation of Queen Elizabeth II in Britain in 1953 and the 1954 football World Cup tournament in Switzerland, both distributed by the European Broadcasting Union (EBU). Even if German broadcasters have concentrated on Germany in producing TV shows, German television is part of a globalized television market.

Television and Globalization

The internationalization of television was driven, among other things, by the fact that the medium was considered an extension of radio by the addition of pictures. Thus television was more or less fitted into the existing organizational structure of radio broadcasting. An international broadcasting organization, the OIRT, was founded in the Eastern Bloc as early as 1946. Its members were Austria, Bulgaria, Czechoslovakia, Finland, East Germany, Hungary, Poland, Romania, and the Soviet Union. The OIRT, also known as Intervision, was responsible for the international exchange of programs. Four years later an analogous body was formed in Western Europe: the European Broadcasting Union (EBU), based on the southern coast of England. Broadcasting agencies in twenty-three countries joined the EBU. The EBU's purpose was to promote the exchange of news between these countries' broadcasting agencies. In 1954, the EBU founded the Eurovision network for the exchange of other programs besides news. One of the network's earliest joint activities was the Eurovision Song Contest, which was first broadcast in 1956. After the dissolution of the Eastern Bloc, the members of OIRT joined the EBU in 1993. The founding of the Cannes programming trade fair MIPTV in 1963 may also be seen as evidence of the early importance of international trade.

These early examples of international cooperation for the purpose of programming exchange illustrate the international orientation and organization of television from its inception. But technical developments like satellite technology and digitalization, the deregulation of TV in Europe, the end of the Cold War, and the economic impact of the international entertainment industry have undergone a transformation of television.

Technical developments have brought with them numerous changes in the world of media. Multinational media conglomerates have grown up that operate throughout the world and merge together the film, television, telecommunications, and computer industries (Artz and Kamalipour 2007; Kunz 2007; Wasko 1994). The classic Hollywood studio system (Schatz 1988) has also changed, mainly because under these conditions—that is, in a globalized media industry (Barker 1997; Havens 2006; Miller et al. 2005; Straubhaar 2007)—films are no longer produced just for the cinema, but also for television (Gomery 2005; McDonald and Wasko 2008; Wasko 2003). The processes of globalization were driven by technological advances, including satellite technology (Parks 2005; Straubhaar 2007: 119ff.) and the introduction of new information and communication technologies that have facilitated worldwide networking (Castells 2000), and by political innovations, including the deregulation of the broadcasting sector and the subsequent introduction of private-enterprise television, first in most of the Western European countries, and after the collapse of the Eastern Bloc, in Eastern European countries as well (Straubhaar 2007: 93ff.).

Globalization refers to the world-wide fusion of economic, political, and cultural units to form transnational spaces of cultures and lifestyles (Robertson 1992). Globalization creates imagined communities of social actors who are connected to one another by the Internet and other information and communication technologies. The concept of imagined community originated with Benedict Anderson, who developed it in the context of his studies on nationalism. Anderson's central thesis was that "nation" can be understood as an imagined political community. Imagined, because most members of a nation, even a very small one, never have an opportunity to meet, much less know, most other members (Anderson 1991: 6). Yet they still have a mental image of the nation that they feel they belong to. In the course of the globalization discussion, Arjun Appadurai has expanded the concept of imagined community to speak of imagined worlds. These are multiple worlds, scattered across the globe, created by the historically situated imagination of persons or groups (Appadurai 1994). Appadurai locates these imagined worlds in five "dimensions," which he describes as fluid landscapes: ethnoscapes, mediascapes, technoscapes, finanscapes, and ideoscapes

(Appadurai 1994). The global streams of finance (finanscapes) play a part in the global distribution of the media (mediascapes) and technology (technoscapes)—and are at the same time made possible by them. Global finance also favors human mobility (ethnoscapes), which is made possible by political systems such as national governments and international organizations (ideoscapes). The electronic media especially favor the tendencies toward globalization in all the other dimensions because they permit "new form of global mass culture, very different from ... the cultural identities associated with the nation-state in an earlier phase" (Hall 1994: 52). Stuart Hall sees satellite television as the epitome of this new form of culture: "Not because it is the only example but because you could not understand satellite television without understanding its grounding in a particular advanced national economy and culture, and yet its whole purpose is precisely that it cannot be limited any longer by national boundaries" (Hall 1994: 52). Almost all television stations can be received via satellite from anywhere the world. Indian ZEE-TV is available in England, for example; the German network RTL can be received in the Sahara; Chinese CCTV can be seen in Australia.

Satellite technology was improved enormously during the 1960s, and major sports events played an important role in this development. The 1964 Olympic games in Tokyo saw the first television images broadcast throughout the world via satellite (Abramson 1987). In reality, worldwide broadcasting was not quite that simple, since the images were transmitted by satellite only from Japan to the United States. The signal was sent from a Japanese ground station in Kashima to the Syncom III satellite. The relayed signal was received in California and broadcast from there in North America and Canada. In Montreal the broadcasts were recorded on magnetic tape, which was then sent aboard jet airliners to Hamburg, where the Europe broadcasts originated (Abramson 1987). Just a short time later, in April 1965, the Intelsat I satellite went into orbit to relay television signals between Europe and the United States. The first such transmission, on 25 May 1965, was the boxing match between Cassius Clay and Sonny Liston. Technical progress also improved the television broadcasts of the 1966 football World Cup tournament in England.

As early as the late 1960s, new and more powerful satellites had been launched into orbit. Now it was possible to transmit television programs via satellite direct to home sets equipped with satellite receivers (Abramson 1987). This also permitted the international distribution of television programs on a large scale. It wasn't until the 1980s, however, that technical and administrative regulations allowed satellite television to become popular worldwide. In the early 1980s, the first US television channels were transmitted internationally via satellite to cable television networks in other countries. Thus American television became available to viewers in Canada and the Caribbean (Straubhaar 2007: 120). Mainly, however, satellite technology was used in countries with large area, such as Brazil, China, India, the Soviet Union, and the United States, and in island countries like Indonesia and Malaysia, to distribute the national television programs domestically (Straubhaar 2007: 120).

The liberalization of national television markets that accompanied the international distribution of television channels via satellite led to the introduction of private commercial television in numerous countries. This drastically changed the national and international television industry in most Western countries.

As in other European countries new private media consortiums entered the stage in the 1980s "to exploit the technological opportunity presented by satellite and cable transmission" (King 2003: 97). Private commercial television began in the Federal Republic of Germany in 1984. Like public service broadcasting, the private networks are integrated in Germany's federal system. Before this could be accomplished, there were technical, legal, and political issues to be resolved. A 1981 decision by the federal Constitutional Court, known as the FRAG decision, stipulated that private-sector broadcasting was basically constitutional since the public airwaves fall under the sovereignty of the individual Länder. This cleared the way for media legislation at the level of the Länder to permit the licensing of private networks. Furthermore, thanks to advances in cable and satellite technology, the technical groundwork for distributing more television channels was also in place. As early as November 1980, the minister-presidents of the Länder had agreed to test the feasibility and the acceptance of cable television in four pilot projects. These pilot projects were to be accompanied by scientific studies. They were financed by a portion of the radio and television fees collected by the Länder. On 1 January 1984, the age of private television financed entirely by advertising revenue in Germany began with the launch of the pilot cable project in Ludwigshafen and the founding of West Germany's first commercial television network, Satelliten Fernsehen GmbH (SAT.1). RTL plus, which had been transmitting from Belgium up to then, also began broadcasting in Germany. The Munich pilot project started three months later, followed in June and August 1985, by pilot projects in Dortmund and Berlin.

In the years that followed, more and more private networks were added, broadcasting their programs with varying success. Networks with complete programming offerings attained a larger audience than those with specialized programming. In the 1990s numerous private networks were founded. Today Germany has some forty networks that can be received nationwide, as well as numerous regional networks and local stations. Some of these networks' programs can only be viewed over digital television by paying subscribers, however. The first network to be financed through subscription fees rather than advertising was Premiere (now Sky), which introduced pay TV in Germany on 28 February 1991. The new networks were mainly held by large publishing companies, such as Axel Springer, Heinrich Bauer, Holtzbrinck, and the WAZ group (Westdeutsche Allgemeine Zeitung), but also by media conglomerates such as Bertelsmann and the film distributor Leo Kirch.

In licensing private television networks, government agencies were to ensure that individual companies' interests in several networks did not result in an unbalanced power over public opinion, since private-sector television is constitutional only if a plurality of opinion is assured under market conditions. Nonetheless, because operating private television networks is an expensive business, some concentration took place. As a result three major families of television channels dominate the market: (1) the public service broadcasters ARD, ZDF, and the regional channels of the ARD plus theme channels like Phoenix, Kika, Arte, 3sat; (2) the channels of the ProSiebenSat.1 Media Group, formerly owned by Leo Kirch; (3) the channels of Bertelsmann's RTL Group. This system of the German TV market is still settled even if there were some transformations following the digitalization of television in the 1990s.

The dual broadcasting system, in which public and commercial television networks coexist, became the norm. Yet the television market continues to be regulated by national laws (although in the European Union, for example, the Audiovisual Media Service Directive that followed theTelevision Without Frontiers Directive" creates an international framework). The globalization of television is subject to national, local limitations.

This is also true of international media conglomerates, which run up against national restrictions again and again, including not only national media laws, but also different production cultures and sometimes the widely varying cultural conditions that audiences live in. Moreover, national information and communication policies are challenged, or perhaps even threatened, by international developments in the media field. "The remarkable global expansion of media corporations, facilitated by liberalization and privatization of media systems worldwide and the development of cable and satellite technologies, has reduced states' ability to exercise power and maintain information sovereignty" (Morris and Waisbord 2001: ix.). Nonetheless, states can still regulate the free expansion of global media conglomerates through regulations in national, bilateral, or multinational territories, and can regulate the global free exchange of cultural commodities, of which television formats are an example. The European Audiovisual Media Service Directive is one such regulation. Others include the national media laws in European and other countries, and the state media laws in the West German Länder (on regulations in Europe, see also Chalaby 2009; Iosifidis, Steemers, and Wheeler 2005: 57ff.; Schlesinger 2001).

In the global media market, however, states cannot adopt decisions and regulations independently. They are interdependent in many ways. Thus developments such as the deregulation and liberalization of television in Europe have taken place not just in one country, but in nearly all countries almost simultaneously—although different phases of development are distinguishable (Iosifidis, Steemers, and Wheeler 2005: 35ff.). The first phase took place from the 1970s to the mid-1980s, primarily in Italy, Germany, and France. The second phase began in the late 1980s with the introduction of commercial television in Spain, Portugal, Greece, Scandinavia, and the Benelux countries, and was also marked by changes in the British market. The third phase, that of digitalization, began in the late 1990s. The digital platforms and technologies permit "the combination of new or different information services, including an expanded choice of television channels and interactive offerings such as e-mail, Internet access and home shopping" (Iosifidis, Steemers, and Wheeler 2005: 46). This has created a "multi-channel environment" in which the viewers are no longer addressed as citizens, as in the days of public television or state broadcasting monopolies, but as consumers (Moran 2005). Most importantly, the television networks are confronted with new technologies that permit more interactive use.

Where the licensing of commercial networks had led to expanding programming, digitalization gave a significant boost to that trend. Specialized channels for news (CNN), culture (arte), sports (Eurosport), and music (MTV) have been joined by numerous niche channels, such as specialized channels for sportsmen, gourmets and wine lovers, exercise and health, travel and weather. The more television channels there are, the more content, i.e. television shows, must be produced. The explosion of channels has made content a scarce resource. The globalization of the television industry and the accompanying international networking have made program content a commodity that is increasingly traded worldwide (Bielby and Harrington 2008; Havens 2006; Moran 2009a, 2009b; Moran and Malbon 2006; Oren and Shahaf 2012; Steemers 2004). Albert Moran (2005: 294) found: "The most clearly visible dynamic seems to be one of adaptation, transfer and recycling of narrative and other kinds of content." One reason for this is that commercial television broadcasters' goal is to make the highest possible profit with the lowest possible investment. The international exchange of programming, which began in the 1950s, has grown into a global television market characterized by intense competition for the few globally successful programs. National television channels have never relied on their own productions alone, but have always bought programs from other countries. Since the 1990s, however, the market has taken on a new momentum. The international trade in formats has become a big business.

International Format Trade

Countries that introduced television in the 1950s looked at existing programs for ideas for their own productions, and sometimes bought programs from other countries. The Soviet Union was the model for other countries in the Eastern Bloc, while Western European and Latin American countries patterned their programming primarily after the United States, although Great Britain was a secondary model. Hollywood film studios were critical of television at first. As a result, companies that had sponsored radio serials, such as the soap and detergent producers Procter & Gamble and Colgate-Palmolive, were able to enter the new television market. The studios soon abandoned their aloof stance, however—especially after they discovered that money could also be made by exporting television programs to Latin America and Europe. In the first wave of globalization, which Timothy Havens (2006) situates in the years from 1957 to 1972, the proportion of the US television industry's total revenues that was earned through export sales increased to over 40 percent, while in Europe the exchange of programs in the Eurovision network increased from 440 hours in 1960 to 1,138 hours in 1972. In the Eastern Bloc, programming exchange in the Intervision network also increased, from 170 hours in 1960 to 1,124 in 1972 and 2,759 in 1980 (Eugster 1983). These figures alone show that television programming was being increasingly internationalized. Moreover, the figures do not include domestic productions based on ideas taken from other countries—that is, imitation, or what would today be called format theft. Thus in the 1960s several popular Australian television programs were unlicensed imitations of BBC serial formats (Havens 2006). In Japan, American and British shows were frequently imitated and adapted to Japanese culture (Straubhaar 2007). The same is true of German television, which imitated a number of US and British entertainment shows. Buying family and detective series was part of day-to-day business for the two public networks in West Germany.

The formatting of television programs began in this period, although the term *format* for television programs was not established until the 1990s. Latin American telenovelas as a specific narrative form evolved from Cuban adaptations of American radio soap operas, whereas television soaps in the United States continued the original tradition from American radio. Other genres specific to television also crystallized, including game shows, quiz shows, talk shows, music shows etc., not only in the United States and Latin America, but also in Europe and Asia (Straubhaar 2007). Programs that followed the conventions of these genres were distributed around the world, under license and in the form of unlicensed adaptations. Television producers learned of these shows at fairs such as the MIPTV mentioned above, at which television programs have been bought and sold since 1963. In the 1960s and 1970s, the MIPTV fair was dominated by US programs (Havens 2006). Accordingly, the proportion of US-produced shows in the other countries' television programming was high. In 1972, the proportion of US programs in Brazil was 44 percent, in Australia 48 percent, in Jamaica 62 percent, in Hong Kong 28 percent, in South Korea 19 percent, in Lebanon 41 percent, and in France 3 percent (Straubhaar 2007).

According to Havens (2006), there was little change in the globalization of television between 1973 and 1985. The share of revenue from programming exports in the US television industry stagnated, and declined in some years. One important reason was that, by this time, production capacities had been established in many countries, and consequently the national television networks were able to draw more heavily on domestic productions.

Even into the 1980s the television market in Germany remained very simple, since the introduction of private-sector broadcasting was no more than a proposal discussed in political circles. The programming executives of the public networks, ARD and ZDF, were free to shop around for new stock in Great Britain and the United States. After ARD scored a major hit in 1981 with the US series *Dallas*, ZDF followed two years later with the competing product *Denver-Clan* (original title: *Dy-*

nasty), likewise imported from the United States. Until then, series had not been particularly successful in prime time. After these hits, however, the networks tried to pull domestic productions onto the series bandwagon. In the mid-1980s, when RTL and SAT.1 went on the air as Germany's first private television broadcasters, their initial programming schedules were filled mainly with American series. Even then, all the networks on the German television scene were trying to take advantage of the same programming trends. It was rather rare for native German formats to attain international popularity. The show *Wetten dass ...?* (US title: *Wanna Bet?*) was sold to several countries, however. But the only major German hit was the detective series *Derrick,* which was shown in over ninety countries.

In view of the development of domestic series, the international programming market didn't collapse, but it did stagnate. This changed in the mid-1980s, however, as the deregulation of the television market and the introduction of privately owned networks created new growth, which was again boosted by digitalization in the mid-1990s. The second wave of globalization drastically changed the international television market (Havens 2006) and led to tremendous growth due to the proliferation of channels. More formats than ever were traded at the television fairs. Although the total revenues are rising as shows are bought and sold, however, there are also changes in the power structure of the industry. In the US television industry, international format sales no longer earn the share of revenue that they did in the 1960s (Havens 2006). As the demand for programs has boomed, the number of domestically produced shows has also grown in many countries (Straubhaar 2007). As a result, the share of US productions in almost all national television markets has declined from 1972 to 2001—from 44 percent to 19 percent in Brazil, from 48 percent to 29 percent in Australia, from 62 percent to 53 percent in Jamaica, and from 19 percent to 6 percent in South Korea. Only in France, the market share of US productions grew from 3 percent to 18 percent (Straubhaar 2007). The share of US programs in German Television for the year 2001 was 10.4 percent for the ARD, 5.5 percent for ZDF, 13.5 percent for RTL, 13.7 percent for Sat.1, 33.6 percent for ProSieben, 17.8 percent for Vox, 28.8 percent for RTL II, and 37.7 percent for Kabel 1. The private channels had an higher average of US-based TV shows in their schedule than the public service channels ARD and ZDF.

A completely new trend began with the boom of reality TV at the beginning of the twenty-first century. After *Hans Meiser* met with relative success in 1992, numerous other afternoon talk shows were launched—

at one time up to ten such shows ran on various channels in the early afternoon. Similarly, the popularity of *Richterin Barbara Salesch* in 1999 started a boom in courtroom shows. Also in 1999, the extreme popularity of *Wer wird Millionär?* (original: *Who Wants to Be a Millionaire?*) led to many more quiz shows on all the major networks (Armbruster and Mikos 2009). In 2000, *Big Brother* marked the beginning of the trend towards reality shows, likewise with many imitations. Just a short time later, *Popstars* and *Deutschland sucht den Superstar* (original: *Pop Idol*) launched the wave of talent or casting shows, which has continued with *Germany's Next Topmodel* (original: *America's Next Top Model*) since 2006, and continues to be an audience favorite. The "life improvement" formats boomed with *Avenzio—Schöner leben, Einsatz in vier Wänden, Die Super-Nanny,* and *Raus aus den Schulden*.

All of these programming trends have one feature in common: they are based on concepts or ideas that did not originate with German producers or networks. These are all licensed formats, acquired on the international television market and adapted for the national market. Any licensed format that met with a degree of success was copied and imitated by other networks. In this way the German television market developed a certain momentum that is driven mainly by licensing and imitating international formats. The new shows were specified as a framework that consisted of an idea and its stylistic and dramaturgical realization, yet left room for local adaptation (Mikos 2002a). The licenses for locally adaptable reality formats were a logical response (even if by chance rather than consciously) to the constraints that had limited the international marketing of television formats. These constraints are evident in the local assimilation of internationally marketed films and television formats (Thussu 1998). Tamar Liebes and Elihu Katz (1993) for example were able to show in a study in the late 1980s how the series *Dallas* was differently received and assimilated in Israel, Japan, and Morocco.

In the moment of assimilation, the global marketing of films and television formats encounters national and local borders. The American media scholar Silvio Waisbord (2004: 378) stated, "Format television shows glocalization at work." In the same context, the American television researcher Joseph D. Straubhaar (1991; 2007) coined the term "cultural proximity" to describe the way in which countries and cultures tend to prefer their own local and national films and television formats.

However, in the fragmented markets of the early twenty-first century, this is true only for some milieus and target groups, not in general. The concept of cultural proximity also refers to linguistic regions.

That is, films and television formats are easier to distribute in countries where the same language is spoken. Films from other linguistic regions are adapted by dubbing or subtitling. The introduction of DVDs has made it possible to watch the same film in different language versions. DVDs often include subtitles in a choice of many languages. This is one way in which films can be adapted for other cultures.

The changes in the global film and television market have also led to a reorganization of media power. It is true that the United States continues to be "the leading exporter of cultural products" (Thussu 2007: 15), and that the entertainment industry is among the greatest sources of export revenue. Moreover, Europe is the largest market for the American media industry. Yet American television programs are marketed elsewhere as well: they can be seen in more than 125 countries (Thussu 2007). The United States retains the dominant position in the worldwide marketing of television programs, with a market share of about 70 percent of all sales, but that position is built primarily on fictional series. In the show format segment, Great Britain has become the largest exporter. Formats such as *I'm a Celebrity—Get Me Out of Here!*, *Supernanny*, *Pop Idol*, and *Who Wants to Be a Millionaire?* originated in Britain, which is also the largest importer of German television formats (Schmitt, Bisson, and Fey 2005). The Netherlands have also conquered a relatively large share of this market, primarily thanks to the production company Endemol, whose worldwide success began with *the Big Brother* format. Brazil and Mexico, furthermore, are the leaders in the worldwide marketing of telenovelas.

We can identify three varieties of format marketing in the global television market (Mikos 2002a; Mikos and Perrotta 2013):

(1) One marketing variant entails selling *broadcast rights* for fully produced series or, more commonly, for individual seasons. Albert Moran (2009a) and Silvio Waisbord (2004) called this type "canned program." These series then compete under their titles as brand names for the television networks of foreign countries. The buyer acquires the broadcast rights to a finished product and performs no modification except subtitling or dubbing. The salability of the product depends on the dominance of its format and on the openness of the narrative to interpretation. Furthermore, the narrative openness of a television series is formally rooted in the structure of its patterns. The 1980s series *Dallas* is perhaps the best known example of the sale of rights to a fully produced format. More recent examples include drama and sitcom series such as *Ally McBeal, CSI: Miami, Emergency Room, Friends, Gilmore Girls, Grey's Anatomy, Heroes, Lost, My Name Is Earl, Sex and the City, Game*

of Thrones, The Sopranos, Fringe, How I Met Your Mother,* and *Boardwalk Empire.*

(2) Another type of format marketing involves selling the *rights to a series concept and a format outline.* In this variant no finished content is sold. Instead each buyer produces the series, adapting it to local conditions within the limits of the agreed outline. For example, the German daily soap opera *Gute Zeiten, schlechte Zeiten* (1992–) is an adaptation of a Dutch adaptation of an Australian serial titled *The Restless Years* (1977–1981) (Moran 1998: 109; O'Donnell 1999: 56–57). *Ugly Betty,* with its various international adaptations, is a more contemporary example (Mikos and Perrotta 2012).

(3) The third marketing variant is the licensing of *rights to quiz shows, game shows, and reality shows.* In this case individual programs are international brands. Well-known examples are *Big Brother, America's Next Top Model, The Swan, Pop Idol,* and *Who Wants to Be a Millionaire?.* These shows have a brand that is used uniformly throughout the world, and their presentations, from dramaturgy to character constellations to design, follow uniform rules across all adaptations. Only the contestants, the games, and the quiz questions adapt to local conditions. The uniform dramaturgical and aesthetic elements are specified in a format "bible." The shows are then produced to the same specifications by different production companies in the various local markets.

There is a fourth form of licensing: sports rights. But this is a special case that cannot be compared with the other ones.

In the global television market, series and shows are marketed worldwide. The formatting makes it easier to buy and sell new programs with a minimum of risk. Only large television markets like the United States, the United Kingdom, or Germany generate revenues that cover the production costs for developing a format. Program creators located in smaller television markets must thus depend on international marketing. The advantages of format business for the television networks are self-evident. The networks save development costs, and at the same time they acquire a product that has been proven successful in one or more other national television markets. Furthermore, when networks buy a license for a television format, they acquire the corresponding expertise of the original production. Thus the purpose of acquiring format licenses is not only to obtain a product or an idea, but also to obtain the benefit of the experience gained in the production and broadcasting of the format in other local television markets.

However, while licensed formats may minimize the risk of a market launch, they do not offer absolute protection against flops: it has been shown "that formats do not guarantee success" (Lantzsch 2008: 132). While "glocalization" may be an advantage, it can also have its drawbacks. A format that is successful in one country may flop in another due to local and national differences in the viewers' culture, self-image, and television habits. Thus the makeover show *The Swan* was by all means a success in the United States, but the German adaptation, *The Swan — Endlich schön!* was poorly received — partly because the German audience has a different relationship to the subject of cosmetic surgery than the US audience, and the format provoked an agitated debate over the protection of minors, in which it was seen as a potential moral danger to young female viewers. If the format adaptation is successful, however, there are benefits for both parties, the licensor and the licensee:

> As with any other branded product, this fulfills the prerequisites for a twofold image transfer: every national version benefits from the strength of the global brand, and the market value of the global brand increases with each successful national adaptation. ... The ideal to which each adaptation aspires is a production that does justice to the idiosyncrasies of the national (media) culture and is oriented towards national audiences, yet at the same time remains the national version of a globally branded product. (Hallenberger 2004: 161)

The practice of format trade brings with it a global networking of the market participants: the television broadcasters, media conglomerates, license and format traders, and production companies.

Formats are bought and sold at the annual programming fairs. There is a fair almost every month of the year, beginning with NAPTE in January, held in Las Vegas since 2004. MIPTV takes place in March or April in Cannes, and the Los Angeles TV Screening is held in May. The most important market for fictional series is MIPCOM, held in Cannes in September or October, and MIP Asia/TV Asia takes place every December in Singapore. Participation in these fairs increased drastically until the mid-1990s, and has been fairly constant since then (Havens 2006). Buyers and sellers of all sizes are among the participants.

The market is dominated by a few large companies, but there is room for independent producers as well. The producers with the largest international revenues in the television format market, such as Endemol, FreemantleMedia, ITV, Strix, and the BBC, are also the ones who invent and bring to market the most new formats (Moran and Malbon 2006; Schmitt, Bisson, and Fey 2005; Jäger and Behrens 2009). Conversely, those who are most successful in selling new formats internationally are the producers with the highest revenues. The Swedish company Strix for example achieved its market position by inventing the format *Expedition Robinson*, which became very popular in the United States as *Survivor*. Endemol significantly expanded its position through the success of *Big Brother*. In most countries that have a relatively large national television market to supply, a few leading producers dominate that market (Schmitt, Bisson, and Fey 2005; Jäger and Behrens 2009). In Germany, the leaders are Brainpool, MME and Tresor, Grundy UFA (part of the FremantleMedia empire), Endemol Germany, and ITV Germany (formerly Granada). Alongside these, distribution companies have also become established that do not develop or produce formats, but simply trade in licenses, such as Absolutely Independent. Some producers have founded their own distribution companies, such as the BBC's BBC Worldwide.

Imported Format Television in Germany

Since the beginning of German television, the makers of programs have imitated show ideas and concepts from those countries that, like Great Britain and the United States, had a decade more experience with programming and the invention of individual shows or series. As West German television was thus influenced by Britain and the United States, the Soviet Union played an analogous role for East German television. Eurovision in the West and Intervision in the East were forums for programming exchange, and platforms for the joint production of shows such as the Eurovision Song Contest. Buying family and detective series was part of day-to-day business for the two public networks in West Germany. In the 1960s and 1970s, their programming was replete with serials such as *Auf der Flucht* (original: *The Fugitive*), *77 Sunset Strip*, *Die Zwei* (*The Persuaders!*), *Mit Schirm, Charme und Melone* (*The Avengers*), *Tennis, Schläger und Kanonen* (*I Spy*), *Bezaubernde Jeannie* (*I Dream of Jeannie*), and comedy series such as those of *Marty Feldman* and *Benny Hill*. There were also some adaptations of foreign formats. *Ein Herz und eine Seele*, an adaptation of the British sitcom *Till Death Us Do Part*, was very successful. Also some American entertainment and quiz shows were adapted, such as *Alles oder Nichts* (original: *The $64,000 Question*), *Das Elternspiel* (original: *Parent's Game*), and *Gut gefragt ist halb gewonnen* (original: *Twenty Questions*).

In the 1980s the television market changed by the introduction of commercial channels. In the beginning commercial TV imported American series, American sitcoms, and American entertainment shows with a commercial appeal. German audiences were introduced to shows like *Glücksrad* (original: *Wheel of Fortune*), *Familienduell* (original: *Family Feud*), and *Der Preis ist heiß* (original: *The Price Is Right*).

After the major success of *Dallas* and *Denver-Clan* (original: *Dynasty*) at the public service channels ARD and ZDF, they tried to establish domestically produced serials. ARD created *Lindenstrasse* for early Sunday evening, modeled after the British *Coronation Street,* while ZDF brought *Diese Drombuschs* and *Die Schwarzwaldklinik* to the screen, two of the most popular series in Germany, followed by *Das Erbe der Guldenburgs,* after the American pattern of intrigue and complex relationships among the characters. Thus a new programming trend, the evening family series, was established.

These tendencies have continued until the twenty-first century. There are domestic serials and series like *Um Himmels Willen, In aller Freundschaft, Tatort,* and *Balko* on the public service channels, but at the same time there are a lot of American series and sitcoms, especially on the commercial channels, such as *CSI: Miami, Hawaii Five-O, Desperate Housewives, Grey's Anatomy, Fringe, The Mentalist, Homeland, Game of Thrones, How I Met Your Mother,* and *New Girl.*

Most of the programming trends have one feature in common: they are based on concepts or ideas that did not originate with German producers or networks. These formats are licensed, acquired on the international television market, and adapted for the national market. Any licensed format that met with a degree of success was copied and imitated by other networks. In this way the German television market developed a certain momentum that is driven mainly by licensing and imitating international formats. The result is a twofold convergence in the programming of the large (and some less large) networks: not only the networks' program structures, but also the formats themselves tend to become standardized. Yet if everyone is doing more or less the same thing, the individual networks can't develop a distinctive profile.

And the format merry-go-round spins faster and faster; the programming fads follow one another in rapid succession. This increases the pressure of competition, and the accelerated adaptation of formats leads to occasional flops. For example, the format *Hire or Fire* with Jon de Mol was cancelled after the first episode because it didn't attain the projected market share. Another format, *Big Boss,* flopped because the national adaptation did not reflect the professionalism of the American original, *The Apprentice* with Donald Trump. Sometimes a format fails on the overheated German television market in spite of international success because the networks have to adapt it not only to the national audience, but also to please supervisory agencies such as the state media boards and politicians who frequently voice opinions about television shows, ostensibly in the public interest. Thus formats such as *Big Brother, Deutschland sucht den Superstar* (original: *Pop Idol*), *Ich bin ein Star — Holt mich hier raus!* (original: *I'm A Celebrity, Get Me Out of Here!*), *The Swan — Endlich schön!* (original: *The Swan*), *Germany's Next Topmodel* (original: *America's Next Top Model*), or *Das Supertalent* (original: *Britain's Got Talent*) are often the object of debates about "trash TV," in which the protection of minors becomes a pretext for airing aesthetic issues.

The effects of this are not positive, neither for the German television market nor for its position in the network of international relationships that makes up the global format business. For this reason, German television has been left behind internationally as far as format development is concerned by smaller television markets such as the Netherlands and Sweden. The German market is considered a difficult one, and people hesitate to do business with German networks.

Nonetheless, there are some programming trends in Germany that are based on domestic creations and that are now making their way to the international market through licensing: comedy and knowledge shows. The knowledge show trend began with *Galileo* in 1998. In 2004 the genre was given a makeover by *Clever — Die Show, die Wissen schafft*. The latter format was billed as an original creation, although it was based on a Belgian model. The comedy boom began in 1993 with *RTL Samstag Nacht*. Although this show was modeled after the US *Saturday Night Live*, it and the subsequent SAT.1 offering *Die Wochenshow* brought forward numerous comedians who later graced the screen with formats of their own. Probably the most successful of these were Anke Engelke, whose *Ladykracher* format was licensed internationally, and Olli Dittrich, who earned numerous television awards for *Dittsche* and, together with Engelke, for the improvisational comedy show *Blind Date*. After these hits, German television was populated by more and more comedians, with varying degrees of success. Few formats have been able to achieve international recognition, as expressed in the form of license sales. The latest to make the jump was the improvisational comedy *Schillerstrasse*. Although these two programming trends originated with domestic creations, it is the numerous imitations that have made them trends. Of the entertainment shows, at least ProSieben's *Schlag den Raab* was sold internationally. The Swedish adaptation *Vem kan slå Filip och Fredrik?* attracted a large audience in 2008.

A cursory glance at the programming trends in German entertainment television reveals that there is no German television market outside the global television market. Programming innovation is realized primarily through license acquisitions, which are then adapted to the German market. These provide a stylistic differentiation that the audience can perceive as innovation. The quiz show *Wer wird Millionär?* (original: *Who Wants to Be a Millionaire?*) is surely the most prominent example. The competition on the national television market, which is supplied by the international market, puts an inescapable pressure on the networks to innovate. But because they lack both the money and the time to experiment with truly innovative programming, they draw primarily on the global television market, trying imitations of successful formats on the domestic market. Of course, format television is the main practice of commercial channels that have a bigger share of formatted television than the public service channels (Esser 2010). Even if there is actually still a share of more than 75 percent domestically produced programs in the public service channels ARD and ZDF (Die Medienanstalten 2013), and a domestic market share of about 50 percent at the main commercial channels RTL and Sat.1., the smaller channels have more imported programs. And if we look at the prime time programs there a lot of imported formats on all channels. Between 2006 and 2008 German channels imported 121 different TV formats (Jäger and Behrens 2009). At the same time they exported only 37 different formats. In Sweden the relation is nearly equal (57 imported formats to 41 exported formats); Japan has imported one single format but exported 29 formats. Whereas the United Kingdom has imported 66 formats during that period, but exported 275 different formats. France, Italy, and Spain have a nearly similar relationship of imported and exported formats like Germany. It is a tradition since the introduction of television that German channels are one of the main importers of television format from foreign countries. There were more informal adaptations in the beginning, but since the growth of the international format trade, imported formats and TV shows are licensed and have a prominent place in the schedule, especially in the commercial channels. Like France, Italy, and Spain, Germany is a country of format import, and less a country of format export.

Lothar Mikos is Professor at the Filmuniversität Konrad Wolf in Babelsberg. His publications include *Nordic Noir. Skandinavische Fernsehserien und ihr internationaler Erfolg* (UKV, 2014) co-authored with Lea Gamula,

Innovation im Fernsehen am Beispiel von Quizshow-Formaten. Reihe Alltag, Medien und Kultur 3 (UVK, 2009) and *Film- und Fernsehanalyse* (3rd edition, UVK/UTB, 2015). He has edited and written fifteen other books on film and television.

Chapter 9

HERITAGE, *HEIMAT*, AND GERMAN HISTORICAL "EVENT TELEVISION"

Nico Hofmann's teamWorx

Paul Cooke

During the last decade, high-cost miniseries, invariably sold to the viewing public as must-see TV "event movies," have become a mainstay of German television programming. The trend began in 2001 with *Der Tunnel* (The Tunnel, Roland Suso Richter/Johannes W. Betz), produced for Sat1, telling the true story of a group of friends attempting to escape from the GDR shortly after the building of the Berlin Wall. This was followed by a string of productions focusing on a variety of historical moments, including ARD's portrayal of the 1944 plot against Hitler, *Stauffenberg* (Jo Baier, 2004), Sat1's story of the Berlin Airlift, *Die Luftbrücke—Nur der Himmel war frei* (The Airlift, Dror Zahavi/ Martin Rauhaus, 2005), RTL's account of the 1962 flooding of Hamburg *Die Sturmflut* (Storm Tide, Jorgo Papavassiliou, 2006), reaching a high point of popular success with films such as *Dresden* (Roland Suso Richter, 2006),—ZDF's melodramatic love story of a German nurse and a British airman set against the backdrop of the bombing of the city—and *Die Flucht* (March of Millions, Kai Wessel, Gabriela Sperl, 2007), ARD's equally melodramatic account of a group of expellees escaping the encroaching Red Army at the end of the War. *Dresden* achieved an audience of 12.7 million on its first night (5 March 2006), constituting a massive 32.6 percent of the viewing public, the best ever ratings for this type of drama in the country's history ("Feuersturm mit Millionenpublikum" 2006). Almost as impressive was *Die Flucht,* with 11.2 million viewers on its first night (4 March 2007), 29.5 percent of the audience

("Auch zweiter Teil" 2007). As Rainer Wirtz notes, such historical dramas would typically expect to attract between 7 percent and 12 percent of the television audience, normally between 2 and 5 million viewers (Wirtz 2008: 11). More recently, the trend has appeared to be on the wane. Sat1's *Die Grenze* (The Frontier, Roland Suso Richter/ Christoph und Friedemann Fromm), for example, which twisted the historical format to present the story of a regional East German government attempting to recreate the GDR in the form of a breakaway socialist republic, was deemed by the press to have flopped, only attracting 4.7 million viewers on its first night (16 March 2010) and this despite a huge marketing campaign (Müller and Tuma 2010). That said, this still represented 14.2 percent of the audience. The following year, a spectacular, fictionalized account of the 1937 Hindenburg disaster (*Hindenburg*, Philipp Kadelbach/ Johannes W. Betz and Martin Pristl) also showed that there is still life left in the format, this two-part drama providing the private channel RTL with its most successful broadcast to date (7.8 million viewers, 20.9 percent of the audience on its first night, 6 February 2011) (Weis 2011). Similarly impressively, ARD's biopic of Rommel (*Rommel*, Niki Stein, 2012) beat *The Voice of Germany*, the German version of the international talent show, in the battle for ratings, attracting 18.8 percent of the audience (6.4 million viewers) when it was broadcast during the primetime 20.15 slot on 1 November 2012.

The driving force behind these and many other such miniseries has been the extraordinarily successful partnership of Nico Hofmann's UFA subsidiary teamWorx and the German television industry giant Jan Mojto, whose production and distribution companies EOS Entertainment and Beta Film (which rose from the ashes of the Kirch Media group after its dramatic collapse in 2002) regularly support teamWorx's endeavors.[1] This has been a hugely significant alliance for the industry, bringing about a step change in television production and more than fulfilling the predictions at its conception that it would, in Ed Meza's words, give rise to "big-budgeted, big-event, border-crossing productions" the like of which the country had never seen before (Meza 2006a). At home these productions have a far greater impact on the population as a whole than most German films produced for the cinema. The 12.7 million people who tuned into *Dresden*, for example, easily puts into the shade the 6.5 million German spectators that went to see Wolfgang Becker's *Good Bye, Lenin!* (2003) on its theatrical release, a film that was, nonetheless, considered a major domestic hit for German cinema.[2] Moreover, the ability of the series this partnership has produced to cross borders and go beyond the domestic sphere has been profound. *Stauffenberg,* for example, was sold to 82 countries, *Dresden* to over 100 (Gangloff 2006; Urbe 2006). The underlying reason for their international success, it should be noted, is attributable to the stability of television financing compared with the precarious world of cinematic film funding. It is relatively easy for "small screen historical epics," in particular, to find both buyers and backers among television networks across the globe, since such productions are considered to have longer shelf lives than feature films aimed at the cinema and can thus more readily amortize their initial costs (Meza 2006a). However, this is not the sole reason for teamWorx's success. In this chapter I wish to show how such productions also play into international trends in the production of historical drama in both their form and content. Specifically, I examine the extent to which the films can be seen as part of the move towards the production of what has been termed "heritage" drama. At the same time, and seeming to work against these films' international credentials, I suggest that such films also resonate with that most peculiarly German of production trends, the *Heimat* film, and the impulse to create a community of viewers rooted in a shared understanding of the German past. To begin, however, I shall discuss the way in which the concept of the television "event" itself plays an important role in these dramas' success, the company's very approach to marketing their films as "events" reflecting this tension between international appeal and national specificity.

Constructing the TV "Event"

The concept of the "television event," now much discussed by commentators, is not new to the small screen in Germany. In the 1950s and 1960s certain episodes of popular West German police dramas such as *Stahlnetz* (Net of Steel, Jürgen Roland, Wolfgang Menge, 1958 to 1968) or numerous Francis Durbridge adaptations (e.g., *Das Halstuch*/The Scarf, Hans Quest, Francis Durbridge, Marianne de Barde, 1962; Tim Frazer, Hans Quest, Francis Durbridge, Marianne de Barde, 1963) exhibited many of the qualities associated with the kinds of exceptional moments in the German mass media that are often now described as "events." At the time, however, they were termed *Straßenfeger* (street cleaners), due to their apparent ability to clear the streets of people, often attracting over 90 percent of the viewing public and offering, in the process, a communal celebration of this young medium. This was, of course, a time long before the increased competition between broadcasters introduced by the dual system in the 1980s, competition that has intensified with the proliferation of media channels in our present digital age. It is almost impossible for a single broadcast to achieve such an audience share today. That said, far fewer people had television sets at that point (just over 1 million at the end of the 1950s compared with well over 51 million today). Consequently, while audience shares have generally decreased, the total number of viewers has increased, allowing certain television broadcasts to have a comparable impact on public consciousness. One thinks, most obviously, of major soccer games in Germany, which at times come closest to achieving the audience share of earlier decades. The 2010 World Cup semifinal between Germany and Spain, for example, was watched by 31 million people—the largest number of viewers the country has ever seen—83.2 percent of the television audience (Niemeier 2010).

In the past two decades, a great deal of academic research has been undertaken on the nature and impact of media events. Whatever the content, be it a television drama or sport, such events are generally conceptualized as exceptional, disruptive moments in the mediascape that generate a sense of shared experience amongst the public, allowing the whole of society to feel part of a community, the television, in particular, acting as what Daniel Dayan and Elihu Katz describe in their groundbreaking study of such moments as a community's "ceremonial center" (Dayan and Katz 1992: 15). Recently, scholars have particularly begun to discuss the increased volume of media phenomena that have been defined as "events," along with what has been described as an increasingly common process of "eventization," that is, the self-conscious construction of media events.[3] Henry Jenkins, for example, discusses the present level of coordination and convergence across media channels, leading to the "multichannel marketing" of entertainment and the concomitant emergence of "transmedia storytelling" strategies.[4] In a media world larger and more diffuse than ever before, production companies regularly attempt to coordinate content across platforms (television, cinema, the Internet, DVD, mobile phones etc.) in order to create the kind of disruptive events that seemed to be generated less deliberately in the predigital age, when consumers had fewer viewing options.

Within the trajectory of German post–World War II *Vergangenheitsbewältigung* (working through the past), the concept of the television event, specifically, has played a particularly visible role. In 1979, the screening of Marvin J. Chomsky's and Gerald Green's four-part miniseries *Holocaust*, for example, had a huge, and unpredicted, impact on the German public. While there had already been intense discussion of the Holocaust and the question of German culpability for the nation's crimes in certain sections of society, the melodramatic story of the German-Jewish Weiss family ripped apart by Nazi persecution had an emotional resonance across the whole of society never seen before. To say that the impact of *Holocaust* was unpredicted does not, however, mean that it was not itself constructed, to a degree, as an event. Siegfried Zielinski writes of the way "public institutions began to prepare almost feverishly for the coming event," from the Bundeszentrale für politische Bildung (Federal Agency for Civic Education) to all the public broadcasters, such institutions publishing books and screening documentaries "designed to prepare the viewing public for the coming film" (Zielinski 1980). In the last decade, Nico Hofmann's production company teamWorx has taken the self-conscious construction of history as a television event to an unprecedented level, making its name through producing a string of similarly melodramatic historical miniseries that are, somewhat counterintuitively perhaps, regularly marketed as exceptional moments in the German mediascape, to the extent that it has turned "event television" into a new genre of broadcasting. Throughout the company's output, one sees particularly clearly the shift from the television event to the "eventization" of television, with teamWorx using a range of media deliberately to construct the sense of a mass viewing community.[5] In so doing, the company in fact tries to emulate the impact of the so-called event movie, a label frequently attached to those huge budget Hollywood blockbusters designed to be sold the world over and thus operating on a far larger scale than teamWorx can.

The nature of the teamWorx project, along with the scale of Hofmann and Mojto's ambition, is of course hinted at in the name of Hofmann's company. And just in case anyone missed the significance of this allusion, Mojto makes it clear: "We will be the DreamWorks of Europe," he tells us, suggesting that the partnership intends to emulate the success of Jeffrey Katzenberg, David Geffen, and Steven Spielberg's mammoth US production company (Meza 2012). Although this remains a distant goal for the company, Hofmann and Mojto would appear to be moving in the right direction, as can be seen in the growing number of territories that purchase their productions mentioned above. teamWorx is increasingly a company with international impact. Crucially, with *Dresden* they made the breakthrough into the English-speaking market, which has always been, as Scott Roxborough and Mimi Turner note, the "toughest to crack" for German language productions (Roxborough and Turner 2006). This achievement was then consolidated with *The*

Sinking of the Laconia (2011), a BBC coproduction about the sinking of a British passenger liner by a German submarine—the first German-British television coproduction for decades. Written by the well-known British dramatist Alan Bleasdale (*The Monocled Mutineer,* Jim O'Brien, 1986; *G.B.H.,* Robert Young, 1991) and starring major German and British actors (Andrew Buchan, Lindsay Duncan, Thomas Kretschmann, and Franka Potente), the miniseries was heralded by the company as marking yet another important watershed moment in its international development (Meza 2006). And efforts to take further steps in this direction continued with *Hindenburg.* Although an all-German production, it was filmed in English. Like *Laconia,* it included an international array of actors (Greta Scacchi, Stacy Keach, Lauren Lee Smith) and also like *Laconia* was showcased at Cannes in an attempt to ride the wave of growing interest beyond Germany in the nation's television productions. Nonetheless, *Hindenburg* also highlighted some of the challenges faced by teamWorx within the English-speaking market. For its North American distribution, for example, it in fact had to be resynchronized. The original English voice track was considered too "unnatural" by the broadcasters. Consequently, the live voices of the German actors were replaced by native English speakers (Festenberg 2011).

Like Spielberg, teamWorx sets out to produce big-budget, mass entertainment with high production values. Its films regularly cost in excess of €10 million, an enormous sum of money for a television production in Germany. The budgets themselves, moreover, often become a central plank in the marketing campaigns that invariably precede their broadcast. As Tobias Ebbrecht notes in his examination of contemporary German historical event television, it is a notable aspect of the phenomenon that the "event" also "encompasses its own production process." In a similar fashion to Hollywood event movies, "through extra-textual events (documentaries, talks and 'making ofs') the film becomes embedded in an ensemble of telecasting" (Ebbrecht 2007: 230). The production costs of films such as *Dresden, Die Flucht,* or *Hindenburg* are repeatedly referred to both by the company itself in its publicity and throughout the broader media coverage, highlighting the fact that these films are not run-of-the-mill television productions.[6] teamWorx's historical event television is always presented as a prestige project, epic in scale. The company also tends to emphasize this aspect in its marketing campaigns by drawing attention to the use of special effects, which often accounts for the majority of the production costs. Their films exploit the kind of CGI that—although nowhere near as expensive or sophisticated as those to be found in a Spielberg production, for example—allow brief moments of spectacle that one would not normally find in television productions, be it an image of a burning airship crashing to its destruction in *Hindenburg,* or the reproduction of the firestorm that engulfed the city in *Dresden.* The ostensibly exceptional nature of these television event films is then finally also underlined in their marketing by highlighting the number of major figures and rising stars of domestic, and increasingly nondomestic, television and film that make up their cast, as can be seen from the list of people involved in the English-language productions *Laconia* and *Hindenburg* already mentioned. Notably, these productions are also not afraid to cast stars against type in order to make the most of an actor's immediate celebrity and to increase the hype around their broadcast. Felicitas Woll, for example, who starred as the German nurse Anna in *Dresden,* was at that point best known for her role as Lolle in ARD's very successful romantic comedy series *Berlin, Berlin* (2001–2004). The affection with which younger viewers in particular held her served, as the production company hoped, to attract a portion of the German audience that might not immediately tune in to a historical drama.

Thus far, all the kinds of marketing techniques outlined here, while clearly aimed at the construction of teamWorx's output as must-see "events," are not necessarily unique to its productions. More distinctive is the use of the Internet to enhance the hype around a given film. As one would expect, this tends to be carefully constructed as part of an orchestrated "multichannel" marketing campaign, to return to Jenkins's terminology. However, more importantly, it is also used to create the sense that these television events are embedded within a communal viewing experience that uses the representation of past historical traumas to reinstate the kind of integrative and (as we shall see later in this chapter) reconciliatory impulse that Dayan and Katz consider central to their understanding of media events. All of teamWorx's productions have a developed web presence, at times simply designed to enhance further the sense that these broadcasts are significant media events that are part of a wider sociopolitical debate. Ebbrecht, for example, points to the way ZDF's website linked its production of *Dresden* to the controversy surrounding the publication of Jörg Friedrich's book *Der Brand* (The Fire: The Bombing of Germany, 1940–1945, 2008) and its discussion of the status of the Allied bombing campaign in Germany as a war crime by including a video debate between Friedrich and a German-Jewish survivor of the bombing, Ralph Giordano. It also allowed visitors to play a multimedia "history game," built around repackaged archive footage, introduced by the station's head historian and leading historical documentary maker, Guido Knopp, a figure who features in much of the extratextual material that surrounds many of these broadcasts (Ebbrecht 2007: 231). However, the use of social networking sites such as Facebook and Twitter as well as online discussion fora also tend to go beyond this process of embedding in order explicitly to create, and advertise the existence of, a community of active participants in—rather than passive consumers of—these events. Along with the usual collage of images from the film and interviews with the cast and crew on the production website, *Hindenburg*, for example, prominently features its Facebook site on its front page, and in particular the names and profile pictures of people who have signed up to its fan group.[7] More developed than this are the discussion groups on the websites for *Dresden*, *Die Flucht*, and *Laconia*. Here we often find vibrant examination of the films and their relationship to the experience of discussants as well as the contemporary cultural and political significance of their approach to the representation of the past.

At times, website postings tend to reflect the kind of "authenticity" debates to be found in the wider media and academic reception of many contemporary German historical films.[8] Here one might mention the extended debate on the blog of Knut Loewe, the production designer on *Laconia*, about whether the use of incorrect insignia on the sailors' uniforms in the film invalidates the entire production, or the discussion on the same blog around the representation of Polish soldiers as violent thugs who were willing to allow the Italian prisoners of war incarcerated on the ship to drown as it sank (Loewe 2011). Similar remarks can be found on *Die Flucht*'s web forum "Erinnerungen, Erlebnisse, Eindrücke" (Memories, Experiences, Impressions). Yet significantly here the prominent trend is for younger people to use the forum to discuss the place of this period of history in their own families' collective memory. At times, participants lament the fact that their grandparents would never talk about this period in their lives. At times they use the forum as a space to present an account of their family's experience of the war. In so doing, they both participate in, and also extend, the archival basis upon which this account of history is built, thereby further increasing the significance of this particular television event ("Erinnerungen" 2011). But whether participants in these discussions like or loathe the films themselves, whether they see them as a chance to share their family history with others or as a missed opportunity accurately to depict an important historical moment, their participation in the discussion of these productions creates the sense of a communal engagement with the past and the continued significance of television

as society's "ceremonial center," to recall Dayan and Katz once more—
even as the significance of this medium is challenged by the specific
nature of their engagement, via the Internet.

From Heritage to *Heimat*

The construction of a viewing community is central to the success of
teamWorx's productions as "events." As can be seen by the international array of participants in some of the Internet discussions these
dramas generate, as well as the success of many of these productions
internationally, this is a community that has the potential to speak to
the specific issues of German history while also engaging audiences
beyond this national context. The complementary nature of the relationship between the national and the international is, furthermore,
reflected in both the form and content of the films themselves. As commentators have pointed out, generically, many of the most successful of
these films adopt international conventions of mainstream genre filmmaking. These conventions are wide ranging, from their use of melodrama to their invocation of Hollywood epics like *Gone with the Wind*
(Victor Fleming, 1939) and *Titanic* (James Cameron, 1997).[9] However,
one aspect of their generic make up that has not yet received much
discussion is the way in which these productions circulate within an
international context of heritage filmmaking.

As Lutz Koepnick argues, many contemporary German history films
can be viewed as part of an international trend towards the production
of heritage cinema, films that typically present the past as what might
be termed a spectacular museum that can be easily consumed by the
present-day spectator: "What typifies heritage filmmaking is the production of usable and consumable pasts, of history as a site of comfort
and orientation"(Koepnick 2002: 49). The concept of the heritage film
was first used to describe a number of highly successful British historical dramas, most notably those produced by the Merchant Ivory film
company, such as *A Room with a View* (James Ivory, 1986) and *Maurice*
(James Ivory, 1987).[10] These were films that seemed to wallow in the lost
world of the British Empire, focusing on the experience and lifestyles
of a past elite. It was also identified as the defining aesthetic impulse in
many of the United Kingdom's most internationally successful television dramas, such as the commercial broadcaster ITV's Evelyn Waugh
adaptation *Brideshead Revisited* (Charles Sturridge and Michael Lindsay-Hogg/ Derek Granger, 1981), a trend that continues to the present

with the same channel's international smash hit *Downton Abbey* (Brian Percival, Julian Fellowes, Shelagh Stephenson, Tina Pepler, 2010–2015), the story of the aristocratic Grantham family negotiating the first decades of the twentieth century, which has been sold to over 200 territories worldwide (Midgley 2013).

Whether they are made for television or the cinema, such heritage films tend to privilege setting over the stories they tell in their painstaking recreation of an authentic image of the past, producing dramas that celebrate, in the cases mentioned here, the continuity of British imperial heritage culture—as signified most notably by their presentation of the British "country house"—into the postimperial present. Indeed, the opulent celebration of its setting, and in particular its showcasing of the best of the English National Trust's country house portfolio, has seen *Downton Abbey* described as "the pinnacle of period porn" (Hislop 2012). Alessandra Stanley suggests provocatively in the *New York Times* that this series is almost reminiscent of *Fifty Shades of Grey* in the way it allows the viewer unashamedly to indulge in an nostalgic fantasy of a lost past, the sexual fetishism of E. L. James's best seller replaced here with an obsession for "breeding and heritage" (Stanley 2013).

The closest German television production comes to this kind of "period porn," as Eckart Voigts-Virchow notes, is in the long-running and very successful series of dramas produced by ZDF based on the romantic novels of the British author Rosamunde Pilcher. This series began in 1993 with the broadcast of *Stürmische Begegnung* (The Day of the Storm, Helmut Förnbacher) and has led to over 100 productions by the broadcaster that present interchangeable stories of romantic intrigue set on British country estates that are even more indulgently sugary than their British counterparts. "Pilcherland," as Voigts-Virchow terms the world these films create, offers German audiences a form of "Ersatz-heritage" unavailable within the context of German history, using British heritage culture to present a "globalised fantas[y] of national identity (Virchow 2009: 133–35).[11]

At the same time these films, with their construction of idyllic, nostalgically charged, rural communities, along with the exuberant use of long takes showcasing their countryside setting, firmly place them within a specifically German tradition of *Heimat* filmmaking. *Heimat* is a notoriously difficult word to translate into English. Loosely equivalent to the English "home" or "homeland," *Heimat* is a heterogeneous concept that, as Elizabeth Boa and Rachel Palfreyman outline in their examination of the historical trajectory of the term, has been used to reflect a wide range of positions in discussions over the years around the role of place, belonging, and identity in German culture as the nation has attempted to reconcile the tensions between modernity and tradition (Boa and Palfreyman 2000). *Heimat* film production reached its zenith in the 1950s when West German audiences flocked to cinemas to watch films such as Hans Deppe's *Schwarzwaldmädel* (The Black Forest Girl, 1950) and *Grün ist die Heide* (Green Is the Heath, 1951). These offered escapist, brightly colored images of Germany in which dirndl-clad women and lederhosen-wearing men fell in love to a soundtrack of German *Volksmusik*, providing a cinematic embodiment of idealized German family values that celebrated a fully integrated German community that had overcome the trauma of the war (Moltke 2005).[12] The *Pilcher* series relocates the German *Heimat* fantasy to Britain. As such, it can be seen part of a wider trend in contemporary *Heimat* film production which sees the German rural *Heimat* community shifted to a variety of non-German locations, from Poland to Kenya, providing a specifically German take on the tendency towards the globalization of identity fantasies identified by Voigts-Virchow above.[13] Its indulgence of the British heritage tradition would, however, appear to be more unique within contemporary German film production.

While filmmakers have been influenced by the popularity of the heritage film, the German variation often differs in a number of important ways from the British form. This is due, fundamentally, to the nature of the history depicted. Although there is clearly a tendency to turn the past into a kind of readily consumable museum in many contemporary German historical dramas made for both television and cinema, the very status of German history as a past to be consumed and its relation to the present-day spectator is more problematic. An image of a British country house is not the same as that of a war-torn German building adorned with swastikas such as we find in numerous contemporary historical dramas. Instead, in many of these productions, we see a rejection of the concept of "heritage" as a nation's physical inheritance, which is, as Andrew Higson points out, central to the concept in the British film tradition (Higson 2003: 28). In many German heritage films, the audience is similarly allowed to enjoy the materiality of the history presented, specifically in this case, indulging the continued popular fascination with the pageantry of fascism and the public's seemingly insatiable appetite for depictions of the war along with other aspects of Germany's authoritarian history. However, it is on the level of narrative where the particular nature of the German "inheritance" is to be found. Throughout, one finds the presentation of a sense of "Germanness" based on an Enlightenment humanist tradition, which is both older than National Socialism and can look beyond the latter's barbarity, creating instead an inclusive, multicultural, and democratic version of the German *Heimat*, where the nation can work in harmony with the international community, pointing forward to the Berlin Republic that is to come. Thus, although different in their frame of reference, such films like the *Pilcher* narratives mentioned above, often also conflate the concept of heritage and *Heimat*, a connection summed up in Georg Seeßlen's rejection of this recent wave of historical filmmaking as part of a disturbing "neuen deutschen Supergenre der Heimat-geschichtsfamilien-Feel-Good-Movies" (new German supergenre of *Heimat*-historical-family-feel-good movies) (Seeßlen 2008: 26). Or, as Wirtz puts it, making explicit the link to ZDF's heritage/*Heimat* cycle, contemporary German heritage dramas focus on the authentic material reproduction of the past, over which "eine 'Pilcher-Sauce' gegossen [wird]" (a "*Pilcher* Sauce" is poured) (Wirtz 2008: 15). Leaving aside the debate about the ethical value of German heritage films as representations of the past, a debate that, as can be inferred from these comments, dominates the critical reception of this cycle of filmmaking, in the rest of this chapter I wish to examine some of the ways in which teamWorx productions highlight the dynamic between heritage and *Heimat* filmmaking, and with it their presentation of a complementary dynamic between national and international concerns in the stories these films tell.

The explicit connection to the British heritage aesthetic in the team-Worx cycle is shown most obviously in their foregrounding of the materiality of history, constructing the past as a museum exhibit into which the viewer is directly sutured. For example, a crane shot of the Hindenburg passenger terminal, which provides a panorama of the physical scale of Zeppelin's operation, immediately gives way to a jerky shot that positions the viewer as a passenger boarding the flight, the camera following the various characters we will later encounter on the voyage as they pass through the hanger and onto the ship. Similarly, a wide shot highlighting the overwhelming scale of the refugee trek westwards in *Die Flucht* is juxtaposed with a close-up of the faces of trouble-worn women taking shelter inside a farm from the snowy conditions outside, the viewer positioned as if she or he were one of the refugees staring at those around them. Through the use of such subjective camera work that attempts to generate empathy between the viewer and the characters on screen, the past is presented almost as a form of virtual reality into which the viewer is directly placed. The use of jerky close-up shots in *Hindenburg*, for example, seems to suggest the sense of indexicality offered by the sort of handheld camera footage one might typically find in a documentary. That said, these sequences are not to be confused with the type of cinéma vérité techniques one finds throughout European film production, from Andreas Dresen to Lars von Trier. The rich veneer of a form of filmmaking that aspires to the production values of Hollywood is never lost entirely to the type of gritty realism of these low-budget European films. Yet teamWorx productions often do at least allude to this type of realist aesthetic. They also, at times, recall the types of documentary images and sounds that are now the dominant form in which these periods of history are generally accessible to audiences. *Hindenburg* recreates in detail the shots of the burning airship crashing to the ground, famous from the newsreel footage of the time, accompanied by a reenactment of Herbert Morrison's equally famous emotional radio commentary. This detailed recreation is then interspersed with images of the cameras shooting this footage, and of Morrison's obvious distress at the tragedy he is witnessing, all of which creates the impression that we are being given a behind-the-scenes view of the events as we know they really happened from the well-known media images and sounds. In line with the broader strategies of eventization in German television outlined in the previous section, the film implicates the viewer. We become witnesses in the construction of the historical record, rather than the passive consumers of a television film. In *Dresden*, this is taken one step further. We see, for example, a British fighter pilot filming his colleagues boarding a plane, a shot that is immediately followed by a piece of period footage of a similar group, which is in turn followed by a shot inside a plane of the fictional airmen climbing on board, suturing us to the point of view of one of the crew. Here, historical documentary footage is sandwiched between the two constructed shots, the use of continuity editing creating the illusion that the entire sequence is historically accurate and that we are ourselves part of the documentary. Later, as Anna and Robert, her British airman (John Light), walk through the destroyed city the day after the bombing, the film incorporates real footage of the city: a disturbing grainy black and white shot of charred bodies lying motionless on the street, obviously taken at the time (Crew 2007: 126).[14] The use of black and white then continues into the subsequent shot as we return to the couple walking through the ruins, suggesting that the whole sequence has been taken from a documentary newsreel. All of these strategies attempt to create what Axel Bangert defines in his discussion of *Die Gustloff* (Joseph Vilsmaier and Rainer Berg, 2008)— another heritage television "event film" that, although not produced by teamWorx draws heavily on the company's approach—as a strategy of "immersion" that seeks to recreate a sense of immediacy for the viewer, giving the illusion that he or she is really "there," allowing the audience an empathetic point of connection with the past (Bangert 2011: 311).

By encouraging the viewer to empathize with the main protagonists, such films also highlight the continued relevance of this past event for the present-day viewer, creating an emotional bridge between the historical narrative on the screen and the experience of the viewing audience. It is here where we see the notion of a specifically German heritage invested in the sensibilities of individual characters who represent a form of Enlightenment humanism that can see beyond the barbarism of National Socialism to the values of the present-day nation. In these characters, a universal and good Germany is implied, one that could resist contamination by Nazism. This is a form of "heritage," moreover, that evokes the German *Heimat* tradition and the construction of a wholesome German community uncontaminated by the dark side of German history and that is embedded within a wider international democratic community of nations.

The invocation of the *Heimat* tradition within the teamWorx cycle is perhaps at its most explicit in *Die Flucht*. At the start of the narrative, Lena (Maria Furtwängler), the estranged daughter of a nobleman from East Prussia, returns home to her family estate, the war in its final months. As the opening credits role, she gets off a train and picks her way through the smoke of the station, a crowd of men in grey uniforms on their way to a pointless war that offers no hope of victory and a group of anxious women seeing them off. Once off the platform, the noise and dirt of the modern world is quickly replaced by the romantic swell of strings accompanying Lena's journey by horse and cart to her home. The sun shines on a verdant landscape as an aerial point-of-view shot zooms over the treetops taking us to the family's country estate. This is Lena's *Heimat*, a provincial idyll, where enlightened German values exist—embodied largely in the women who now look after the house—even as they are challenged by a Nazi ideology that indoctrinates children into fighting for a lost cause, on the one hand, and by an outmoded aristocratic system that did nothing to prevent the Nazi takeover, on the other. Of course, as we know before we even turn on the television to watch the drama, Lena is destined to lose her home, situated as it is east of the Oder-Neisse line. Thus, as is typical of the *Heimat* genre, the depiction of her home is immediately imbued with a sense of nostalgia. She will leave this world behind her, leading the trek westwards of those who work for her family, through the harsh winter under constant threat of attack, until they reach safety in Bavaria in the spring of 1945 and a beautiful landscape that is immediately recognizable from the 1950s *Heimat* film cycle. However, unlike the images of a landscape that was home to a fully integrated German community that dominated the genre in the postwar period, here the countryside is punctuated by placards warning expellees such as Lena to keep moving. They are not welcome here. Thus the film, on one level, challenges the trite nostalgia of the 1950s cycle, presenting the "reality" behind the images of the period that would be well known to the audience of *Die Flucht* in Germany, just as we see in the hyperrealistic presentation of the airship's destruction in *Hindenburg*, along with the film's portrayal of the disaster's contemporary media representation, outlined above.

Nonetheless, ultimately the comfortable sense of integration we find in the 1950s *Heimat* films is reinstated, the countryside once again imbued with the idyllic potential of her lost East Prussian *Heimat*. Crucially, however, the narrative resolution involves implicating the German *Heimat* landscape within a broader sense of international reconciliation and integration for the nation. The ending of *Die Flucht* promises a new meritocratic future for Lena. She will escape Germany's lost aristocratic past to find love with a former French prisoner of war, François (Jean-Yves Berteloot). François previously labored on her father's land and now works for the Americans, helping to bring Nazi war criminals to justice. After a long search François finds Lena, and in the final moments of the film the couple declare their love for each other in a quintessential *Heimat* setting, sheltering from a light summer rain shower beneath a tree as the sun sets and the romantic strings of the film's opening credits return. This is a love that seems to offer hope not only to Lena but to the whole nation, an example of the potential for reconciliation between former enemies united in their shared values and their common disdain for Germany's past crimes.

The narrative of *Die Flucht* is typical of teamWorx productions, which frequently present the efforts of the central female protagonist to escape the constraints of a stiflingly traditional and—in the case of teamWorx's best known productions—invariably nationalistic past in the hope of embracing a new understanding of *Heimat*. As we can see from the burgeoning relationship between François and Lena, that new understanding is generally conceptualized as the beginning of the country's democratic, outward-looking future the present-day viewer knows will come. Similarly, in *Hindenburg* the free-spirited German engineer Merten Kröger (Maximilian Simonischek), liberates Jennifer van Zandt (Lauren Lee Smith) from the corruption of her American industrialist father, as well as the dangerous exploitation by her boyfriend Fritz (Andreas Pietschmann) for the Nazi war effort. Once again, the aesthetics of the *Heimat* tradition are invoked when we first meet Merten. We see him set off in a glider over a beautiful patchwork of fields and woodland, his casual regard for his own safety as he soars through the air (he has never flown before) acting as a counterpoint to the destructive manipulation of technology embodied in the Nazi Fritz and his henchmen. Equally in *Dresden*, although we are now in an urban setting, as in *Die Flucht*, we are allowed to indulge in a typically nostalgic presentation of a lost *Heimat* in the film's opening black and white footage of the city when it was still the "Florence of the Elbe," before it was destroyed in the firestorm unleashed by the Allies, but which was ultimately caused, we are left in no doubt in the film, by German nationalistic folly. And, while the affair between Anna and Robert is itself doomed to failure — having survived the bombing, Robert dies on a journey back to his lover in the immediate aftermath of the war — we learn that Anna is expecting his baby, a child who points the way to a future utopia, in which a unified Europe will surely prevent any future European civil conflicts. Thus, all these productions create the sense of their narratives being rooted within a postauthoritarian, often multicultural *Heimat*, a community of belonging symbolized in the type of international bonds generated in the resolution of their romantic plotlines and that the German nation has long sought to foster, especially across Europe.

Constructing a television "event" out of a romantic narrative that suggests the resolution of the nation's past along with the repositioning of the nation in the present also often highlights the ritualistic, ceremonial function of the television event as conceptualized by Dayan and Katz. These are symbolically laden productions, constructing Germany as part of an international community, a community that is also evidenced in the way the films are presented to consumers discursively through the company's use of "multichannel" marketing techniques, as well as in their actual consumption. The impulse to embed these narratives within an international context while also foregrounding their German specificity is also reflected in the aesthetic strategies they employ. These are strategies that often play to the conventions of heritage and other forms of international mainstream genre filmmaking on the one hand and the particular German sensibilities of the *Heimat* tradition on the other. Throughout, the traumas of Germany's past become a repository of images and experiences through which the present-day nation can redefine and reconfigure itself. The aesthetics of the heritage film become a vehicle for the construction of a sense of *Heimat* rooted in the material presentation of Germany's problematic past, allowing the viewer to indulge the seemingly insatiable popular appetite for stories about the nation's history, while also celebrating its transcendence of this past and its present-day position as a valued member of the international community.

Paul Cooke is Centenary Chair of World Cinemas at the University of Leeds. He has written four monographs, including *Contemporary German Cinema* (Manchester: Manchester University Press, 2012) and *Representing East Germany: From Colonization to Nostalgia* (Oxford: Berg, 2005), edited or coedited twelve other books, and published widely on film and television. He is currently working currently working on a project looking at the relationship between European Heritage Cinema and the wider Heritage Sector.

Notes

1. teamWorx was set up in 1998 by producers Nico Hofmann, Ariane Krampe, and Wolf Bauer. Bauer is also chief executive officer of UFA Film and TV Production. The company has to date made over 240 television productions and is known across Europe for its hugely popular "Event TV" productions, mainly but not exclusively, set in the past. For further information on the history of the company see http://www.teamworx.de/ueber-uns/unternehmen.html.
2. Figures for *Good Bye, Lenin* taken from the Filmförderungsanstalt, Filmhitliste: Jahresliste (international) 2004, http://www.ffa.de/, accessed 9 February 2007.
3. See for example Hepp 2004; Hitzler 2011.
4. For further discussion, see Jenkins 2006.
5. For a more extended discussion of this aspect of teamWorx productions see Cooke 2013.
6. See, for example, Fuhr 2011.
7. "Hindenburg—RTL," http://www.rtl.de/cms/unterhaltung/hindenburg.html, accessed 10 June 2011.
8. For further discussion of "authenticity" debates in German heritage films see Cooke 2012: 88–120.
9. For further discussion see Cooke 2008; Bergfelder 2010.
10. For a more detailed discussion of such historical dramas as heritage films and the debates this description has generated see Higson 2003; Monk 2011.
11. This is, of course, not the only example of such a tendency in German film history. One might also mention the representation of Britain in Rialto's 1960s Edgar Wallace films. For further discussion see Bergfelder 2005: 172–206.
12. For further discussion of *Heimatfilme* see Moltke 2005.
13. For further discussion, see Cooke, Contemporary German Cinema, pp. 258–63.

14. As David Crew points out, this image also recalls "the gruesome photographs of corpses taken by Heinz Kröbel before February 20, 1945 when many of the people who had been killed on the streets of Dresden were cremated in huge piles on the Altmarkt. Kröbel's graphic photographs appeared in 1995 in a new exhibition on the destruction of Dresden sponsored by the Stadtmuseum bearing the symptomatic title 'Burned beyond Recognition'" (2007: 126).

Chapter 10

ONCE UPON A CRIME

Tatort, Germany's Longest Running Police Procedural

Bärbel Göbel-Stolz

Tatort is like a Hydra. No matter how many heads you cut off, everything will grow again. The directors will be new, the actors will be new, and the inspectors new, stories new, and places will be new, over and over again. Everything is new and yet the same. The format stands, but is brought to life with new artistic vision, new personalities, new angles.
—Gunther Witte (2009)

The German police procedural *Tatort* (Scene of the Crime) premiered in November 1970 and has been broadcast for forty-six years; an end is not in sight.[1] At the time of the drama's inception, the militant left-wing Red Army Faction held Germany in a grip of fear; extended media coverage and wanted signs at post offices alerted the nation's citizens to the imminent danger of domestic terrorism. Germany was deeply divided into supporters and opponents of the group that sought to fight capitalism, consumerism, and Americanism (Aust, 1997). Gunther Witte, creator of the *Tatort* series, claimed in an interview that national upheavals and politics played only a small part in the decision-making process for those in charge at the ARD (Consortium of public-law broadcasting institutions of the Federal Republic of Germany); it was "just business." The ongoing political unrest, however, may have ensured that funding through government channels was easily received for a tale dealing with crime, morality and ethics.

After a decade of ARD's being the sole television station in the nation, over 50 percent of viewers had wandered off to the newer, more culture- and entertainment-oriented ZDF (Witte 2009). *Tatort,* with twelve episodes in the 1970–71 season, brought a new regional, yet national program into play that was part of the already widely successful crime television genre (Brück, Viehoff 1996), and amassed over 50 percent of Germany's national audience for episode premieres (Hartling et al, 1997). One cannot help but wonder about the timing of this massive, German-wide production of tales of crime and punishment against a backdrop of national turmoil. At least on Sunday evenings, for ninety minutes law and order were restored in German living rooms.

The series began its now forty-four-year run at a time when *Fernsehspiele*, government-funded television films, were at the height of artistic development. Fassbinder, Schlöndorff, and other well-known film directors of the German New Wave movement offered viewers critical television series and films that questioned the social constructs in Germany and the nation's World War II history. *Tatort*, in contrast, was conceptualized from the beginning as not artistic in its style, but rather a straightforward police procedural. At its inception Gunther Witte had drafted a rulebook, an outline for the series commonly known as the "*Tatort* bible." Today format bibles are generally used for format series, such as *Who Wants to Be a Millionaire* or *Big Brother*, which sell to different international territories, yet always try to follow the basic construct of the series' original run. Much in the same vein as today's TV bibles, *Tatort's* bible described the general look, narrative style, character presentation, and subject matter for the series. The series had a distinct recipe.

No one predicted (Gunther Witte certainly did not) that the series, originally based upon earlier optioned scripts and crime novels, would become the crown jewel of Germany's public television programming. *Tatort* has remained one of the most popular programs in Germany throughout the long history of the series. By comparison, the two longest running American primetime drama series each ran for twenty years (*Gunsmoke*, 1955–1975, CBS; and *Law & Order*, 1990–2010, NBC). Only soap operas, newscasts, specials, and sportscasts have reached the forty-year mark. ARD used *Tatort* to maintain its leading position among audiences even with the shifting media environments in Germany over the years. Following World War II, Germany relied solely on public broadcasting until the early 1980s, when the dual system, with public and commercial broadcasters functioning side by side, was introduced. With the reunification of Germany in 1990, a vast new market opened that allowed commercial stations to expand quickly and successfully, establishing them as competitors to public broadcasting — but these commercial stations required cheap programming, and thus imported much US and European product.

Tatort is, in many ways, not American drama. The series has a unique format—part series, part anthology, part franchise, as well as a peculiar history of what we will here, tentatively, call censorship. Over nearly five decades, *Tatort* created and still provides entries into a visual archive of German society and its morals—1970 to the present. *Tatort* arguably contains a cultural history of Germany in televisual format.[2] This chapter will review the series format, discuss the episodes removed from circulation, and investigate case studies illuminating the cultural importance of the police procedural.

Textual Form in *Tatort*

The *Tatort* series form allows for plots to be complex and literate in nature, while maintaining an episodic structure. Each episode is ninety minutes long, shot on 16 mm film,[3] and presents well-rounded characters that a German audience can easily relate to, especially because the series is currently divided into fifteen different detective teams and regions. The series premiered in November 1970 and during its first season (1971–72), contained eleven episodes, featuring seven investigators in seven cities. The division into regions is part of the textual make-up of *Tatort*.

Tatort airs on Sunday nights, primetime, on one national station, Das-Erste, run by the ARD. Although there is only one time slot, 8:15 p.m. on Sunday—much like the US show *CSI* (CBS), which has a Las Vegas, Miami, and New York location, each with their own team and cases—several locations are utilized in *Tatort*. All teams and locations share an airtime, meaning they are rotated from week to week. This results in each team airing episodes only a few times a year, up to four episodes per annum with specific team. Some locations are bound to regional stations that have a lower budget, and thus these locations, while still airing episodes in the series line-up, will only be featured once a year. The production structure of *Tatort* thus provides a microcosm of the combination of regional and national, typical of German television.

The number of episodes and formats grew throughout time, but while each new decade brought changes, there were no significant alterations to the basic format. This means that the basic set-up, genre specifics, and narrative structure have remained intact for the series as a whole. Rather than changing the base structure of the series, individual regions will attempt to alter the concept by experimenting with only one detective, or even only one episode, at a time. This also holds true for foreign contributors such as Austria and Switzerland. Recently Switzerland agreed to join the *Tatort* line-up again,[4] and the regional caster HR added a new team to the line-up. German actor of Hollywood fame Til Schweiger (*SLC Punk*, 1998; *Driven*, 2001: *Inglorious Basterds*, 2009) premiered as a new detective for the north German pubcaster NDR in Hamburg in 2013. This shows that the *Tatort* brand is alive and well; its combination of generic stability with small variation has managed successfully to hold audience loyalty.

When *Tatort* was created, many rules were established to ensure that the series could have a recognizable brand image, despite the numerous producers, actors, writers, and directors involved in the different regions. After all, the individual stations did not have to work together and in fact usually would not (Henke, 2009).[5] This meant that certain rules established to define the series were not always rigorously followed. For example, one rule created to maintain an artistic value is the exclusion of flashbacks in the series, and it is the one violated most often (Witte 2009). More importantly, to maintain viewers, *Tatort* had to be distinctly German, rather than American, in its televisual style. This aided in the series' success when foreign products flooded the market in the dual broadcasting age. *Tatort* was distinctive, yet it was something audiences had known for years and could relate to more easily than the playing with stereotypes typical of David Hasselhoff and *Knight Rider* (RTL). Chases, explosions, and unrealistic plots were to be avoided at all cost. Yet, despite the level of multiple detective teams at work in the series, several actors became synonymous with *Tatort*.

Figure 10.1. Hypermasculine homicide detective Horst Schimanski.

The most infamous *Tatort Kommissar*, Schimanski (Götz George), worked from 1981 to 1997 within the format-family. He was everything earlier *Tatort* detectives, who were mostly conservative employees of the state, were not. Schimanski episodes broke *Tatort*'s basic rules several times. He swore, drank, and was a womanizer, yet offered a new platform for younger audiences to identify with, one who was not an authoritative parental figure. He was thus easier to relate to than the conservative older detectives of the 1970s. Action sequences such as chases contributed to his popularity. Consequently, ARD established a spin-off series, *Schimanski*, sharing *Tatort*'s Sunday nighttime slot roughly once every other year. Schimanski's apartment is filled with empty beer bottles and his kitchen area is cluttered with dirty plates and glasses. This man is a prototypical bachelor, and his breakfast consists simply of raw eggs in a glass, highlighting his "hypermasculinity." This *Kommissar* is not merely an aloof investigator, he is also a human and a man. For those familiar with Scandinavian detective series, or hardboiled detective literature from the United States, it comes as no surprise that author of the *Wallander* series Henning Mankell, after meeting one of the actors for *Tatort*, wrote two treatments for *Tatort* (Heinze 2009). Schimanski was not an inherently German detective, but instead reflected a renewed international move towards a different perception and construction of masculinity.

Schimanski's figure represents an "expansion of emancipation, autonomy, democracy, indulgence, spontaneity and the expression of emotional needs" (Brück et al. 2003). The former reflection of German ideology speaking of obligation to the system, its discipline, abstinence, and obedience then was displaced from the central character to those characters on the sidelines, or, in this case, to Schimanski's partner, Detective Thanner. The team creates an ongoing and lively debate over moral values through the contrast of these two characters. Schimanski, for all that he is not well educated, has the opportunity to explain his actions to his partner as best he can: He is a complex kind of detective, and a rather crude human being.

The Schimanski character has received much attention from writers and researchers; his episodes are rerun more than those of many other notable detectives. ARD pushed to exploit the format even further, extending its reach to movie theaters. The episode "Zahn um Zahn" (A Tooth for a Tooth, 1985/1987), directed by Hajo Hies, was the first *Tatort*, and the first Schimanski episode, to be released to movie theaters before its premiere airdate on ARD. To clarify again: all *Tatort* episodes are roughly ninety minutes in length and shot on 16 mm film; thus no specific changes had to be made during production for this release format. There would be two more theatrically released Schimanski "films" following, and a few non-Schimanski episodes that would air in specific regional theaters, rather than receiving a nationwide theatrical release. Schimanski broke the rules and thereby found a large following, but some "common" rules cannot be broken without consequences.

In 1977, *Tatort* received criticism from viewers and critics alike, for a particular episode that stood out from the rest. "Reifezeugnis" (Proof of Maturity, 1977) is often voted the favorite episode in *Tatort*'s history and made both lead actress Nastassja Kinski and director Wolfgang Petersen (*Das Boot*, 1985; *Outbreak*, 1995; *Troy*, 2004) famous in the media industry. "Reifezeugnis" is the story of Sina Wolf, the sixteen-year-old daughter of a wealthy family. She has secretly been dating her teacher, Mr. Fichte. When Sina's classmate Michael, who is in love with the girl, finds out, he tells friends of the forbidden relationship and tries to blackmail Sina into sleeping with him. Sina, however, manages to grab a stone and beats Michael to death. Fichte ends their relationship, leaving town with his wife and trying to outrun the spreading rumors. Sina,

Figure 10.2. A fifteen-year-old Nastassya Kinski portraying student Sina in the episode "Reifezeugnis" (1977).

turned murderer and feeling abandoned by her teacher, Fichte, then attempts to drown herself. When the detectives and Fichte find her, she declares sadly: "But I can swim, so I always swam back."

While soft-porn films with titles such as *School Girl Report* (1970), or *Housewife Report* (1971), were nothing new to Germany at the time, the bare breasts of then fifteen-year-old Nastassja Kinski on a public station at primetime received mixed reviews from audiences. However, the sex scenes, later cut a few frames from their original length, attracted audiences, and Kinski became famous overnight (Maurer, 2008) The idea that those in positions of authority, in this case a teacher, could take advantage of a minor was not outlandish, and many viewers could empathize. Sina's parents are portrayed as often absent, but caring and devoted nonetheless. At a time when the nuclear family and its values had changed relative to the first half of the century, this episode presented a topical warning to parents of the potential consequences of parental neglect.

The well-written, haunting script and the performances in this episode made it stand out with *Tatort* audiences, and thus the episode was available in the United States through a variety of video rental stores, such as Blockbuster. Tatort episodes hardly ever cross the language barrier (and if so, then only as individual films), making the fact that "Reifezeugnis" is still available in English on sites such as Amazon, under the title "For Your Love Only," speak volumes about its continued success with an international audience.[6] Henceforth, *Tatort* became more risqué, as subsequent episodes illustrate.

The series became well known for pushing the envelope, yet it did not do so successfully all the time. Well received by some members of the audience, certain episodes fell out of favor with too many of its viewers, or influential viewers. Episodes such as "Drei Schlingen" (Three Nooses, 1978; reissued 2003), as a result, encountered a different fate than the mildly edited "Reifezeugnis." Neither the editing of nudity in "Reifezeugnis" nor the actions described in the following discussion, should be mistaken for censorship per se, as all discussed episodes first aired in their original and unaltered state. Only after negative audience response triggered the network's shelving process would an episode be edited for further circulation or removed from broadcast rerun cycles entirely. We may compare this practice to that of the FCC in the United States. The FCC does not preregulate or fine for disruption of content on television. Instead, the agency reacts to viewer comments. The more viewers complain or alert the FCC, the more likely a fine will follow. In other words, this circumvents actual censorship and is rather a protection tool inspiring self-censorship in the United States.

The media, especially when publically funded, are meant to serve the masses, not disturb the peace.

The Poison Locker

Democratic power is thus quite visible in *Tatort*'s history, especially when episodes are removed, periodically or ultimately, from circulation upon viewer request. With almost 950 episodes to date, only six episodes are currently shelved, or "locked away" in what Germans refer to as the "Poison Locker."[7] The reasons for the removal from circulation of these episodes, which span all decades, are varied. For example, "Geisterbahn" (Tunnel of Horror, 1972) is under licensing disputes, and therefore shelved solely for economic reasons. The other five episodes faced various degrees of repudiation of their visual and narrative "quality" (certainly a value judgment), as well as issues concerning thematic content. I will present an overview of episodes here, but will discuss one specific episode and its reason for occupying the *Tatort* poison locker in greater detail.

Reasons for negative audience reviews vary greatly. Insufficient clarity of narrative, qualities of plot, and technical issues have all led to removal of episodes from syndication.[8] Each station is relatively autonomous in its production of *Tatort*; although it is part of the federalized system, its relative sovereignty allows each station to make independent decisions. Josephine Schröder-Zebralla, programming director at the RBB, the regional station servicing Berlin and the Brandenburg state, was responsible for two of the poison locker episodes (Schröder-Zebralla 2009). The episodes in question received negative audience responses in part as a response to the changed visual aesthetics of the series. The producers at the relatively small regional station saw a possibility to save roughly €50,000 per episode by using Beta Cam instead of 16 mm film.[9] The RBB received enough negative feedback from viewers for it to resume filming all new episodes for the team in question in 16 mm. The detective team had, due to the visual quality difference, lost a sizable portion of their audience, and the actors' contracts were not renewed (Schröder-Zebralla 2009). With newer technologies and an audience starting to view programs and films on their home computers, experiments with *Tatort*'s visual format continue to spark negative audience reactions.

While this part of the program's history marks a failed experiment, it does reflect how ARD's stations react to customer demand. The RBB is one of Germany's smallest regional stations. Since GEZ (*Gebühre-*

neinzugszentrale) fees are distributed among the individual stations according to their viewership, this means that even one *Tatort* episode, running at approximately €1.3 million, can be a financial challenge to produce. RBB regularly receives funding from Degeto and finances its *Tatort* via the same. The station generally produces two *Tatort* episodes per year (three in 2005), but the Roiter team premiered episodes four times a year for three consecutive years, which was unusual for a station of this size and made the Beta option a valuable saving. Audiences not only complained about the cheap look (Werner 2009) but found the often-confusing narratives unacceptable, often violent, and the sexual content unrelated to the narrative (Henke 2009).

The RBB, by removing the episodes that received the most negative responses, and by editing others, self-controlled its rerun output. ARD and its nine supporting channels thereby manage to maintain a "quality control" of the brand, removing what would alienate audiences and endanger the series' marketability. This form of quality control is thus an important measure to maintain viewers and the funding based on them. The following chart lists some of the withdrawn episodes and brief reasons for their withdrawal.

Table 10.1. *Tatort* withdrawn episodes

Title	*Station/Airdate*	*Reason for Removal*
"Der Fall Geisterbahn" (The Case of the Tunnel of Horrors)	HR— 12 February 1972	Licensing Dispute
"Der gelbe Unterrock" (The Yellow Petticoat)	SWF— 10 February 1980	Narrative structure highly fragmented; appealing murder fantasies assumed to affect young viewers
"Mit Nackten Füssen" (With Bare Feet)	HR— 9 March 1980	Epileptics are shown as predisposed to criminal behavior—outraged audiences
"Tod im Jaguar" (Death in a Jaguar)	SFB— 9 June 1996	BETA_CAM Ads hinted at anti-Semitism
Krokodilwächter (Crocodile Keepers)	SFB— 10 November 1996	BETA _CAM brutality/torture led to minister of media control giving a statement
Wem Ehre Gebührt (Where Honor Is Due)	NDR— 23 December 2007	Scenes of incest in a Turkish minority family led to protests from audiences in several cities

Three episodes made by the Roiter team are worth mentioning here, since they garnered much attention on important websites, such as www.tatort-fundus.de. Although all of the episodes shot on video came under scrutiny, "Tod im Jaguar" (Death in a Jaguar, 1996) and "Krokodilwächter" (Crocodile Warden, 1996) both were pulled from circulation, and "Ein Hauch von Hollywood" (A Breath of Hollywood, 1998) has never been aired in the 8:15 p.m. prime time slot, but only during late-night programming. According to the Fundus website, "Tod im Jaguar" received, due to a false press release, the negative image of being an anti-Jewish episode; "Krokodilwächter" was shelved after a senator critiqued the unusual depiction of extreme brutality towards women, the episode's gratuitous sexuality, and its confusing plot.

Tatort had its loyal audience, but if it wanted to keep it and still generate new audiences, the producers had to listen to viewer complaints. Even in this changing market geared towards niche programming, it is the larger audiences that secure the show and therefore the station and dual television system. One strategy that has proven successful for *Tatort* over and over again was to make use of its multi-detective format and create new teams and detectives to join the already successful ones in their quest for new audiences, while phasing out less successful teams at the same time.

Removed from Circulation

"Drei Schlingen" was the first *Tatort* episode to be removed from circulation for its specific content. Ten years ago, it was edited to be rerun in its shortened version; it lost less than 24 frames, less than one second. "Drei Schlingen" (Three Nooses, 1978—reissued 2003) encountered a different fate from most problematic episodes, by being shelved, or, as the term is used in Germany, stashed in the poison locker, only temporarily. The select few episodes sharing the poison locker space remain there indefinitely.

The episode opens with an attack on a money transport. Young Finke and his older colleague Schiesser are separated during a delivery, and during the attack Finke is shot and killed. Haferkamp and Kreutzer, detectives on the case, find a connection to a judo studio and thus Schiesser who trains there, but they need a lead on the team that attacked the transport. Two male martial arts students, involved romantically with each other, are found dead. Although this sexual preference is not a reason given for shelving the episode (nor has it been edited out), content of sexual nature did cause the episode to be removed from the rerun cycle for an extensive period of time. Haferkamp and Kreutzer find the walls of one of the men covered in heteronormative pornographic posters, videos, and calendars. After reviewing the edited and unedited versions of the episode, it is clear that the mass of pornographic material did not cause the stir, but a single shot. One shot provides a slow tilt, the camera moving upwards on a poster, revealing first the legs and then the genitals of a black woman. Only a few frames were eliminated, deleting the genitalia elements from the shot.

Although there is no hard evidence available, Henke has suggested that it is the audiences and their actions (phone calls, mail etc.) that can lead to the removal of episodes from circulation (Henke 2009). In this case, the decision was made after the ARD received a large number of phone calls from viewers who were indignant about the images shown. However, the resurfacing of this episode in 2003 also proves that ARD and *Tatort* are able to adapt to changing morals, periodically review their former decisions, and reintroduce episodes that may no longer shock viewers. One reason the ARD may have attempted to work with shock value in the first place was the imminent introduction of private television to the German market place at the time. Since these stations had small budgets, in comparison to the GEZ-fed ARD and ZDF, they would be focusing on purchasing US and other, relatively cheap, foreign programming. ARD was under pressure to at least offer some more sensational programming to not hemorrhage viewers.

The Charlotte Lindholm episode "Wem Ehre Gebührt" (To Whom Honor is Due, 2007) received a large amount of critical praise. National and regional newspapers, according to *Tatort-Fundus*, stated that the characters were multidimensional, the plot layered, and the murderer was not easily revealed to the episode's audiences (Gamer 2007). A young German-Turkish woman, Afife, is found dead. Her family and husband Erdal are Alevi, a specific Islamic ethnic group in Turkey, often ostracized by the more prominent Sunni. Charlotte Lindholm, a female detective coming to terms with working in a team and from behind a desk, is shown as suspicious, because residents and citizens of Turkish descent have often been accused of "honor killings." Afife's sister Selda, who is very religious, tells Charlotte anonymously that her sister was, in fact, murdered and that she fears for her own life. Selda is pregnant, and soon Charlotte begins to realize that her "honor killing" theory does not hold, but follows the clues only to find Selda dead. Selda's murderer is her own father. It is Selda's father who is also the father of Selda's child.

Figure 10.3. Detective Charlotte Lindholm with Selda Özkan in "Wem Ehre Gebührt" (2007).

This particular episode shook Germany, because the Alevi felt that it incited ethnic prejudice and reinvigorated century-old stereotypes. Despite its acclaimed quality in narrative, character development, and performances, this episode has been shelved since its original airdate and is not scheduled to be rerun. *Tatort-Fundus* has supplied a detailed breakdown of the events surrounding the episode's controversy:

Mid November 2007: NDR releases the press kit with a preview DVD of "To Whom Honor is Due"

Mid-December 2007: Alevi protest against ARD airing the episode. They are offered a discussion appointment, for January 2008.

Later, ARD begins airing trailers for the upcoming episode of *Tatort*, "To Whom Honor is Due"

22 December 2007: Up to 1,800 calls a day are recorded at the ARD, in protest of the episode scheduled for 23 December

23 December 2007: ARD opens the episode with a disclaimer: "The following story is fictive. The following episode is not meant to instill prejudices toward the Alevi community."

Only 6.59 million viewers tuned in, which is below an average of roughly 9 million for any given Lindholm *Tatort*;

Minutes after the episode airs, Tatort-Fundus receives the first emails, outraged by the depiction of Alevi; some even threaten the website administrator Werner, although the site is not linked to ARD or any of its substations

27 December 2007: The ARD receives notification of being sued in court; Alevi protesters assemble at ARD headquarters in Berlin; later, protests spread through Germany and to Austria; almost 20,000 German-Turkish and European Alevi assemble in Cologne on 28–29 December

The Alevi community demanded that the episode be removed from circulation and requested an official apology from ARD. The station proceeded with press releases restating the opening disclaimer and promising to take the protest claims seriously.

The issue of a child-murdering father was not at stake, but rather the idea of incest in an Alevi family. The Sunni, the opposing ethnic group, often used alleged incidents of incest in their hate speeches against the Alevi, a "fact that escaped the 'Tatort' team" (Wehn 2002). As a result of this oversight, Alevi felt their ethnic group was being slandered by the ARD. In fact, their protests prior to the premiere of the episodes were ignored. ARD pointed out the favorable critiques published by such reputable papers as the *Frankfurter Allgemeine Zeitung,* in defending its "ignorance." In an interview, the episode's director Angelina Maccarone stated that she was sorry about not coming across the incest-related history in her research, and that she was only trying to tell a story that could happen in any family. She also claimed that she was attempting to work against the stereotype of "honor killings" so prevalent in German-Turkish relations in Germany (2007). German authors began demanding a clarification of the protests' relevance to free speech, stating that one specific group feeling ostracized cannot and should not hinder their freedom of producing art. Other voices stated that the film had only shown one family, not the Alevi as a whole (Brück et al. 2003). Moreover, one could argue that the Alevi were shown in a favorable light as forward-thinking Muslims who have adapted to their environment. However, the controversial issue remained: a well-established stereotype that had been part of oppressive behavior against the Alevi was (no matter how unwittingly) reiterated.

The decision about the future of "Wem Ehre Gebührt" was sealed in March 2008, when it was placed in the poison locker. Members of the Alevi community were finally appeased by the episode's removal from circulation. The Alevi protests are a reminder of how many Turkish-German citizens and immigrants there are in Germany, who consider themselves as affected by and participating in society's cultural and media discourse. And as audience members they can, likewise, voice their opinion and find leverage with the broadcasters. It also demonstrates how influential *Tatort* programs are both in the dominant culture and ethnic communities, as well as how recent identity politics have come to regulate how certain minorities may or may not be depicted. This episode and the societal discourse surrounding it could be at the heart of an independent research project, especially considering the well meant but delayed reaction to the protests. It may be a strong foundation for a sociopolitical analysis that could deepen our understanding not only of German-Turkish relationships, but also the regulation of their depiction on screen.

Cultural Representation

Following the Alevi crisis, *Tatort* introduced German-Turkish investigator Cenk Batu (Mehmet Kurtulus), the first lead investigator of Turkish heritage, while not the first immigrant, and the first undercover operative the series offered. Batu is well dressed, in great physical shape, a loner. Volker Herres, programming director of the NDR, the regional station in charge of Cenk Batu, stated in a DasErste.com press release in 2007 that the station took pride in featuring the "long overdue" first Turkish investigator on the show (2009). However, the actor Kurtulus said that he had not foreseen the cultural significance of his acceptance of the role. "I don't see myself as the figurehead for German-Turkish society" (quoted in Berger 2009). The implications of being the first German-Turkish detective in a leading role, if I may be more specific than Mr. Herres, were far more than he anticipated.

While many newspaper articles mentioned the fact that an ethnic detective had been introduced, there is a lack of significant discussion of what this might mean for German-Turkish relations specifically. Instead, according to Kurtulus, it becomes obvious that where integration is concerned, "we have not come very far in this country" (Berger 2009). The discussion appears to assume that full integration has succeeded and that there is no imbalance in the cultural offerings of television. That Batu remains a loner and outsider within the structure of the series may be an indicator of the limits of Turkish integration.

Moreover, the attention given to Batu's/Kurtulus's cultural and ethnic background seen as representative shifts the focus away from another change to the *Tatort* format: "The character of Inspector Cenk Batu has given *Tatort* an entirely new narrative perspective. Batu is a loner, without an office and regular office hours. In the episodes with him therefore there will be none of the typical *Tatort* scenes in police headquarters or the forensics lab. Instead the spectator is treated like an insider, always knowing what Batu knows" (Berger 2009). These two new developments—an undercover agent and the first Turkish lead detective—clearly show that the long-running German series is once again updating its profile and brand. However, the latest move to a faster, thriller-like format, especially in the last decade and the inclusion of a German-Turkish lead has not resulted in any significant ratings increase. The Batu *Tatort* episodes received the weakest ratings, lower even than the ratings from the neighboring detective in Vienna, Austria (produced by the ORF in partnership with the ARD); the possible audience-related reasons for this are manifold, but beyond the scope of this series overview.[10] But his creation for the north German pubcaster is not surprising: the NDR is known for its contemporary detectives and episodes, echoing what is perceived as the current Zeitgeist and socially and politically relevant topics. Yet, the trend did not work for Batu's audiences, as Kurtulus's engagement with *Tatort* ended after only six episodes. His character nonetheless opened up possibilities for the series and its reflection of cultural policies in Germany (Buchner 2007).

Catering to Audience Wishes

Tatort is a police drama that takes itself seriously to a certain degree and adjusts to audience trends, as seen above, exchanging and updating individual elements (or *Kommissare*) of its brand, maintaining its validity with contemporary viewers. Occasionally, in its long history, the series experimented with adapting to specific international trends as they occurred. This strategy often worked quite well in an entertainment industry that licensed a significant portion of foreign material to begin with, and thus had an open and willing audience. Sometimes, however, while these experiments did not end up in the poison locker specifically, these "different" approaches to *Tatort* were simply forgotten and ignored by schedulers, while marking true efforts in providing for the audience.

In 1993, Fox network aired the first episode of *The X-Files*. The series follows the FBI agents Mulder and Scully, who work on mysterious and unsolved paranormal cases. Mulder is a believer and Scully an intellect-driven scientist. The series was sold to German station PRO7 in Spring 1994 and premiered in September. *The X-Files* became popular with

German audiences very quickly, and is often considered to have visibly changed the mystery television landscape (Koven, 2010). The craze that it started did not fail to affect Germany, and *Tatort* producers, and viewers, as well. Plausible, fact-based scenarios of murder and crime generally drive the genre of crime television. Considering the stipulations of the format bible (Appendix 2), it is clear that *Tatort* took extreme pride in its devotion to realism and actuality. The episode "Tod im All" (Death in Space, 1995), ignoring many of the format's unspoken rules, plays not only with the conventions of the crime drama, but also those of science fiction.

The plot revolves around the stumbling investigation of the nonbeliever Odenthal, and her believing partner Kopper. The episode clearly emulates the base structure of *The X-Files*. Thomas Bohn directed the episode that reached 17.8 percent of German audiences (6.91 million),[11] but also resulted in audiences calling the station to complain about the deviation from *Tatort*'s format (Henke 2009). The episode opens with an unusually lively night sky, reminiscent of a Van Gogh painting, and then moves into a dimly lighted 911 police-call station. The eerily lighted room is not only unusual for the depiction of police work in *Tatort*, but creates a look that lends the feel of a station better suited to *The X-Files*. The anonymous caller tells the officer that the sci-fi writer van Deeling was murdered a week ago and that it is time for investigations to begin.

Over the course of the episode there are many intertextual references to the sci-fi genre, and the two detectives, each taking an opposing side, spar about whether aliens could be involved or not. The episode ends, after the murder has been solved, with Odenthal standing at the same phone booth that inspired the police's involvement in the writer's disappearance. She is looking at a water tower. After a final call, thanking the detective for her help in finding peace for van Deeling, there is a brief, eerie silence. The water tower's top section then lifts off from the main tower and the detective watches it disappearing in the night's sky.

The episode received much negative feedback, but is a curiosity nonetheless. The episode has rerun only nine times in the fifteen years since its premiere. This, by comparison, is a low number for reruns for a *Tatort* episode in general, but especially so for Odenthal episodes as she is not only the longest running detective (team) featured in the series' line-up but one of the most viewed, according to ratings provided on Tatort-Fundus. *Tatort* viewers appear to have their limits when it comes to experimenting with their show.

All for One

As we have seen, the shifts *Tatort* underwent during each decade of its existence are closely related to social, technological, and democratic policies, from changes in family structure to the introduction of private television to the integration of Turkish-Germans. However, these changes have always been implemented to maintain viewership. During the 1980s and 1990s it was quite clear that changes were forced upon the series as a result of ARD's battle against the new commercial stations. This period also saw ARD's loss of their number one position in German television. Later on, however, ARD's regaining of that spot proved that endurance and maintenance of a program can pay off, especially with an appealing lead character like Schimanski. The commercialization of a station's output therefore makes it a better-suited competitor in a dual television system market, where public and commercial broadcasters exist side by side.

Even during its first decade, with no commercial competitor, audiences were considered in programming choices, as is demonstrated by the removal of certain episodes from circulation and their placement in the poison locker. Similarly, the positive reviews for "Reifezeugnis" (Proof of Maturity) by critics did not save it from losing a few shots of Nastassja Kinski's naked body, after audiences had remarked about the level of nudity.

In the 1990s, ARD and ZDF lost their lead position in domestic production and looked to highly rated programs from the United States, such as the *X-Files*. Merging the science fiction style of the *X-Files* with *Tatort* did not prove successful, but demonstrated ARD's commitment to catering to their audiences. The stations had begun to embrace contemporary representations of gender, ethnicities, and society as a whole, reflected in the constantly changing representations of German police detectives, as for example the character of Lena Odenthal, who was a power-house female lead detective.

The representation of shifting relationships of society, crime, and police are demonstrated by the introduction of the undercover cop genre as well as the debut of *Tatort*'s first Turkish-descent investigator. The technological changes of the past decade have made the generational gap of audience members more evident for ARD and pressured the network into taking action. ARD needed to engage in new technologies and provide TV-on-DVD options for the series, as well as online access to their *Tatort* episodes for tech-savvy viewers. Even though youth protection laws apply and streaming options are only temporary for each episode, the *mediathek,* ARD's online streaming service, is a promising new tool to engage young viewer's interest in the public broadcast's offerings.

According to a survey conducted several years ago by the Alexander von Humboldt Foundation, there are specific (stereotypical, but true) German traits. Some of these can be found in *Tatort's* textuality, especially in its detectives: "orderliness, punctuality, efficiency, discipline, adherence to rules and regulations" (unless we're talking Schimanski of course).[12] By trade, crime shows in general focus less on the positive attributes such as "friendliness, openness, helpfulness, [and a] genuine interest in guests." *Tatort's* real strength, however, lays in its "reliability, a sense of responsibility and duty," namely, that responsibility towards an audience, creating for them a space that fulfills expectations held each Sunday evening. *Tatort,* even though experimenting with contemporary styles and forms and always updating its content, is German public television's "preservation of traditional values" and ongoing "Eurocentri[c]" interrogation of crime and national morals.

Bärbel Göbel-Stolz is Visiting Assistant Professor of Communication and Culture at Indiana University. She received her PhD from the University of Kansas in 2011, with her dissertation: "'In Search of the Audience'—Forty Years of German Public Television and its Audience Driven Commercialization" in 2011. Publications include "Fiction Programming on German Pay TV," in *Tutta un'altra fiction. La serialità pay in Italia e nel mondo. Il modello Sky,* ed. Massimo Scaglioni and Luca Barra (Rome: Carocci, 2013) and "Public Industry: The Commercialization of Public Broadcasting," in *Media Economies,* ed. Marcel Hartwig and Günther Süß (Trier: WVT, 2013). Her ongoing research focuses on the investigation of media artifact trading and marketing, as well as exhibition practices of US television in European markets.

Appendix A. Tatort Format Bible (Translation)

Translated from Original Redraft Provided by Gunther Witte (roughly 1982–83)

Tatort
Concept and Profile of the ARD Crime-Series
By Gunther Witte

Initial Agreement:
- Every station establishes their stories within their individual region. The diversity of regions creates a specific charm for the series.
- The stories have to be plausible in reality. This does not mean naturalistic representation of police work and does indeed offer the possibility to move away from reality within some boundaries (as for example in Schimanski).
- The detectives (and their teams) are to be the center of the narratives, that may be presented from the detectives' or omniscient narrators' points of view.

Criteria for the *Tatort* format/genre
- The episodes of the series tell suspenseful and entertaining crime-oriented stories, that are meant to reach a large audience. Different from concepts such as *Derrick* or *Der Alte,* and especially in contrast to US series creations, (*Tatort*) concentrates on individual stories. This is an important measurement to protect the series from signs of wear.
- *Tatort* episodes are not individual films and do not have artistic intent. They should not be used for cinematic experiments/expressions.
- The series should present understandable, clearly arranged—and naturally suspenseful—cases. Complicated stories will not be accepted by the audience, no matter how artistically correct the execution (see: "Schwarzes Wochenende" (Black Weekend), by Dominik Graf)
- Stories that address explosive political and sociopolitical topics are well placed in the series as long as they are offered in a crime genre specific fashion. Didactic, documentarian, or heavily dialogue driven material is therefore not effective.
- *Tatort* episodes deal with capital offenses, such as any level of homicide.
- Representations of violence, considering the current sensitivity around violence debates, have to be handled with care. The amount of violence shown needs to translate to the level of violence connected directly to the mediation of the crime to the viewer. Excessive or spectacular images of violence should also be avoided because audiences avoid such depictions and will change the station. Calls for crime drama void of depictions of violence or dead bodies are, however, counterproductive, unrealistic, and foreign to the genre.

- The opening sequences of the episodes have to be attractive, fast paced, and captivating. Research has proven that viewers decide within the first few minutes whether they remain with the program or not. Opening has to mean capturing!
- Tempo and rhythm of the episodes have to orient themselves along the crime genre. An artistic or poetic slow pace is inappropriate.
- Artistic choices, for example camera techniques, should only take liberties with the standard model if it serves the narrative. An experimental or independent camera style is incongruous.
- The characters in each episode should be clearly defined by perpetrator/victim stereotypes (but naturally include "riddles" for the audience to solve).
- The private life of the detective may, of course, be included in the episode, but only if it is linked directly to the case and does not develop its own narrative.
- Subtitles, flashbacks, and voice overs are to be avoided, if they diminish the acceptance of the episode.
- *Tatort* episodes should all use the joint end credits design of the cross hairs. The absence of the cross hairs usually documents the directors wish to be clearly separated from the series.

According to Gunter Witte, the original format concept, or "bible," for the *Tatort* program, had become less important to the series' producers after its early years had brought the procedural much praise. This study discusses a variety of experiments with the *Tatort* format. Many of these experiments act against direct guidelines as you see them formulated here. Not before too long the *Tatort* bible had lost its guiding relevance and soon thereafter was declared lost. When this investigation began, several producers and creators of *Tatort* told this researcher the bible had been lost; others stated they had never seen it and thought it a myth. *Tatort* coordinator Prof. Dr. Henke provided more specific answers, in stating that the paper was created to guide people that, simply put, hundreds of episodes later, no longer needed guidance in creating material for the well-established format. The series creator, after he supplied the document you see translated above, stated that: "They do not really adhere to the rules all the times, but [these rules] provide a guideline to audience success" (Witte 2009), implying that crew and creators of the series have access, but Henke's point is well made: over 800 episodes into the process, guidelines serve only as rare reminder of what made this series outstanding among its German television peers.

Once Upon a Crime 213

Appendix B. Ratings[13]

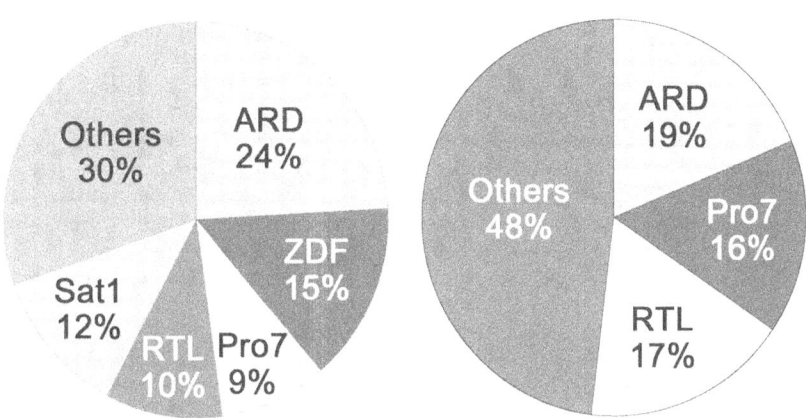

Figure 10.4. *Tatort* general audience ratings percentages, September 2010.

Figure 10.5. *Tatort* ratings percentages for ages 14–49, September 2010.

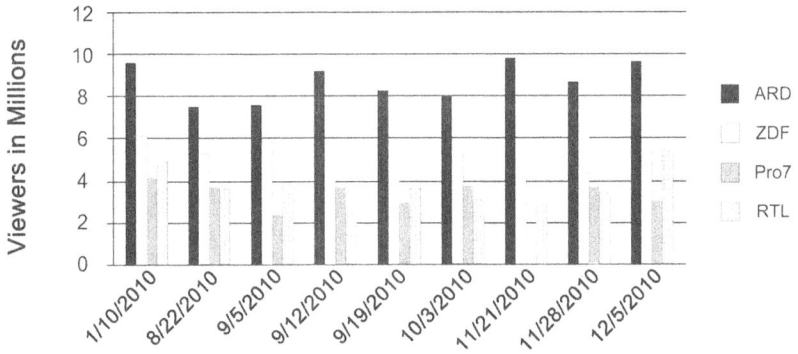

Figure 10.6. 2010 *Tatort* ratings, general audiences.

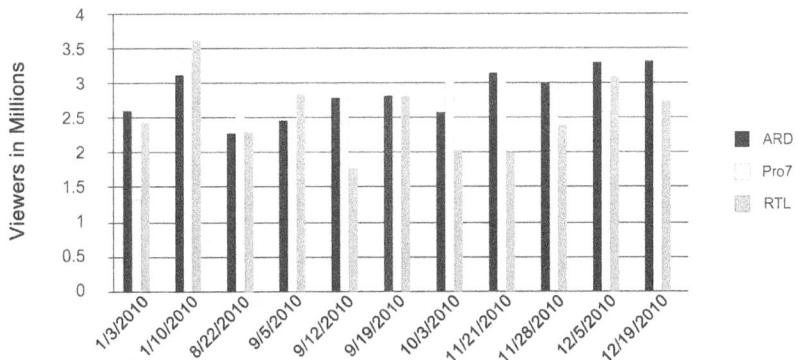

Figure 10.7. 2010 *Tatort* ratings, Ages 14–49.

Notes

1. This chapter is in part a reworking of various chapters of this author's PhD dissertation (Göbel-Stoltz 2011).
2. For example, for more on *Tatort* as historical archive and its regional versatility and use of urban spaces, see Griem and Scholz 2010.
3. Only a handful of episodes were shot on Beta, in Berlin. All episodes are no longer aired and have received negative audience feedback (Heine 2009).
4. Switzerland stopped producing *Tatort* in 2001 and rejoined the brand in 2011.
5. The original format bible has vanished, but detailed translations of the currently existing rewrite from the early 1980 can be viewed in the Appendix section.
6. It has to be noted, however, that often the dates given on these copies vary from 1970–1976.
7. As of 14 January 2013, 872 episodes have premiered.
8. Different from the term *syndication* in US television, it needs to be clarified here that the rerun episodes air both on regional stations and on the main station DasErste, either during midseason and season breaks or in the late night schedule.
9. A *Tatort* episode in 2010 cost roughly € 1.3 million.
10. "Mehmet Kurtulus bleibt unpopulärster 'Tatort-Kommissar'," digitalfernsehen.de, http://www.digitalfernsehen.de/Mehmet-Kurtulus-bleibt-unpopulaerster-Tatort-Kommissar.46534.0.html.
11. Tatort-Fundus: http://www.tatort-fundus.de/web/folgen/chrono/3/1997/350-tod-im-all.html.
12. http://www.mpibpc.mpg.de/137167/stereotypes. March 10, 2011.
13. All data on ratings has been accumulated over the course of 2010 using the following primary sites: www.quotenmeter.de, www.kress.de, and www.digitalfernsehen.de.

Bibliography

Abramson, Albert. 1995. *Zworykin, Pioneer of Television*. Urbana: University of Illinois Press.
———. 1987. *The History of Television, 1880–1941*. Jefferson, NC: McFarland.
Ackermann, Anton. 1951. "Zum 5 jährigen Bestehen der DEFA." In *Deutsche Film-AG: Auf neuen Wegen: Fünf Jahre fortschrittlicher deutscher Film*, 5–18. Berlin (DDR).
Adorno, Theodor. 1997a. *Negative Dialektik, Gesammelte Schriften 6*. Frankfurt: Suhrkamp.
———. 1997b. "Prolog zum Fernsehen," *Eingriffe. Neun kritische Modelle, GS 10.2*. 507–17.
Agde, Günter. 2001. "Die langen Schatten danach. Texte nichtrealisierter Filme der DEFA 1965/66." Berlin: DEFA-Stiftung.
ALM, ed. 2001. *Programmbericht zur Lage und Entwicklung des Fernsehens in Deutschland 2000/01*. Konstanz: UVK.
"Alexander Kluge—Begründung des Stifters." 2010. Retrieved 1 April 2013 from http://www.grimme-institut.de/html/index.php?id=1059&0=.
Almereyda, Michael. 2003. "Pirate Movies Weren't Always Shipwrecks." *New York Times*, 6 July.
"A New Realism." 1975. *Film Comment* 11(6): 14–17.
Altman, Rick. 2004. "Crisis Historiography." In *Silent Film Sound*, 15–23. New York: Columbia University Press.
Anderson, Benedict. 1991. *Imagined Communities. Reflections on the Origin and Spread of Nationalism*. London/New York: Verso.
Andriopoulos, Stefan, Gabriele Schabacher, and Eckhard Schumacher, eds. 2001. *Die Adresse des Mediums*. Cologne: DuMont.
Appadurai, Arjun. 1994. "Disjuncture and Difference in the Global Economy." In *Global Culture. Nationalism, Globalization and Modernity*, edited by Mike Featherstone, 295–310. London: Sage.
Armbruster, Stefanie, and Lothar Mikos. 2009. *Innovation im Fernsehen am Beispiel von Quizshow-Formaten*. Konstanz: UVK.
Artz, Lee, and Yahya R. Kamalipour, eds. 2007. *The Media Globe. Trends in International Mass Media*. Lanham, MD: Rowman & Littlefield.
"Auch zweiter Teil der 'Flucht' erfolgreich." 2007. *Der Spiegel*.
Baecker, Dirk. 1999. "Kommunikation im Medium der Information." In Maresch, Rudolf and Werber, Niels, eds. *Kommunikation Medien Macht*. Frankfurt: Suhrkamp. 174–191

Bailey, Kenneth D. 1990. *Social Entropy Theory*. Albany: State University of New York Press.
Bangert, A. 2011. "Zwischen 'Traumschiff' und Titanic: Der Untergang der Wilhelm Gustloff im zeitgenössischen deutschen Fernsehen." In *Die 'Wilhelm Gustloff': Geschichte und Erinnerung eines Untergangs*, edited by B. Niven, 305–27. Halle: Mitteldeutscher Verlag.
Barker, Chris. 1997. *Global Television. An Introduction*. Oxford and Malden, MA: Blackwell.
Barkoff, Jürgen, Hartmut Böhme, and Jeanne Riou, eds. 2004. *Netzwerke: eine Kulturtechnik der Moderne*. Cologne: Böhlau.
Beier, Martin. 1996. *Film, Video und HDTV: die Audiovisionen des Wim Wenders*. Berlin: Köhler Verlag.
Beniger, James. 1986. *The Control Revolution: Technological and Economic Origins of the Information Society*. Cambridge, MA: Harvard University Press.
Benjamin, Walter. 1980. *Ursprung des deutschen Trauerspiels. Gesammelte Schriften*, ed. Rolf Tiedemann and Hermann Schweppenhauser. Vol. 1: Abhandlungen. Frankfurt: Suhrkamp.
Bente, Garry, and Bettina Fromm. 1997. *Affektfernsehen. Motive, Angebotsformen und Wirkungen*. Opladen: Westdeutscher Verlag.
Berger, C. 2009. "A Reluctant Figure of Integration: 'Tatort'—Inspector Mehmet Kurtulus." *Goethe-Institut e.V. Online Redaktion*. http://www.goethe.de/wis/med/rtv/for/en4176359.htm.
Bergfelder, Tim. 2005. *International Adventures. German Popular Cinema and European Co-Productions in the 1960s*. New York: Berghahn.
———. 2010. "Shadowlands: The Memory of the Ostgebiete." In *Screening War: Perspectives on German Suffering*, edited by Paul Cooke and Marc Silverman, 123–42. Rochester, NY: Camden House.
Berling, P. 1992. *Die 13 Jahre des Rainer Werner Fassbinder: Seine Filme, seine Freunde, seine Feinde*. Bergisch Gladbach: Lübbe.
"Besondere Ehrung des DVV für Alexander Kluge." 2010. Retrieved 1 April 2013 from http://www.grimme-institut.de/html/index.php?id=1042&0=.
Beutelschmidt, Thomas. 2008. *'Audiovisuelle Literatur'. Datenbank der Adaptionen epischer und dramatischer Vorlagen im DDR-Fernsehen*. Leipzig (MAZ 30 mit Datenbank CD-Rom).
———. 2009. *Kooperation oder Konkurrenz? Das Verhältnis zwischen Film und Fernsehen in der DDR*. Berlin: Schriftenreihe der DEFA.
———. 2010. *Die Auftragsproduktionen des DEFA-Spielfilmstudios für das DDR Fernsehen von 1959–1990*. Berlin. (http://defa-stiftung.de/cms/beutelschmidt).
———. 2013. "Grenzüberschreitung intern: Die Zusammenarbeit zwischen der DEFA und dem DDR-Fernsehen." In *DEFA International*, edited by Michael Wedel, et al., 93–112. Wiesbaden: VS Springer Verlag.
———, ed. 2007. *Das literarische Fernsehen. Beiträge zur deutsch-deutschen Medienkultur*. Frankfurt: Peter Lang.
———, and Wrage, Henning, eds. 2004. *"Das Buch zum Film, der Film zum Buch" : Annäherung an den literarischen Kanon im DDR-Fernsehen*. Leipzig : Leipziger Universitätsverlag.
Bielby, Denise D., and C. Lee Harrington. 2008. *Global TV. Exporting Television*

and Culture in the World Market. New York and London: New York University Press.
Bignell, J., and A. Fickers. 2008. *A European Television History*. Oxford: Wiley-Blackwell.
Blessing, Benita. 2009. "Once Upon a Game—Game Theory and the Failure of the SED." Panel Presentation. *CONFRPT: Between Compulsion and Persuasion: Cultural Authority in the GDR (GSA 2009)*. H-German. Accessed 1 March 2012.
Boa, Elizabeth, and Rachel Palfreyman. 2000. *Heimat—A German Dream: Regional Loyalties and National Identity in German Culture 1890–1990*. Oxford: Oxford University Press.
Bolter, J. David and Grusin, Richard. 1999. *Remediation: Understanding New Media*. Cambridge: MIT.
Brandis, Helmut. 1957. *Mehr Filme, billigere Filme, bessere Filme*. Berlin (DDR) 28.9. (BArch DR 1/4479), 2 and 7.
Brecht, B. 2000. "The Radio as a Communications Apparatus." In *Brecht on Film and Radio*, edited and translated by M. Silberman. London: Methuen.
Brosius, Hans-Bernd. 1995. *Alltagsrationalität in der Nachrichtenrezeption. Ein Modell zur Wahrnehmung und Verarbeitung von Nachrichteninhalten*. Opladen: Westdeutscher Verlag.
Brück, Ingrid and Viehoff, Reinhold, eds. 1996a. *Der Westdeutsche Fernsehkrimi: Anmerkungen Zur Forschungslage*. 50 Jahre Deutscher Fernsehkrimi. Halle (FRG): Institut für Kommunikationswissenschaften Universität Halle.
———, eds. 1996b. *Crime Genre and Television. From Stahlnetz to Tatort: A Realistic Tradition*. Hallische Medienarbeiten 8. Halle, Dept. für Kommunikationswissenschaften, Universität Halle.
Brück, I., et al. 2003. *Der Deutsche Fernsehkrimi*. Ulm: Metzlersche Verlagsbuchhandlung Poeschelverlag.
Buchner, K. 2007. "Der Erste Türke Als 'Tatort'—Kommissar." *Stern*. http://www.stern.de/kultur/tv/mehmet-kurtulus-der-erste-tuerke-als-tatort-kommissar-587765-print.html.
Buchner, K. 2009. Schleichwerbung Im Tatort?" *Stern*, 26 February.
Buchwald, M. 1999. "Fernsehen Im Wettbewerb." *Rundfunkpolitik in Deutschland: Wettbewerb Und Öffentlichkeit*, edited by D. Schwarzkopf, 615–643. Munich: Deutscher Taschenbuch Verlag.
———. 1999. "Öffentlich-Rechtlicher Rundfunk: Institutionen—Auftrag—Programme." *Rundfunkpolitik in Deutschland: Wettbewerb Und Öffentlichkeit*, edited by D. Schwarzkopf, 316–407. Munich: Deutscher Taschenbuch Verlag.
Burchell, Graham, Colin Gordon, and Peter Miller. 1991. *The Foucault Effect: Studies in Governmentality*. Chicago: University of Chicago Press.
Burns, R. W. 1998. *Television: An International History of the Formative Years*. London: IEE.
Butler, J. G. 2010. *Television Style*. New York, Routledge.
Castells, Manuel. 2000. *The Rise of the Network Society*, 2nd ed. London: Blackwell.
Cavell, Stanley. 1982. "The Fact of Television." *Daedalus* 111, no. 4 (Fall): 75–96.
Chalaby, Jean K. 2009. *Transnational Television in Europe. Reconfiguring Global Communications Networks*. London and New York: I. B. Tauris.

Christensen, Jerome. 2012. *America's Corporate Art: The Studio Authorship of Hollywood Motion Pictures.* Stanford, CA: Stanford University Press.
Classen, Christoph. 2010. "DDR-Medien im Spannungsfeld von Gesellschaft und Politik." In *Wie im Westen, nur anders: Medien in der DDR*, edited by Stefan Zahlmann, 385–407. Berlin: Panama Verlag.
Collins, Richard. 2004. "'Ises' and 'Oughts': Public Service Broadcasting in Europe." In *The Television Studies Reader*, edited by R. Allen and A. Hill. London: Routledge.
———. 1994. *Broadcasting and Audio-Visual Policy in the European Single Market.* London: John Libbey.
———, and Porter, Vincent. 1981. *Westdeutscher Rundfunk and the Arbeiterfilm: Fassbinder, Ziewer and Others.* London: BFI Publishing.
Cooke, Paul. 2005. *Representing East Germany Since Unification: From Colonization to Nostalgia.* Oxford and New York: Berg.
———. 2008. "*Dresden* (2006), TeamWorx and *Titanic* (1997): German Wartime Suffering as Hollywood Disaster Movie." *German Life and Letters* 61: 279–94.
———. 2012. *Contemporary German Cinema.* Manchester: Manchester University Press.
———. 2013. "Reconfiguring the National Community Transnationally: teamWorx, Television, and the Eventization of German History." *Modern Languages Review* 108: 597–617.
Crew, D. 2007. "Sleeping with the Enemy? A Fiction Film for German Television about the Bombing of Dresden." *Central European History* 40: 117–32.
Dasgupta, S. 2012. "Policing the People: Television Studies and the Problem of 'Quality'." *NECS-US: European Journal of Media Studies* 1. http://www.necsus-ejms.org/policing-the-people-television-studies-and-the-problem-of-quality-by-sudeep-dasgupta/.
Davidson, John E. 2012. "Industry in Idealized Form: The Work of Movies in Film's First One Hundred Years." *PMLA* 127(4): 879–89.
Davis, Sam. 2000. *Quotenfieber: Das Geheimnis erfolgreicher TV-Movies.* Bergisch Gladbach: Lübbe.
Dayan, Daniel, and Elihu Katz. 1992. *Media Events: The Live Broadcasting of History.* Cambridge, MA: Harvard University Press.
"dctp." Retrieved 1 April 2013 from http://www.dctp.de/index.php. 2013.
Deeken, Annette. 2004. *Reisefilme : Ästhetik und Geschichte.* Remscheid: Gardez! Verlag.
Die Medienanstalten, eds. 2013. *Programmbericht 2012. Fernsehen in Deutschland. Programmforschung und Programmdiskurs.* Berlin: Vistas.
Dienst, Richard. 1994. *Still Life in Real Time.* Durham, NC: Duke University Press.
Dimendberg, Edward and Kaes, Anton. 2010. "Film and Television.". In *The United States and Germany During the Twentieth Century: Competition and Convergence*, edited by Christof Mauch and Kiran Klaus Patel, 194–201. Cambridge: Cambridge University Press.
Dittmar, C. and Vollberg, S., eds. 2004. *Alternativen im DDR-Fernsehen? Die Programmentwicklung 1981 bis 1985.* Leipzig: Leipziger Universitätsverlag.
Doelker, Christian. 1989. *Kulturtechnik Fernsehen: Analyse eines Mediums.* Stuttgart: Klett-Cotta.

During, Simon. 2005. *Cultural Studies: A Critical Introduction*. London: Routledge.
Ebbrecht, T. 2007. "History, Public Memory, and Media Event: Codes and Conventions of Historical Event-Television." *Media History* 13(2): 221–34.
Eckert, Gerhard. 1953. *Die Kunst des Fernsehens*. Emsdetten: Lechte Verlag.
Eco, Umberto. 1984. "A Guide to the Neo-Television of the 1980s," *Framework* 25: 18–25.
Eifert, M. and W. Hoffmann-Riem. 1991. "Die Entstehung und Ausgestaltung des Dualen Rundfunksystems." In *Rundfunkpolitik in Deutschland: Wettbewerb und Öffentlichkeit*, edited by D. Schwarzkopf, 50–117. München, Deutscher Taschenbuch Verlag.
Elsaesser, Thomas. 1996. *Fassbinder's Germany: History, Identity, Subject*. Amsterdam, Amsterdam University Press.
———. 2005. *European Cinema: Face to Face with Hollywood*. Amsterdam: Amsterdam University Press.
Elsner, Monika, Müller, Thomas, Spangenberg, Peter. 1998. "Early German Television: The Slow Development of a Fast Medium." In *Materialities of Communication*, edited by Hans Ulrich Gumbrecht and Karl Ludwig Pfeiffer, Karl Ludwig, 108–143. Stanford: Stanford University Press.
Engell, Lorenz. 2012. *Fernsehtheorie zur Einführung*. Hamburg: Junius Verlag.
———. 2009. "Fernsehen mit Unbekannten. Überlegungen zur experimentellen Television." In Grisko, Michael and Münker, Stefan, eds. *Fernsehexperimente. Stationen eines Mediums*. Berlin: Kadmos. 16-45.
———, Bernhard Siegert, and Joseph Vogl, eds. 2004. *1950*. Weimar: Universitätsverlag.
———. 1989. *Vom Widerspruch zur Langeweile. Logische und temporalie Begründungen des Fernsehens*. Frankfurt: Peter Lang.
Epstein, M. M., et al. 2007. *Quality Control: The Daily Show, the Peabody and Brand Discipline*. London, I. B. Tauris.
"Erinnerungen, Erlebnisse, Eindrücke." 2011. Retrieved June 10, 2011, from http://www.daserste.de/dieflucht/.
Esposito, Elena. 2002. *Soziales Vergessen*. Frankfurt: Suhrkamp.
Esser, Andrea. 2005. "Formatiertes Fernsehen. Die Bedeutung von Formaten für Fernsehsender und Produktionsmärkte." *Media Perspektiven* (11): 502–514.
Eugster, Eugen. 1983. *Television Programming Across National Borders: The EBU and OIRT Experience*. Dedham, MA: Artech House.
Fahle, Oliver, and Lorenz Engell. 2006. *Philosophie des Fernsehens*. Munich: Fink.
"Fast 3.000 Sendungen ….". 2010–2015. Retrieved 1 April 2013 from http://www.kluge-alexander.de/fernsehen.
Fehlig, Werner. 1955. *Gedanken zu einer Dramaturgie der Fernsehkunst*. Berlin (DDR). BArch. DR 8/3.
Finke, Klaus. 2007. *Politik und Film in der DDR*. Oldenburg: Bis Verlag.
Festenberg, N. v. 2011. "RTL-Zweiteiler *Hindenburg*: Friedlicher Riese, leicht entflammbar." *Der Spiegel Online*.
"Feuersturm mit Millionenpublikum." 2006. *Der Spiegel*.
Fischer, R., ed. 2004. *Fassbinder über Fassbinder: Die ungekürzten Interviews*. Frankfurt am Main: Filmverlag der Autoren.
Fley, Matthias. 1997. *Talkshows in deutschen Fernsehen—Konzeptionen und Funktionen einer Sendeform*. Bochum: Brockmeyer.

Flusser, Vilem. 1997. "Für eine Phänomenologie des Fernsehens." In *Medienkultur*, edited by S. Bollmann. Frankfurt am Main: Fischer.
———. 2004. "On the Theory of Communication." In *Writings*, translated by E. Eisel, edited by A. Ströhl. Minneapolis: University of Minneapolis Press.
French, J. *Die Probleme des Dualen Rundfunksystems Der Bundesrepublik Deutschland und die Zukunft Seiner Öffentlich-Rechtlichen Säule*. München, Grin Verlag. 2008
Fuchs, M. "Der Erfinder: Gunther Witte." *DU—Zeitschrift für Kultur* 8(779). 2007
Fulbrook, Mary, ed. *Power and Society in the GDR 1961–1979: The Normalisation of Rule?* New York: Berghahn Books, 2009.
Funiok, Rüdiger. 2007. *Medienethik. Verantwortung in der Mediengesellschaft*. Stuttgart: Kohlhammer.
Freud, S. 2010. *The Interpretation of Dreams*. New York, Sterling.
Frey-Vor, Gerlinde, and Rüdiger Steinmetz, eds. 2003. *Rundfunk in Ostdeutschland. Erinnerungen—Analysen—Meinungen*. Konstanz: Universitätsverlag Konstanz.
Gast, Wolfgang, and Gerhard R. Kaiser. 1977. "Kritik der Fernsehspielkritik: Das Beispiel von Fassbinder's *Acht Stunden sind kein Tag*." In *Literaturkritik—Medienkritik*, edited by J. Drews, 103–16. Heidelberg: Quelle & Meyer.
Gehrau, Volker. 2001. *Fernsehgenres und Fernsehgattungen: Ansätze und Daten zur Rezeption, Klassifikation und Bezeichnung von Fernsehprogrammen*. Munich: Reinhard Fischer.
Fuhr, E. 2011. "Liebesgeschichte im Luftschiff: Der TV-Zweiteiler *Hindenburg* will an den Kinoerfolg vom *Untergang der Titanic* anknüpfen." *Berliner Morgenpost*.
Gamer, K. 2007. "Innendienst, Schwangerschaft Und Ehrenmord." *Tatort-Fundus*. http://www.tatort-fundus.de/web/folgen/chrono/4/2007/684-wem-ehre-ge buehrt/filmkritik.html.
Gangloff, T. P. 2006. "Herr der Katastrophen; TV-Produzenten Nico Hofmann weiß, wie man mit Geschichte Quote macht." *Die Welt*.
Geisler, Michael. 1999. "From Building Blocks to Radical Construction: West German Media Theory since 1984." *New German Critique* 78 (Autumn): 75–107.
Giesen, R. 1994. "Die Renaissance des Sadisten: *Martha*, ein sogennter Frauenfilm von Fassbinder, wir ausgegraben." *Frankfurther Rundschau*.
Giessmann, Sebastian. 2005. "Netzwerke als Gegenstand von Medienwissenschaft. Abgrenzung und Perspektiven," *MEDIENwissenschaft* 4: 424–29.
———. 2006. *Netze und Netzwerke: Archäologie einer Kulturtechnik, 1740–1840*. Bielefeld: Transcript.
Göbel-Stolz, B. 2011. "'In Search of the Audience'—Forty Years of German Public Television and Its Audience Driven Commercialization." PhD dissertation, University of Kansas.
Gomery, Douglas. 2005. *The Hollywood Studio System. A History*. London: BFI.
Grisko, Michael, and Stefan Münker, eds. 2009. *Fernsehexperimente: Stationen eines Mediums*. Berlin: Kadmos.
Griem, J., and S. Scholz, eds. 2010. *Tatort Stadt: mediale Topographien eines Fernsehklassikers*. Frankfurt: Campus Verlag.
Gröhler, H. 1971. "Rainer Werner Fassbinder über Film, Fernsehen und Theater." *Kölner Stadt Anzeiger*.

Gruber, K., and C. Schulte. 2007. "Die Bauweise von Paradiesen. Für Alexander Kluge." *Maske und Kothurn* 53(1): 137–92.

Grünewald, T. 2005. "Reframing Islam in Television: Alexander Kluge's Interviews on Islam and Terrorism since 9/11," *seminar* 41(3): 325–44.

Grundsätze sozialistischer Kulturarbeit im Siebenjahrplan. 1960. In: Kulturkonferenz 1960. Protokoll der vom Elektrokohle Berlin abgehaltenen Konferenz, 431. Berlin (DDR).

Gumbert, Heather R. 2014. *Envisioning Socialism: Television and the Cold War in the German Democratic Republic.* Ann Arbor: University of Michigan Press.

Habermas, Jürgen. 1985. *Der philosophische Diskurs der Moderne.* Frankfurt: Suhrkamp.

——— and Niklas Luhmann. 1971. *Theorie der Gesellschaft oder Sozialtechnologie.* Frankfurt: Suhrkamp.

Hagen, Wolfgang. 2004. *Warum haben Sie keinen Fernseher, Herr Luhmann?* Berlin: Kadmos.

Hall, Stuart. 1994. "Das Lokale und das Globale. Globalisierung und Ethnizität." In *Rassismus und kulturelle Identität*, 44–65. Hamburg and Berlin: Das Argument.

Halle, Randall. 2008. *German Film After Germany. Toward a Transnational Aesthetic.* Urbana: University of Illinois Press.

Hallenberger, Gerd. 2004. Fernsehformate und internationaler Formathandel. In *Internationales Handbuch Medien 2004/2005,* edited by Hans-Bredow-Institut, 159–67. Baden-Baden: Nomos.

Halstenberg, A. 1974. "Ein Hauch von Horror: Rainer Werner Fassbinders Film Martha." *Kölner Stadt Anzeiger.*

Haltof, Marek. 2004. *Polish National Cinema.* New York: Berghahn.

Havens, Timothy. 2006. *Global Television Marketplace.* London: BFI.

Heinze, D. 2009. Interview by B. Göbel-Stolz.

Heller, Heinz-B., and Peter Zimmermann, eds. 1995. *Blicke in die Welt: Reportagen und Magazine des nordwestdeutschen Fernsehens in den 50er und 60er Jahren.* Konstanz: Ölschläger.

Henke, G. 2009. Interview by B. Göbel-Stolz.

Hepp, A. 2004. "Radio and Popular Culture in Germany Comedy and Eventization." In *More Than a Music Box: Radio in a Multi Media World,* edited by A. Crisell, 189–212. New York: Berghahn.

Hickethier, Knut. 2003. "Gibt es ein mediengeschichtliches Apriori? Technikdeterminismus und Medienkonfiguration in historischen Prozessen," Behmer, Markus; Krotz, Friedrich; Stöber, Rudolf; Winter, Carsten, eds., *Medienentwicklung und gesellschaftlicher Wandel. Beiträge zu einer theoretischen und empirischen Herausforderung.* Wiesbaden: Westdeutscher Verlag. 39–52

———. 2002. "Von anderen Erfahrungen in der Fernsehöffentlichkeit." In C. Schulte and W. Siebers (ed.), *Kluges Fernsehen: Alexander Kluges Kulturmagazine.* Frankfurt am Main: Suhrkamp.

———. 2001. *Medienkultur und Medienwissenschaft. Das Hamburger Modell. Vorgeschichte, Entstehung, Konzept.* Hamburg: Zentrum für Medien und Medienkultur.

———, and Hoff, Peter. *Geschichte des deutschen Fernsehens.* Stuttgart: Metzler, 1998.

———. 2000. "Das 'Hamburger Modell' der Medienwissenschaft. Binnendifferenzierung oder Abspaltung - zum Verhältnis von Medienwissenschaft und Germanistik." In Heller, Heinz-B.; Kraus, Matthias; Meder, Thomas; Prümm, Karl; Winkler, Hartmut, eds., *Über Bilder sprechen. Positionen und Perspektiven der Medienwissenschaft*. Marburg: Schüren. 35–56

———. 1980. *Das Fernsehspiel der Bundesrepublik. Themen, Form, Struktur, Theorie und Geschichte, 1951–1977*. Stuttgart: Metzler.

Higson, A. 2003. *English Heritage, English Cinema: Costume Drama since 1980*. Oxford: Oxford University Press.

"Hindenburg-RTL." Retrieved June 10, 2011, from http://www.rtl.de/cms/un terhaltung/hindenburg.html.

Hislop, E. 2012. "Review: *Downton Abbey* Christmas Special." Retrieved 28 December 2012, from http://www.cherwell.org/culture/reviews/2012/12/27/review-downton-abbey-christmas-special.

Hitzler, R. 2011. *Eventizierung: drei Fallstudien zum marketingstrategischen Massenspaß*. Wiesbaden: VS Verlag.

Hjort, Mette. 2010. "On the Plurality of Cinematic Transnationalism." In *World Cinemas, Transnational Perspectives*, edited by Natasa Durovicova and Kathleen Newman, 12–33. New York: Routledge.

Holzweissig, Gunter. 2003. "DDR-Medien und Medienpolitik." In *Bilanz und Perspektiven der DDR-Forschun*, edited by Rainer Eppelmann, Berdn Faulenbach, and Ulrichs Mahlter, 113–116. Paderborn: Schöningh.

Hörisch, J., ed. 1997. *Mediengenerationen*. Frankfurt am Main: Suhrkamp.

Horst, Sabine. 2006. "Schlimme Schurken! Fluch der Karibik und Hollywoods Traum vom Piratenleben." *epd Film* 8: 20–25.

Humphreys, P. 1990. *Media and Media Policy in West Germany: The Press and Broadcasting Since 1945*. New York: Berg.

Iden, P., ed. 1974. *Rainer Werner Fassbinder*. Reihe Film. Munich: Carl Hanser.

Iosifidis, Petros, Jeanette Steemers, and Mark C. Wheeler. 2005. *European Television Industries*. London: BFI.

Jäger, Elfi, and Sonja Behrens. 2009. *The FRAPA Report 2009. TV Formats to the World*. Huerth: FRAPA.

Jäger, Ludwig, Linz, Erkia, and Schneider, Irmela, eds. 2010. *Media, Culture and Mediality: New Insights into the Current State of Research*. Bielefeld: transcript.

Jäger, Manfred. 1994. *Kultur und Politik in der DDR*. Köln: Edition Deutschland Archiv.

Jahn-Sudmann, Andreas. 2009. "Film und Transnationalität—aForschungsperspektiven." Ricarda Strobel u. Andreas Jahn-Sudmann, eds. In *Film transnational und transkulturell. Europäische und amerikanische Perspektiven*, edited by Ricarda Strobel and Andreas Jahn-Sudmann, 15–26, München: Fink.

Jameson, Frederic. 1977. "Imaginary and Symbolic in Lacan: Marxism, Psychoanalytic Criticism, and the Problem of the Subject." *Yale French Studies* 55/56: 338–95.

———. 1981. *The Political Unconscious. Narrative as a Socially Symbolic Act*. Ithaca, NY: Cornell University Press.

———. 1988. "On Negt and Kluge." *October* 46: 151–77.

Jansen, P. W., and W. Schütte, eds. 1975. *Claude Chabrol*. Reihe Film. Munich, Carl Hanser.

Jarausch, Konrad, and Michael Geyer, eds. 2003. *Shattered Past. Reconstructing German Histories*. Princeton, NJ: Princeton University Press.
Jenkins, H. 2006. *Convergence Culture: Where Old and New Media Collide*. New York, New York University Press.
Johnson, Uwe. 1987. *Der 5. Kanal*. Frankfurt: Suhrkamp.
Jung, C. G. 1915. *Theory of Psychoanalysis*. New York: Nervous and Mental Disease Publishing.
———. 1970. *The Collected Works of C. G. Jung*. Princeton, NJ: Princeton University Press, 1970.
Kansteiner, Wolf. 2006. *In Pursuit of German Memory : History, Television, and Politics after Auschwitz*. Athens, Ohio: Ohio University Press.
Karasek, H. 1974. "Eine tödlich perfekte Ehe: Spielredakteur Hellmuth Karasek über Rainer Werner Fassbinders Fernsehfilm *Martha*." *Der Spiegel*: 120.
Kardisch, Laurence, ed. 1997. *Rainer Werner Fassbinder. Published in conjunction with the Exhibition Rainer Werner Fassbinder. The Museum of Modern Art, New York, January 23—March 20, 1997*. New York: Harry A. Abrams.
Kassung, Christian, and Thomas Macho, eds. 2013. *Kulturtechniken der Synchronisation*. Munich: Fink.
Kelleter, Frank. 2012. *Populäre Serialität: Narration-Evolution-Distinktion. Zum seriellen Erzählen seit dem 19. Jahrhundert*. Bielefeld: transcript.
Kilb, A. 1994. "Satansbraten: Nach 20 Jahren erstmals im Kino: Fassbinders *Martha*." *Die Zeit*, 47.
Kilian, H. 1971. *Das enteignete Bewußtsein: Zur dialektischen Sozialpsychologie*. Neuwied: Luchterhand.
King, Anthony. 2003. *The European Ritual. Football in the New Europe*. Aldershot: Ashgate.
Kittler, Friedrich. 1996. "Farben und/oder Maschinen denken." In *Synthetische Welten. Kunst, Künstlichkeit und Kommunikationsmedien*, edited by Eckhard Hammel, 119–32. Essen: Verlag Die Blaue Eule. Online at http://hydra.humanities.uci.edu/kittler/farbe.html (downloaded on 24 August 2014).
———. *Discourse Networks 1800/1900*. Trans. Michael Metteer with Chris Cullens.. Stanford: Stanford University Press.
———. 2010. *Optical Media*. Translated by Anthony Enns. Cambridge: Polity.
Klimke, Martin, and Joachim Scharloth, eds. 2007. *1968: Handbuch zur Kultur- und Mediengeschichte der Studentenbewegung*. Stuttgart: J. B. Metzler.
Kluge, Alexander. 1975. "Kommentare zum antagonistischen Realismusbegriff." *Gelegenheitsarbeit einer Sklavin*. Frankfurt am Main: Suhrkamp.
———. 2003. "Rede zum Büchner-Preis-2003." Retrieved 1 April 2013 from http://www.kluge-alexander.de/zur-person/reden/2003-buechner-preis.html.
———. 2008a. *Seen sind für Fische Inseln* (DVD). Frankfurt am Main: zweitausendeins.
———. 2008b. "Why Should Film and Television Cooperate? On the Mainz Manifesto," translated by S. Liebman. *October* 46: 96–102.
———. 2009a. *Das Labyrinth der zärtlichen Kräfte. 166 Liebesgeschichten*. Frankfurt am Main: Suhrkamp.
———. 2009b. "Die Aktualität Adornos." Retrieved 1 April 2013 from http://www.kluge-alexander.de/zur-person/reden/2009-adorno-preis.html.

———. 2009c. "Fakten, Fakten, Emotionen," *Süddeutsche Zeitung*, 28 May.
———. 2013. *Die Entsprechung einer Oase. Essay für die digitale Generation* (e-Book). Berlin: mikrotexte.
Knop, Karin. 2007. *Comedy in Serie: medienwissenschaftliche Perspektiven auf ein TV-Format.* Bielefeld: transcript.
Koepnick, L. 2002. "Reframing the Past: Heritage Cinema and Holocaust in the 1990s." *New German Critique* 87: 47–82.
Kolditz, Gottfried. 1970. "Derjenige, der z.B. einen heiteren Film gesehen hat und das Kino zufrieden verließ, sieht sich auch einen problemreichen Gegenwartsfilm an." In Manfred Beckmann. "Von der Utopie zum Zuschauer von heute: Ihr Leben—der Film" *Filmspiegel* 5: 11.
Kopper, Gerd. 2006. *Medienhandbuch Deutschland: Fernsehen, Radio, Presse, Multimedia, Film.* Reinbek: Rowohlt.
Kopstein, Jeffrey. 1997. *The Politics of Economic Decline in East Germany, 1945–1989.* Chapel Hill, NC: University of North Carolina Press.
Körte, Peter. 1994. "Unendlich Fremd. Nach 20 Jahren: Rainer Werner Fassbinders *Martha.*" *Frankfurter Rundschau*, 17 November.
Krämer, Sybille. 2004. "Kulturtechniken durch Zeit(achsen)Manipulation. Zu Friedrich Kittlers Medienkonzept im Rahmen einer Historischen Medienwissenschaft." In *Medienphilosophie. Eine philosophische Einführung*, edited by David Lauer and Alice Lagaay, 201–25. Frankfurt am Main: Campus.
Kretschmar, Judith, and Florian Mundhenkel, eds. 2012. *Von der Flimmerkiste zum IP-TV: Umbrüche und Zukunftsperspektiven des Mediums Fernsehen.* Munich: Martin Meidenbauer.
Krüger, Udo. 1998. "Zwischen Konkurrenz und Konvergenz: Fernsehnachrichten öffentlich-rechtlicher und privater Rundfunkanbieter." In *Fernsehnachrichten: Prozesse, Strukture, Funktionen*, edited by K. Kamps and M. Meckel, 65–84. Opladen: Westdeutscher Verlag.
Kunz, William N. 2007. *Culture Conglomerates. Consolidation in the Motion Picture and Television Industries.* Lanham, MD: Rowman & Littlefield.
Künzler, Matthias. 2009. *Die Liberalisierung von Radio und Fernsehen : Leitbilder der Rundfunkregulierung im Ländervergleich.* Konstanz : UVK Verlagsgesellschaft.
Lacan, Jacques. 1981. *Le Séminaire III.* Paris: Seuil.
Lantzsch, Katja. 2008. *Der internationale Fernsehformathandel. Akteure, Strategien, Strukturen, Organisationsformen.* Wiesbaden: VS Verlag.
Latour, Bruno, and Steve Woolgar. 1986. *Laboratory Life: the Social Construction of Scientific Facts.* Princeton, NJ: Princeton University Press.
Lenin, Vladimir I. 1959. "Womit Beginnen?" In *Ausgewählte Werke in Zwei Bänden*, vol. 1, 309. Berlin (DDR): Dietz.
Leschke, Rainer. 2003. *Einführung in die Medienethik.* Stuttgart: UTB.
Liebes, Tamar, and Elihu Katz. 1993. *The Export of Meaning. Cross-cultural Readings of "Dallas".* Oxford and Cambridge, MA: Oxford University Press.
Lindelof, Anja Mølle. 2007. "Look! It's Rock 'n' Roll! How Television Participated in Shaping the Visual Genre Conventions of Popular Music." *Music, Sound, and the Moving Image* 1(2): 141–53.
Loewe, K. 2011. "The Laconia: Sinking an Ocean-Liner Onscreen." Retrieved 10 June 2011 from http://www.bbc.co.uk/blogs/tv/2011/01/the-sinking-of-the-laconia.shtml.

Luhmann, Niklas. 1996. *Die Realität der Massenmedien,* 2nd ed. Opladen: Westdeutscher Verlag.
Maccarone, A. 2007. "Wem Ehre Gebührt." *Tatort.* Germany, ARD: 88:03.
Madarász, Jeannette. 2009. "Economic Politics and Company Culture: The Problem of Routinisation." In *Power and Society in the GDR 1961–1979: The Normalisation of Rule?,* edited by Mary Fulbrook. New York: Berghahn.
Maier, Charles A. 1997. *Dissolution: The Crisis of Communism and the End of East Germany.* Princeton, NJ: Princeton University Press.
Mandelbrot, Benoit. 1982. *The Fractal Geometry of Nature.* San Francisco: Freeman.
McDonald, Paul, and Janet Wasko, eds. 2008. *The Contemporary Hollywood Film Industry.* Malden, MA: Blackwell.
McGee, Laura. 2003. "Revolution in the Studio? The DEFA's Fourth Generation of Film Directors and Their Reform Efforts in the Last Decade of the GDR." *Film History* 15: 444–64.
Meza, E. 2006a. "Mojito's Mojo Working with an Eye towards Hollywood." *Daily Variety*: 1.
———. 2006b. "Territory Reports: Germany." *Daily Variety.*
———. 2012. "German TV companies dip into the past for epic skeins that woo huge auds," *Variety* April 2, Vol. 426 Issue 8: 19.
Midgley, N. 2013. "ITV Plans for Revenue Boost on Downton Abbey Effect." *The Telegraph.*
Michael, F. 1973. "WDR setzt Fassbinders beliebte Familienserie vom Programm ab." *Westfällische Rundschau.*
Mikos, Lothar. 2002a. Freunde fürs Leben. Kulturelle Aspekte von Fußball, Fernsehen und Fernsehfußball, in: Schwier, Jürgen, ed. *Mediensport. Ein einführendes Handbuch,* 27–49. Hohengehren: Schneider Verlag.
———. 2002b. Lokale Orientierung des globalen Fernsehmarktes am Beispiel »Big Brother«. In: Hepp, Andreas & Löffelholz, Martin (eds.), *Grundlagentexte zur transkulturellen Kommunikation,* 436–55. Konstanz: UVK.
———. and Harry Nutt. 1997. *Sepp Herberger. Ein deutsches Fußballleben.* Frankfurt, New York: Campus.
———, and Perrotta, Marta. 2012. "Traveling Style: Aesthetic Differences and Similarities in National Adaptations of *Yo soy Betty, la fea.*" *International Journal of Cultural Studies* 15(1): 81–97.
———, and Perrotta, Marta. 2013. "Global *Ugly Betty.* International Format Trade and the Production of National Adaptations." In *The International Encyclopedia of Media Studies,* edited by Angharad N. Valdivia, Volume II: *Media Production,* edited by Vicki Mayer. Malden, MA: Blackwell.
Miller, Toby et. al. 2005. *Global Hollywood 2.* London: BFI.
Mittell, J. 2001. "A Cultural Approach to Television Genre Theory." *Cinema Journal* 40 (3): 3–24.
Modleski, Tania. 1988. *The Women Who Knew Too Much.* New York: Methuen.
Moe, H. 2009. "Status Und Perspektiven Öffentlich-Rechtlicher Onlinemedien." *Media Perspektiven* 4: 189–201.
Moltke, J. v. 2005. *No Place Like Home: Locations of* Heimat *in German Cinema.* Berkeley: University of California Press.
Monk, C. 2011. *Heritage Film Audiences: Period Films and Contemporary Audiences in the UK.* Edinburgh: Edinburgh University Press.

Moran, Albert. 1998. *Copycat TV. Globalisation, Program Formats and Cultural Identity.* Luton: University of Luton Press.

———. 2005. "Configuration of the New Television Landscape." In *A Companion to Television,* edited by Janet Wasko, 291–307. Oxford: Blackwell Publishers.

———. 2009a. *New Flows in Global TV.* Bristol and Chicago: Intellect Books.

———, ed. 2009b. *TV Formats Worldwide. Localizing Global Programs.* Bristol and Chicago: Intellect Books.

———, and Justin Malbon. 2006. *Understanding the Global TV Format.* Bristol and Portland: Intellect Books.

Morris, Nancy, and Silvio Waisbord, eds. 2001. *Media and Globalization. Why the State Matters.* Lanham, MD: Rowman and Littlefield.

Müller, Martin U., and Thomas Tuma. 2010. "Letzlich geht es nie um Größe." *Der Spiegel,* 17.

Musner, Lutz. 2001. "Kulturwissenschaften und Cultural Studies: Zwei ungleiche Geschwister?" *KulturPoetik,* 1(2): 261–71.

Negt, O., and A. Kluge. 1972. *Öffentlichkeit und Erfahrung: zur Organisationsanalyse von bürgerlicher und proletarischer Öffentlichkeit.* Frankfurt am Main: Suhrkamp.

———. 1993. *Public Sphere and Experience: Toward an Analysis of the Bourgeois and Proletarian Public Sphere,* translated by P. Labanyi, J. Daniel, and A. Oksiloff. Minneapolis: University of Minnesota Press.

Nehmzow, Arthur/Fernsehzentrum. 1954. *Die Aufgaben der Chefredaktion und der Sendeleitung des Fernsehzentrums Berlin.* Berlin (DDR) 11.3. (BArch DR 8/2) .1

Nelmes, Jill, ed. 2011. *Analysing the Screenplay.* New York: Routledge.

Niemeier, T. 2010. "Die Fußball-Weltmeisterschaft: Eine Quoten-Übersicht." http://www.quotenmeter.de/cms/?p1=n&p2=43347&p3.

Nipkow, P. 1885. "Der Telephotograph und das elektrische Teleskop." *Elektrotechnische Zeitschrift,* 6: 419-425.

Nitsch, Cordula. 2011. *Journalistische Realität und Fiktion : eine empirische Analyse des Fernsehjournalismus in deutschen und US-amerikanischen Romanen (1970–2005).* Cologne: Von Halem Verlag.

Norden, Albert. 1959. Referat o. Titel. In *Die Presse—kollectiver Organisator der sozialistischen Umstellung.* 3. Pressekonferenz des ZK der SED 17. Und 18. April, Leipzig. Berlin (DDR). 3–92.

Nowell-Smith, Geoffrey, ed. 1989. *The European Experience.* London: BFI.

——— and Wollen, Tana, eds. 1999. *After the Wall. Broadcasting in Germany.* London: BFI.

Nowotny, Burkhard. 1989. "Germany: The Slow March of Cable." In *The European Experience,* edited by Geoffrey Nowell-Smith, 37–49. London: BFI.

O'Donnell, Hugh. 1999. *Good Times, Bad Times. Soap Operas and Society in Western Europe.* London and New York: Leicester University Press.

Oren, Tasha, and Sharon Shahaf, eds. 2012. *Global Television Formats. Understanding Television Across Borders.* New York and London: Routledge.

Ortner, C. 2007. *Migranten Im Tatort: Das Thema Einwanderung Im Beliebtesten Deutschen TV Krimi.* Marburg, Tectum.

Paech, Joachim, Schreitmüller, Andreas, and Ziemer, Albrecht. 1999. *Strukturwandel medialer Programme: Vom Fernsehen zu Multimedia.* Konstanz: UVK Medien.

Parks, Lisa. 2005. *Cultures in Orbit. Satellites and the Televisual.* Durham, NC: Duke University Press.
Peters, John Durham. 2005. "Die Zurücktreibung der Medien in die Geisteswissenschaften." *Zeitschrift für Kulturwissenschaften* 1: 143–47.
———. 2008. "Strange Sympathies: Horizons of German and American Media Theory." In *American Studies as Media Studies,* edited by Frank Kelleter and Daniel Stein, 3–23. Heidelberg: Winter.
Petro, Patrice. 2007. "The 'Place' of Television in Film Studies." In *Aftershocks of the New,* 13–30. New Brunswick: Rutgers University Press.
Pfetsch, B. 1996. "Convergence Through Privatization? Changing Media Environments and Televised Politics in Germany." *European Journal of Communication* 11(4): 427–451.
Porter, Vincent and Hasselbach, Suzanne. 1991. *Pluralism, Politics and the Marketplace: The Regulation of German Broadcasting.* London: Routledge.
Postman, Neil. 1985. *Amusing Ourselves to Death: Public Discourse in the Age of Show Business.* New York: Penguin.
Prager, Brad. 2012. "Through the Looking Glass: Fassbinder's *World on a Wire.*" In *A Companion to Rainer Werner Fassbinder,* edited by B. Peucker, 245–66. Boston and London: Wiley-Blackwell.
Protokoll Nr. 52/61 der Sitzung des Politibüros des Zentralkommittees am Montag, dem 9.10.1961, hier Anlage 1 zu TOP 4 "Verbesserung des DEFA-Spielfilmproduktion im Jahre 1961/62." Berlin (DDR). SAPMO-BArch DY 30/J IV 2/2/794. 5
Prümm, Karl. "Film und Fernsehen. Ambivalenz und Identität." In Jakobsen, Wolfgang; Kaes, Anton; Prinzler, Hans Helmut, eds. *Geschichte des deutschen Films.* Stuttgart: Metzler, 1993. 499–518.
Pundt, C. 2002. *Mord Beim NDR.* Hamburg, LIT.
Rat der Evangelischen Kirche Deutschlands. 2008. *Das rechte Wort zur rechten Zeit. Mediendenkschrift.* Gütersloh: Gütersloher Verlagshaus. http://www.ekd.de/EKDTexte/mediendenkschrift/medien3.html (Accessed 28 August 2015).
Raundalen, Jon. 2009. *2Mellom Ersatzprodukt og Massenwirksamkeit: Genrefilmen som kulturelt felt i DDR 1966–1976.* Trondheim: NTNU.
Rediker, Marcus. 2004. *Villains of All Nations: Atlantic Pirates in the Golden Age.* New York: Verso.
Reinhard, Elke. 2006. *Warum heisst Kabarett heute Comedy? Metamorphosen in der deutschen fernsehunterhaltung.* Berlin: LIT.
Rentschler, E., ed. 1988. *West German Filmmakers on Film: Visions and Voices.* London and New York: Holmes and Meier.
Rheinberger, Hans-Jörg. 1997. *Toward a History of Epistemic Things: Synthesizing Proteins in the Test Tube.* Stanford, CA: Stanford University Press.
———. 2010. *On Historicizing Epistemology,* translated by David Fernbach. Stanford, CA: Stanford University Press.
Robertson, Roland. 1992. *Globalization. Social Theory and Global Culture.* London: Sage.
Rodriguez, Héctor. 1999. "Ideology and Film Culture." Richard Allen and Murray Smith, eds. In *Film Theory and Philosophy,* edited by Richard Allen and Murray Smith, 260–81. New York: Oxford University Press.

Röhl, W. 1973. "Kommt die Prolet-Welle?" *Konkret* 13: 16–19.
Rorty, Richard. 2000. "Being That Can Be Understood Is Language," *London Review of Books* 22, no. 6 (16 March): 23–25.
Roth, William. 1983 (orig. 1974). "Kommentierte Filmographie." In *Rainer Werner Fassbinder. Reihe Film 2*. Munich: Carl Hanser.
Roxborough, Scott, and Mimi Turner. 2006. "Low-Key MIPTV Lacking Drama." *Hollywood Reporter*.
Scannell, Paddy. 2014. *Television and the Meaning of 'Live.'* London: Polity.
Schatz, Thomas. 1988. *The Genius of the System. Hollywood Filmmaking in the Studio Era*. New York: Pantheon.
Schenk, Ralf. 2009. "Zum Tod des ehemaligen Regisseurs und Defa-Chefs Hans Dieter Mäde." *Berliner Zeitung*, 2 June.
———. 2012. "DEFA 1946–1992." In *Dream Factory: 100 Years of Babelsberg*, edited by Michael Wedel, 114–19. Berlin: teNeues Verlag.
Schreiber, Jens. 1994. "Stop Making Sense," *Computer als Medium*, ed. Friedrich Kittler, Georg Christoph Tholen, Norbert Bolz. Munich: Wilhelm Fink. 91–110.
Schittly, Dagmar. 2002. *Zwischen Regie und Regime: Die Filmpolitik der SED im Spiegel der DEFA-Produktionen*. Berlin: Christoph Links.
Schlesinger, Philip. 2001. "Tensions in the Construction of European Media Policies." In *Media and Globalization. Why the State Matters*, edited by Nancy Morris & Silvio Waisbord, 95–115. Lanham, MD: Rowman & Littlefield.
Schmitt, Daniel, Guy Bisson, and Christoph Fey. 2005. *The Global Trade in Television Formats*. London: Screen Digest.
Schneider, Irmela, Christina Bartz, and Isabell Otto, eds. 2004. *Medienkultur der 70er Jahre*. Göttingen: Vandenhoeck und Ruprecht.
Schneider, Irmela, Torsten Han, and Christina Bartz. 2003. *Medienkultur der 60er Jahre*. Opladen: Westdeutscher Verlag.
Schneider, Irmela, and Peter M. Spangenberg. 2002. *Medienkultur der 50er Jahre*. Göttingen: Vandenhoeck und Ruprecht.
"Schön populär." 1972. *Der Spiegel*, 44: 177, 179.
Schröder-Zebralla. 2009. Interview by B. Göbel-Stolz.
Schrumpf, I. 1974. "Rainer Werner Fassbinder: 'Fleiß ist meine Genie!'." *Berliner Morgenpost*, 15 January.
Schulte, C., ed. 2000. *Die Schrift an der Wand. Alexander Kluge: Rohstoffe und Materialien*. Osnabrück: Rasch.
Schumacher, Heidemarie. 2000. *Fernsehen fernsehen*. Cologne: DuMont.
Seeßlen, G. 2008. "Neue Heimat, alte Helden." *epd Fim*: 22–27.
Shattuc, Jane. 1995. *Television, Tabloids and Tears. Fassbinder and Popular Culture*. Minneapolis: University of Minnesota Press.
Shaviro, Steven. 2009. *Without Criteria: Kant, Whitehead, Deleuze, and Aesthetics*. Cambridge, MA: MIT Press.
Siegert, Bernhard. 1996. "Es gibt keine Massenmedien." In *Medien und Öffentlichkeit. Positionierungen—Symptome—Simulationsbrüche*, edited by Rudolf Maresch, 108–15. Munich: Boer.
———. 2013. "Cultural Techniques: Or, The End of the Intellectual Postwar Era in German Media Studies." *Theory, Culture & Society* 30(6): 48–65.

———. 2015. *Cultural Techniques: Grids, Filters, Doors, and Other Articulations of the Real.* Translated by Geoffrey Winthrop-Young. New York: Fordham University Press.

Soames, Scott. 2015. "David Lewis' Place in Analytic Philosophy." In *The Blackwell Companion to David Lewis*, edited by Barry Loewer and Jonathan Schaffer, 80–98. Oxford: Blackwell, 2015.

Sobchak, Vivian. "What Is Film History?, or the Riddle of the Sphinxes." In *Reinventing Film Studies*, 300–315. London: Arnold, 2002.

Stäheli, Urs. 2000. *Sinnzusammenbrüche: Eine dekonstruktive Lektüre von Niklas Luhmanns Systemtheorie.* Weilerswist: Velbruck.

Stanley, A. 2013. "Refined Titillation, with Breeding as Tease." *New York Times,* 3 January.

Steemers, Jeanette. 2004. *Selling Television. British Television in the Global Marketplace.* London: BFI.

Steinle, Matthias. 2010. "Film und Propaganda in der DDR." In *Wie im Westen, nur anders: Medien in der DDR,* edited by Stefan Zahlmann, 187–213. Berlin: Panama.

Steinmetz, Rüdiger, and Viehoff, Reinhold, eds.2008. *Deutsches Fernsehen Ost: eine Programmgeschichte des DDR-Fernsehens.* Berlin: VBB.

Stott, Rosemary. 2002. "Continuity and Change in GDR Cinema Programming Policy 1979–1989: The Case of the American Science Fiction Import." *German Life and Letters* 55(1): 91–99.

Strathausen, Carsten. 2009. "New Media Aesthetics." In *After the Digital Divide? German Aesthetic Theory in the Age of New Media,* edited by L. Koepnick and E. McGlothlin. Rochester, NY: Camden House, 2009.

Straubhaar, Joseph. 2007. *World Television: From Global to Local.* London: Sage.

———. 1991. "Beyond Media Imperialism: Asymmetrical Interdependence and Cultural Proximity." *Critical Studies in Mass Communication* 8: 39–59.

Suchsland, Rüdiger, and Constanze Alvarez. 2003. "Dandy des Meeres." *FilmDienst* 18: 9.

Thomsen, C. B. 2004. *Fassbinder: The Life and Work of a Provocative Genius.* Minneapolis, University of Minnesota Press.

Thussu, Daya Kishan. 1998. *Electronic Empires. Global Media and Local Resistance.* London: Arnold.

———. 2007. "Mapping Global Media Flow and Contra-Flow." In *Media on the Move. Global Flow and Contra-Flow,* 11–32. London and New York: Routledge.

Torner, Evan. 2013a. "The Genre Expert: Gottfried Kolditz (1922–1982)." In *World Cinema Directory Germany* 2, edited by Michelle Langford, 18–21. London: Intellect Books.

———. 2013b. "The Race-Time Continuum: Race Projection in DEFA Genre Cinema." PhD dissertation, University of Massachusetts Amherst.

Töteberg, Michael, and Leo A. Lensing, eds. 1992. *The Anarchy of Imagination: Interviews, Essays, Notes: Rainer Maria Fassbinder.* Baltimore: Johns Hopkins University Press.

Trzynadlowski, Jan, ed. 1992. *Filmoznawstwo—film—telewizja.* Wroclaw: Uniwersytet Wroclawski.

Uecker, M. 2000. *Anti-Fernsehen? Alexander Kluges Fernsehproduktionen*. Marburg: Schüren.
Ulbricht, Walter. 1954. Die gegenwärtige Lage und der Kampf um das neue Deutschland. Rechenschaftsbericht des Zentralkomittees auf dem IV. Parteitag der Sozialistischen Einheitspartei Deutschlands. *Neue Welt* 8: 979.
———. 1956. Der zweite Fünfjahresplan und der Aufbau des Sozialismus in der Deutschen Demokratischen Republik. In Protokoll der Verhandlungen der 3. Parteikonferenz der Sozialistischen Einheitspartei Deutschlands. Berlin (DDR). 188.
Urbe, W. 2006. "*Dresden* und *Stauffenberg* sind weltweit Bestseller." *Berliner Morgenpost*.
Uricchio, William. ed. 1991. *Die Anfänge des deutschen Fernsehens: Kritische Annäherungen an die Entwicklung bis 1945*. Tubingen: Max Niemeyer Verlag.
———. 1992. "Television as History: Representations of German Television Broadcasting, 1935-1944," in *Framing the Past: The Historiography of German Cinema and Television*, edited by Bruce Murray and Christopher Wickham. Carbondale: Southern Illinois University Press. 167–196.
———. 1998a. "The Trouble With Television," *Screening the Past: An International Electronic Journal of Visual Media and History* 4, no page numbers, online at http://tlweb.latrobe.edu.au/humanities/screeningthepast/firstrelease/fir998/WUfr4b.htm.
———. 1998b. "Television, Film, and the Struggle for Media Identity." *Film History* 10.2: 118–127.
Vater, Hubert. 1981. "Erwartungen eines Lesers an DEFA und Fernsehen. Was ich mir mehr von unseren Filmemachern wünsche." *Neues Deutschland*, 17 November: 2.
Virchow, E. V. 2009. "Heritage and Literature On Screen: *Heimat* and Heritage." In *The Cambridge Companion to Literature on Screen*, edited by Deborah Cartmell and Imelda Whelehan, 123–37. Cambridge: Cambridge University Press.
Waisbord, Silvio. 2004. "McTV: Understanding the Global Popularity of Television Formats." *Television & New Media* 5(4): 359–83.
Wasko, Janet. 1994. *Hollywood in the Information Age*. Cambridge: Polity Press.
———. 2003. *How Hollywood Works*. London: Sage.
Wedel, Michael. 2013. "Risse im 'Erlebnis-System', Tonfilm, Synchronisation, Audiovision um 1930." In *Kulturtechniken der Synchronisation*, edited by Christian Kassung and Thomas Macho, 209–38. Munich: Fink.
———. 2010. *Kinogeschichte als Krisengeschichte*. Bielefeld: Transcript Verlag.
Wehn, K. 2002. *'Crime Time' Im Wandel: Produktion, Vermittlung, Und Genreentwicklung Des West- Und Ostdeutschen Fernsehkrimis Im Dualen System*. Bonn, ARCultMedia.
Weis, M. 2011. ""Hindenburg" meistgesehene Sendung." Retrieved 7 February 2011, from http://www.quotenmeter.de/cms/?p1=n&p2=47574&p3.
Werner, F. 2009. Interview by B. Göbel-Stolz.
White, M. 2003. "Flows and Other Close Encounters with Television." In *Planet TV: A Global Television Reader*, edited by L. Parks and S. Kumar. New York: New York University Press.
Wiebel, Martin, ed. 1999. *Deutschland auf der Mattscheibe: die Geschichte der Bundesrepublik im Fernsehspiel*. Frankfurt a.M.: Verlag der Autoren.

Wiedemann, Dieter and Lohmann, Hans. 1991. "Der DEFA-Spielfilm zwischen Anpassung und Protest." *Zeitschrift für Literaturwissenschaft und Linguistik* 21(82): 38–51.
Wiegerling, Klaus. 1998. *Medienethik.* Stuttgart; Weimar: Metzler.
Willemen, Paul. 2010. "Fantasy in Action." In *World Cinemas, Transnational Perspectives,* edited by Natasa Durovicova and Kathleen Newman, 247–86. New York: Routledge.
Williams, Arthur. 1976. *Broadcasting and Democracy in West Germany.* Bradford: Bradford University Press.
Williams, Raymond. 1981. *Culture.* London: Fontana.
Winkler, Hartmut. 1999. "Die Prekäre Rolle der Technik. Technikzentrierte versus antrhopologische Mediengeschichtsschreibung." In *Medien. Dreizehn Vorträge zur Medienkultur,* edited by Claus Pias, 221–40. Weimar: VDG.
Winthrop-Young, Geoffrey. 2005. *Friedrich Kittler zur Einführung.* Hamburg: Junius.
———. 2000. "Silicon Sociology, or, Two Kings on Hegel's Throne? Kittler, Luhmann, and the Posthuman Merger of German Media Theory." *Yale Journal of Criticism* 13(2): 391–420.
———. 2011. *Kittler and the Media.* Cambridge: Polity Press.
———. 2013. "Cultural Techniques: Preliminary Remarks," *Theory Culture and Society* 30(3): 3–19.
Wirtz, R. 2008. "Alles authentisch: so war's. Geschichte im Fernsehen oder TV-History." In *Alles authentisch? Popularisierung der Geschichte im Fernsehen,* 9–32. Konstanz: Universitätsverlag Konstanz.
Witte, Gunther. 1982–83. "Concept and Profile of the *Tatort* Crime Series." Ed. ARD. Print.
———. 2009. Interview by B. Göbel-Stolz.
Wolf, Dieter. 2000. *Gruppe Babelsberg: Unsere Nichtgedrehten Filme.* Berlin: Verlag Das Neue Berlin.
Woolrich, Cornell. 1969. "Für den Rest ihres Lebens." In *Ellery Queens Kriminal Magazin,* 11–32. Munich: Wilhelm Heyne.
———. 2001. "For the Rest of Her Life". In *Rear Window.* New York: ibooks.
Wrage, Henning. 2008. *Die Zeit der Kunst. Literatur, Film und Fernsehen in der DDR der 1960er Jahre.* Heidelberg: Winter.
Wuss, Peter. 1988. Diskussionsbeitrag ohne Titel auf dem VI Kolloquium des VFF "Film, Fernsehen, Video—Charakteristische Entwicklungen und Probleme". *Beiträge zur Film- und Fernsehwissenschaft* 31: 75–76.
Zahlmann, Stefan, ed. 2010. *Wie im Westen, nur anders: Medien in der DDR.* Berlin: Panama Verlag.
Zeitzeugengespräch: Gerd Gericke. 2002. Berlin: à jour Film- und Fernsehproduktion GmbH. Courtesy of defa-spektrum.
Zielinski, S. 1980. "1980." *New German Critique* 19: 81–96.
———. 1999. *Audiovisions. Cinema and Television as Entr'actes in History.* Amsterdam: Amsterdam University Press.
Zimmer, Jochen. 1998. "Auftrieb für fiktionale Fernsehproduktion in Deutschland." *Media Perspektiven* 1: 2–18.

INDEX

Adorno, Theodor W., 33, 37, 38, 40, 44, 46, 48, 104, 127
aesthetics of television, 11, 42, 53–57, 60, 68, 71, 74, 75, 81, 98, 100–101, 106, 111, 113, 168, 172, 183, 186, 187, 190, 191, 200
ARD, 8, 72, 87, 88, 90, 92, 114, 136, 141, 143–147, 149, 150, 161, 164, 165, 171, 173, 175, 176, 181, 193, 194, 195, 197, 200, 201, 203, 205, 207, 209, 210

Brecht, Bertolt, 115

cable television, 8, 142, 145, 156, 160, 162
catastrophes, 9, 126, 127
Cold War, 3, 6, 8, 55, 64, 66, 72, 73, 79, 80, 83, 134, 135, 158, 221
communication theory, 115, 116
counterpublic spheres, 113, 129
culture, 3, 4, 5, 8, 12, 19, 20, 22, 31, 44, 56, 60, 61, 104, 109, 113, 117, 119, 120, 162, 169, 206, 210, 217, 222, 228, 231

British heritage culture, 184
German culture, 56, 185
Japanese culture, 164
Popular Culture, 221
Mass culture, 40
Ministry of Culture, 75
cultural studies, 2, 35, 39, 54, 126, 219, 225, 226

DCTP (Development Company for Television Program), 117, 118, 124, 125, 129, 218
www.dctp.tv, 7, 123, 124, 125, 126, 129
Deutsche Film-Aktiengesellschaft (DEFA) 9, 53, 54–67, 71–77, 81–83
Deutscher Fernsehfunk (DFF) 10, 54, 58, 61, 62, 64–66, 71, 72, 77, 82, 139–141, 143, 144, 148, 149
democracy, 69, 113, 119, 231
digitalization, 18, 33, 152, 153, 156, 158, 161–162, 165
dual broadcasting system, 114, 161
dual-television landscape, 127

evolution or development of television, 4, 8–10, 23–24, 26, 37, 42, 55–59, 68, 70, 104, 111, 116, 124, 125, 133, 138–141, 143, 145, 151, 158, 159, 161, 162, 168, 172, 180, 194
export/import of television, 8, 9, 70, 59, 61, 73, 110, 154–174

Fassbinder, Rainer Werner 7, 11, 87–108
film, relations to TV of, 54–56, 58, 65, 71, 72, 107
    feature films on TV, 58
    made-for-TV films, 59, 63–84, 87–109, 184, 185
financial crisis, 127
Flusser, Vilém, 37, 115, 116, 128, 220
formats, formatting, 3, 6, 8, 9, 11, 58, 62, 117, 118, 119, 122, 136, 139, 142, 149, 151, 162, 163–174, 176, 193, 194, 195, 197–199, 202, 206–208, 210–212

genres, 10, 13, 60, 75, 77, 112, 119, 142, 164
German-German relations, 6, 53, 55, 56, 63, 70–71, 79, 134–153
globalization, 9, 123, 142, 153, 158, 159, 161, 165, 185, 215
Grimme Institut, 110

Habermas Jürgen, 36–38, 43, 124
Hickethier, Knut, 10, 35, 65, 117, 221

ideology, 39, 41, 56, 60, 64, 84, 88, 112, 197, 227
    Nazi ideology, 188

influence of, competition from, relations with US television, 6, 56, 70, 110, 160, 165, 167, 168, 170, 171, 194–196
institutions, media, 64, 68–69
Internet, 7, 33, 113, 117, 118, 123–127, 139, 142, 150, 152, 153, 158, 162, 178, 181, 183

Kittler, Friedrich, 11, 33, 49, 76, 223, 224, 231
Kluge, Alexander, v, 7, 13, 45, 110–129, 215, 216, 219, 221, 222, 223, 226, 228, 230

Lacan, Jacques 39, 44
Leitmedium, 117, 123
Luhmann, Niklas, 4, 5, 13, 19, 31, 34, 36–38, 42–49, 221, 225, 229

Mainz Manifesto, 128, 223
media laws, 116, 117, 124, 128, 161, 162
media theory, Medientheorie, 1, 5, 10, 13, 34, 36, 37, 38, 41, 44, 45, 49
    German, 11
Mulvey, Laura 39

Negt, Oskar, 7, 114, 124
news, 10, 42, 56, 117, 121, 125, 142, 144, 146, 147, 148, 157, 162, 187, 194, 203

Oberhausen Manifesto, 111, 125

programming, 2, 3, 7, 8, 10, 58, 59, 70, 72, 73, 110, 111, 114–118, 120, 122, 123, 135, 136, 139, 140, 144, 146, 148, 149,

150, 153, 157, 161, 163–166, 169–173, 200, 203, 206, 209, 219, 229
public sphere, 1, 7, 8, 10, 38, 40, 53, 60, 111, 112, 114, 117, 120, 122, 124, 125, 126, 128, 129, 226
Public Sphere and Experience, 7, 114, 116, 124, 226

radio, 1, 11, 23, 31, 54, 55, 56, 57, 61, 71, 115, 133, 134, 135, 139, 140, 141, 148, 149, 152, 157, 160, 163, 187, 217, 221, 224
    American, 164
ratings, vii, viii, 72, 110, 124, 151, 175, 176, 207, 208, 213, 214
    "ratings killers", 117

technology, televisual, 1–3, 5, 17–31, 34, 36–38, 40–42, 45–

47, 59, 68, 100, 111, 114, 115, 121, 125, 134, 145, 158–160, 162, 200, 209, 210
television event 65, 176–183, 185, 187, 190
Thomas, Helmut, 110
Tykwer, Tom, 110

war, 3, 5, 6, 8, 9, 17, 26, 28, 33–37, 39, 40, 48, 64, 66, 72, 73, 79, 80, 83, 96, 113, 114, 119, 127, 133, 134, 135, 158, 175, 178, 181, 182, 185, 188, 189, 190, 194, 216, 221
Williams, Raymond, 2, 36, 117, 231

ZDF, 8, 10, 72, 87, 114, 135, 140, 141, 143–146, 148–150, 152, 153, 161, 164, 165, 171, 173, 175, 181, 184, 186, 194, 203, 209

www.ingramcontent.com/pod-product-compliance
Lightning Source LLC
Chambersburg PA
CBHW072151100526
44589CB00015B/2184